Fellow Guerrilla Marketers Speak Out . . .

"Authors Jay Levinson and Al Lautenslager methodically explain strategies to help all businesses and organizations with their marketing. Spending 30 days with this book could be one of your more profitable actions this year."

—Jack Canfield, author of *Chicken Soup for the Soul,*
The Power of Focus, and *The Success Principles*

"At last, a detailed step-by-step marketing program that doesn't take a lifetime to implement!"

—Roger Parker, author of *Relationship Marketing for the Internet,*
Web Design for Dummies, and onepagenewsletters.com.

"Don't speed read *Guerrilla Marketing in 30 Days.* Read just one chapter in a sitting, no more, and then write down ideas that you can use to improve your business. Now read another chapter the next day and write down ideas. You'll find you'll implement some truly great ideas before you're halfway through the book. Try it."

—Jon Spoelstra, author of *Marketing Outrageously,*
a *Wall Street Journal* best-seller

"If you are strapped for cash as a small business or a business professional and want to turbo-charge your marketing, read *Guerrilla Marketing in 30 Days.*

—Jeffrey J. Fox, best-selling author of
How to Make Big Money in Your Own Small Business

"Only Jay and Al can deliver on the promise to fix your marketing in 30 days. Buying this book and taking 30 days to turbo-charge your company is a no brainer."

—Guy Kawasaki, author of *The Art of the Start*
and CEO Garage Technology Ventures

2nd EDITION

#1 BESTSELLING MARKETING SERIES OF ALL TIME

GUERRILLA MARKETING IN 30 DAYS

- *All the Powerful, Proven Tactics Boiled into 30 Days of Planning*

- *One Dynamic Blueprint to Maximize Profits and Increase Customers*

- *Action Format Guaranteed to Take Your Business to the Next Level Quickly and Cost Effectively*

Jay Conrad Levinson and Al Lautenslager

EP
Entrepreneur Press

Jere L. Calmes, Publisher
Cover design: Beth Hansen-Winter
Composition and production: Eliot House Productions

This publication is designed to provide accurate and authoritative information in regard to the subject matter covered. It is sold with the understanding that the publisher is not engaged in rendering legal, accounting, or other professional services. If legal advice or other expert assistance is required, the services of a competent professional person should be sought.

Library of Congress Cataloging-in-Publication Data

Levinson, Jay Conrad
    Guerrilla marketing in 30 day/by Jay Conrad Levinson and Al Lautenslager.—2nd ed.
        p.   cm.
    ISBN-10: 1-59918-266-1 (alk. paper)
1ISBN-13: 978-1-59918-266-7 (alk. paper)
        1. Marketing. 2. Advertising. I. Lautenslager, Al. II. Title.
    HF5415.L4766 2009
    658.8—dc22   2009013693

Printed in Canada

13 12 11 10 09   10 9 8 7 6 5 4 3 2 1

We dedicate this book to all entrepreneurs who are passionate about investing time, energy, and their imaginations in the growth and success of their businesses and organizations, all in the spirit of guerrilla marketing.

Contents

Acknowledgments

IfEEL PRIVILEGED TO ACKNOWLEDGE Al Lautenslager for working so hard, overcoming so much, reflecting so much "positivity," and putting it all together to produce this book. Few authors have worked so hard to enlighten so many, so much.

—Jay Conrad Levinson

Most of all, I want to acknowledge and thank the inspiration of my life, my daughter Allison. I also want to thank all of my family and friends, especially Julie, Courtney, and Bradley Gessler. They are the reasons I do what I do, and I appreciate all of their love and support. I also want to acknowledge my mother and father, for their belief in me along the way and their support. Sometimes we just don't thank parents enough. Thanks Mom and Dad. I am also grateful for my partnership with Jay Levinson. When I first read *Guerrilla Marketing*, little did I know that someday we would team up to pen our own book. Thank you from the bottom of my heart, Jay. You are a great mentor. To all those who helped me in the publishing process, who believed in me and were generous with their time in guiding me along: Kathy Ross, Nicki Anderson, Konstantine Haralampopulous,

Marilyn Snyder, Jeannie Triezenberg, Grant Hicks, Will Reed, Roger Parker, Orvel Ray Wilson, Mitch Meyerson, Lawrence Katzman, Jacki Abbey, Don Lawler, Kurt Scholle, Mark Landiak, Mark Moore, John Williamson, Heather Wachter, Amy Young, Shane Beard, Brett Fleckinger, Jeff Korhan, Mark Victor Hansen, Vicki Austin, Mike Skarr, Dale Lipp, Jack Canfield, David Handler, Brian Gay, Jeff Glaze, Mark Steisel, Rick Frishman, Jim Vahle, Jere Calmes, Karen Billipp, and Beth Hansen-Winter. There are others, I'm sure, and I look forward to the next book. Thanks to all!

—Al Lautenslager

Preface

AVE YOU EVER WONDERED WHY you don't have all the clients or customers you need? Many times it's because you can't decide where to begin marketing, you aren't sure how to put the pieces together, or you can't stay motivated and focused. You are capable of doing many of the things required for effective marketing, but the real question is, Will you?

This book has the answer. The answer is yes. Know why? It's because *now you can*. It's because now there's a book that leads you by the hand, in slow motion, from wanting to having. There are many books about guerrilla marketing. This book is about action.

Action is what guerrilla marketing is all about.

But where do you start? You start by formulating a set of simple, effective things to do consistently to address today's marketing and sales challenges. *Guerrilla Marketing in 30 Days* will do that for you.

When it comes to marketing, the missing link is often effective implementation. Too many people spend too much time "getting in position to get in position." The Nike motto says it best: "Just Do It."

What can *Guerrilla Marketing in 30 Days* do for you? It provides a starting point for your marketing—a focus and an accountability system. It provides you with in-depth knowledge of the tools, tips, and techniques that you will need to effectively create an action plan to jump-start client acquisition and eventually acquire sales. *Guerrilla Marketing in 30 Days* provides straightforward tips and techniques that will take your marketing to a whole new level.

You will find that marketing is manageable when you have help each step of the way and you are provided with a well-structured process to follow. We have found that some people need the motivation to start marketing, while current marketers need a way to keep their marketing momentum at a high level.

Guerrilla Marketing in 30 Days is a practical guide for expanding your client base with consistent, step-by-step marketing methods and activities. It is your marketing blueprint to increased profits.

Guerrilla Marketing in 30 Days is a collection of proven guerrilla marketing ideas that anyone can use to boost profits.

What can you expect at the end of 30 days? Your marketing will be in full gear, and you will be on your way to a thriving business! This simple, connect-the-dots system can take anyone from no marketing to full marketing in 30 days.

Jay Levinson and Al Lautenslager have extracted material from many guerrilla marketing books and pulled together a step-by-step plan that will enable anyone with a sincere desire and commitment to attain success while making a profit.

You don't have to read *Guerrilla Marketing in 30 Days* in one day. If you commit yourself to reading one easy-to-understand chapter per day, this classic business book will enable you to absorb the material, speak the language, and acquire the confidence and expertise needed in today's competitive business world.

Important guerrilla marketing concepts are crystallized in brief, easy-to-read daily principles and guidelines so you can learn, remember, and see the results while your marketing power and momentum remains high.

You don't have to be an expert. *Guerrilla Marketing in 30 Days* was written with the knowledge that guerrilla marketing concepts and basic fundamentals are clearly written, quite simple, and easy to follow, and when boiled down even further, understood by a wide audience.

We encourage you to spend more than one day on each of the following marketing components if you can. The goal of this primer is to set a program in motion that you are comfortable with and that is easily implemented. Ongoing review and continuous improvement are two guerrilla tactics that will continue to help you in the 30 days covered by this book.

This information is delivered quickly and easily to allow the reader to fully grasp the fundamentals. Summarized essentials cut to the heart of guerrilla marketing clearly and concisely.

The examples, exercises, and key takeaways are all practical and proven, and they have been organized to keep you focused. You will find that *Guerrilla Marketing in 30 Days* will provide you with a disciplined approach while keeping you on track and eliminating inefficient effort.

Winning and keeping customers is the result of effective marketing. It is the key to business survival, growth, and success. Are you ready to begin your 30-day journey?

Introduction

HEN WE FIRST CAME UP WITH *Guerrilla Marketing in 30 Days,* our hopes were to provide a starting point for those challenged with doing any marketing at all. We also wanted to offer a step-by-step marketing blueprint for business owners and organizations to follow. We recognized at the time that one major challenge with small businesses and organizations of any type was implementation—implementation of anything, but especially marketing. Our hopes were to meet this implementation challenge head on, with impact, to the delight of those seeking guerrilla profits.

Our hopes and wishes came true with the first edition of this book. The 30-day concept proved to be a brilliant approach. It definitely worked, with that impact we were hoping for, for those that we were targeting. If more people could read it, more profits would be realized. Hopefully your competition didn't read it before you did.

Little did we know at the time of the initial writing that a few years later the economy would tank. We knew that Guerrilla Marketing is appropriate for any type of market or business condition but even more appropriate for recession-like business conditions. For that reason, this revision is coming out at just the right time.

Is a tough market the right time to be cutting your marketing budget? Not if you want your business to get through the economic downturn and be in the right position for when the economy does improve!

Tough times are actually the most opportune times to reach out to your customers. That's why the timing of this revision is in your favor. Your competitors are probably cutting their marketing as an expense—you'll be a step ahead of them with consistent marketing!

When it comes to marketing, knowing where to start is a challenge for most businesses. Many try to do too much. Many can't find a starting point. Many don't know enough to begin. That is where *Guerrilla Marketing in 30 Days* comes in. You will find that starting point and know exactly where to begin your marketing.

No one has faith in your product, service or business like you do. Let the world know about your products and service, whether times are tough or not. A downturn is the perfect time to reach out and talk to your prospects and customers about current conditions and what will happen once an upswing hits.

Consider the following, all covered in this revision, for tough market conditions:

- *Test markets, test products, test marketing, explore ideas right now.* Build relationships and you will be poised to be at the right place at the right time.
- *Do inexpensive and free marketing now.* Use the internet to generate free marketing and awareness. This includes writing and submitting articles, posting comments on blogs. Issue online press releases.
- *Use e-mail marketing with your own list.* Hook up with a joint venture partner and do joint e-mail marketing. Position you and your business as the go-to resource, the expert in your industry, and as someone who is helpful and valuable at the same time. However, be careful of too much self promotion.
- *Guerilla marketing is using unconventional and free marketing to reach conventional business goals.* Use direct mail. Resurrect your networking. PR works all the time. When employees have idle time, send them to go to a busy area to hand out your marketing material.

- *Figure out any way to put your message directly into the hands of your target market.* Make a compelling offer that will motivate people to take action, to contact you, and to eventually want to buy from you.
- *Market online.* Issue online press releases. Create your own blog. Participate in all the social marketing sites. Drive traffic to your website with an offer of a free report or checklist or guide exemplifying your expertise and value offering.
- *Capture the e-mail addresses of those visiting your website and market continuously to them.* Give a lead, get a lead. Don't forget to ask for referrals.
- *Use fusion marketing—aligning with another business.* Other businesses are looking for creative ways to market as well. Work together with those that have a similar prospect base as you and reach them together. Find other businesses that don't compete with yours and see about exchanging some flyers, trading leads or traffic, or offering brochures or a banner that promotes your respective businesses.
- *Communicating news to the media can be a very effective way to bring attention to your business.* Do this with a press release. If you can't write a press release, contact me. If you don't know who to contact, contact me. Provide information that is of interest to your community: provide news or information of value. Do not submit a press release that is solely promotional or self-serving. Do this continuously and enjoy the fruits of PR.

These are just a few ideas. Find ones that work for you and implement one, two, or three of them. If they work, repeat them. If they kind of work, fix them, then repeat them. If they don't work, get rid of them and do something that works.

The concepts presented originally in *Guerrilla Marketing in 30 Days*, work. Businesses and organizations that implemented them gained new market share and put "making deposits at the bank" on their to-do list more often. Now it's time for you to do the same.

The other thing we realized when researching and writing the first edition of *Guerrilla Marketing in 30 Days* was that while most marketing is evergreen there are still refinements, new twists, and new applications that evolve, especially with any marketing related to technology.

It is primarily because of this that we are revising *Guerrilla Marketing in 30 Days*. This second edition comes to you updated with new, real live examples and applications that we have found, observed, and used since the first edition's release in 2005.

Marketing with technology has exploded since the first edition. We have added a *bonus day* to the 30 Days layout for marketing online and with technology. Since the first edition things like blogging have surged. We offer guerrilla marketing for bloggers in this new edition.

As we speak and present *Guerrilla Marketing in 30 Days* concepts to groups of business owners, organizations, franchises, and associations of all types, around the globe, we often get asked which one or two or three of the 30 days has been the most successful for businesses or have had the greatest impact.

PR, networking, and direct mail are often the answers to that question, but the answers are different for different businesses and organizations. Ask anyone in our audiences or anyone reading this book that has been in business where the majority of their business comes from and the reply is most often, "word of mouth." Word of mouth is slang for referral marketing. Referral strategies are a form of networking. We covered networking extensively in the first edition and in this one but didn't touch much on referral strategies. You are about to be touched now! Referral strategies represent another *bonus day* for you. Perhaps we should change the title to *Guerrilla Marketing in 32 Days*? But wait, there's more.

Presenting this book to new organizations, continuing to operate as a business owner, coach, consultant, speaker, and author allowed us the channels to get feedback on the first edition.

The days/chapters that we thought had less of an impact than others turned out to be big hits, with more success than we had originally envisioned. Now we are offering more of what has been asked for. The days/chapters related to positioning, benefits, and marketing hooks are enhanced along with more real examples of application.

We say it all the time related to anything Guerrilla Marketing: This book is about *action*. This book of action combined with the *Guerrilla Marketing in 30 Days—Workbook* is the perfect combination for any business or organization's marketing. Guerrilla Marketing works and it works over and over and over. Just choose and implement one or two or three things that you can implement properly and completely and that you are comfortable with emotionally and financially and you will be on your way to more profits. We sometimes think that maybe this book ought to be entitled *Guerrilla Marketing, While Making a Profit*. That title is music to all of our ears.

As we said in the first edition, you don't have to read *Guerrilla Marketing in 30 Days, Second Edition* in one day! If you commit yourself to reading one easy-to-understand chapter per day, this classic business book will enable you to absorb the material, speak the language, and acquire the confidence and expertise needed in today's competitive business world.

Important guerrilla marketing concepts are crystallized in brief, easy-to-read daily principles and guidelines so you can learn, remember, and see the results while your marketing power and momentum remains high.

You don't have to be an expert! *Guerrilla Marketing in 30 Days, Second Edition* was written with the knowledge that guerrilla marketing concepts and basic fundamentals are clearly written, quite simple, and easy to follow, and when boiled down even further, understood by a wide audience.

We encourage you to spend more than one day on each of the following marketing components if you can. This primer is to set a program in motion that you are comfortable with and that is easily implemented. Ongoing review and continuous improvement are two guerrilla tactics that follow this startup beyond the 30 days.

Winning and keeping customers is the result of effective marketing. It is the key to business survival, growth, and success. Are you ready to begin your 30-day journey?

The Guerrilla Marketing Mindset

A SENSIBLE MARKETING MINDSET starts with you—not the company, not the marketplace, and not the customers. Your goal is to be market-ready. Tell yourself that. Convey it to the world!

Tough times are actually opportunities to reach out to your customers. That is a tough thing to consider but it really is the only thing to consider related to your marketing. That takes a disciplined mindset. Start this day with discipline and your 30-day journey will be quite fruitful.

Your competitors are probably cutting their marketing as an "expense"—you can be a step ahead of them by continuing with consistent marketing. Your competitors don't have the proper mindset. You do.

Are tough market conditions and an economic downturn the right time to be cutting your marketing budget? Not if you want your business to get through the current economic downturn and be in the right position for when the economy does improve!

Mark Landiak of Corporate Dynamics Inc. of Naperville, Illinois, conveys it to the world. He says (and has written a book by the same title) that customer service is not a department. The same applies to marketing. It is not a department. Marketing is a verb in this case, not a noun. Marketing is action and action leads to profits.

"Just doing it" is more than casual activity or just winging it. Energy, enthusiasm, and passion have to be present. Energy, enthusiasm, and passion come from a mindset.

In the spirit of guerrilla marketing, marketing is everything you do or say that your prospects and customers see and hear from you. This includes everyone you meet, every vendor you contact, every sign you post, every point of contact, and every communication. A guerrilla marketing mindset is thinking about this all the time.

The marketing mindset is dedicated to the idea that each person and every activity in a company or organization should be focused on the following question: How am I building awareness with my prospects and clients through our marketing? Every day that you start working—whether you are in an office, out in the field, traveling on business, or visiting customers and prospects—you should focus on this question. If you have employees in your business, you should develop systems, checkpoints, and accountability so that they also think about this question.

While all employees, including entrepreneurial owners, know what their job is, they might not be able to focus on or even answer this question about their mindset and, in particular, their marketing mindset. If you would like to make several trips to the bank to make daily deposits, then everyone in your organization must think like a marketer in everything they do. The mindset starts with you. Running a business is more than manufacturing products or delivering cost-effective services. We've all heard it before: "Nothing happens until something gets sold." But, you can't sell a product or service no one knows about. Thinking like a marketer, all the time, ensures that never happens.

This should be your mindset from the first of these 30 days to the last—and beyond. This mindset must carry through in all that you do, in all that you aspire to achieve, in all your guerrilla successes, all the way to the bank.

A marketing mindset isn't just thinking about your brochures, signs, messages, or packaging. It is the way you think about how all of these activities and other things work together to achieve your marketing goals. It is about tying all your activity to the mission statement of your company or organization. It is understanding your target market, who will buy from you, and why. It is the measurement of your plan, and it is about relationships with customers and prospects.

Your marketing mindset is your marketing habit for the next 30 days. You will need to think about marketing all the time.

Entrepreneurs, business owners, managers, directors are all typically good at their technical expertise, whatever that is. The plumber that started his own plumbing company is good at plumbing. The chef that started his own restaurant is good at cooking and food preparation. While technically they are experts in their craft, they are really marketers; marketers of the business they own or started. That is a mindset that most entrepreneurs continue to be challenged with. Thinking about creating awareness for their technical expertise is the marketing mindset that goes along with entrepreneurship and ownership.

Whether it's guerrilla marketing, business, or life in general, everyone is basically guided by a certain set of beliefs. One of those beliefs is that you can find a way to achieve something, get something you want or need, or move from point A to point B, according to your desire or plan. Without that belief, you're bobbing on an inner tube in the ocean of life, just waiting for whatever happens to happen, going wherever the tide takes you.

Your beliefs are closely related to your attitudes, with what you say and with what you do. Your attitude shapes where you want to go. In order for beliefs and attitudes to guide you, you must first start with your mindset.

Webster's Dictionary defines mindset in two ways. Both ways are applicable to *Guerrilla Marketing in 30 Days* and beyond:

1. A fixed mental attitude that predetermines a person's responses to and interpretations of situations

2. An inclination or a habit

Think about your marketing in the same way you think about paying your bills. You pay them routinely every month without giving them much thought. Your marketing can be compared to your breathing. You can't live very long on just a single breath. It takes many breaths, one right after another. Marketing works the same way. You won't attract new customers or new business with one marketing initiative. You keep breathing to stay alive. You continue marketing to make more trips to the bank.

If you are making a list of the top three things that would make your business a success today, marketing should be at the top of the list. Pure and simple, if people don't know about you, your products, or your services, they can't buy from you.

Are you born with a mindset? The answer is no. A mindset is a reflection of your beliefs and attitudes, a conditioning. The good news is that a mindset can be learned and developed.

Marketing skills can be learned. The first step in acquiring the skills is to develop a sensible attitude toward marketing—an attitude based on your beliefs, because what we believe determines how we behave.

A positive attitude helps to build enthusiasm and motivates you to create the time to develop new skills and set realistic marketing expectations.

Your guerrilla marketing attitude combines optimism with energy so that marketing tasks are handled with enthusiasm and passion. In the next 30 days, you will be bubbling over with both.

Marketing Attitude Factors

1. Know what you can and cannot do.

2. Get excited about your marketing.

3. Learn new marketing skills.

4. Integrate marketing into other business functions.

5. Involve everyone.

One way to develop more of a marketing mindset is to look around you. Which signs or billboards catch your eye as you're driving around town? Which radio commercials stick in your mind? Which mail pieces do you throw away and which do you keep?

Pay attention to features, headlines, benefits, and calls to action. Which ones work and which ones don't? Doing so will not only become a habit for you after a while, but it will also be a continual contributor to your ongoing marketing mindset.

Tom Antion of Antion and Associates (antion.com) tells his clients to stop whining about receiving spam. He suggests that they pay attention to the headlines and subject lines that get their attention and make them open the spam e-mails and the ones that cause them to hit the delete button. His lesson: Take notice and learn whether the marketing is good or bad. You can't do this without the mindset to "think marketing all the time."

Keeping both your eyes and mind open is the first step in creating the marketing mindset. The next step is learning how these no-nonsense techniques and methods can be used in your business. It will become habit, and habit becomes mindset.

More Ways to Develop a Marketing Mindset

You have many options to help you develop your marketing mindset:

- Seek the help of experts and learn from them.
- Expand your mind by researching books, websites, e-zines, tele-seminars, etc.
- Keep a record of your marketing journey—your activities, successes, and failures.
- Write and help others as you learn.

Your marketing mindset is supported by your focus on customers, on their needs, and on satisfying those needs. This means getting the right products and services to the right customer in the right way at the right value, all while making a profit. Thinking about these issues all the time keeps your marketing mindset fresh and active.

So many brochures, websites, and salespeople talk about "what we offer," "our features," "what we do," etc. A true marketing mindset puts you in the customer's shoes. Ask yourself what's in it for them? How will they benefit?

The mindset must be developed or shifted to be driven by value, a customer-focus, and a strategic approach.

Four Things that Contribute to a Poor Marketing Mindset

1. Thinking in terms of "I make a good living" or "I'm comfortable and my numbers are fine." Complacency is your number-one enemy once competition steps in or a market turns. Not having the right marketing mindset will leave the company in a vulnerable state and a catch-up situation. Many times action comes too late and there is too much to recover from.

2. Thinking in terms of "I already lead in my market." Sooner or later the competition will get stronger. There will be a new competitor in the market and/or there could be technology changes. Some industry factors are beyond your control. Lack of a marketing mindset will put you at risk from those factors beyond your control.

3. Thinking in terms of "I concentrate on the financials; marketing belongs to the marketing department." Marketing starts with the CEO, owner, or director. Taking on this responsibility requires the right marketing mindset. Growth and survival cannot happen without marketing, and marketing can't happen without the proper mindset.

4. Lacking a competitive spirit, not having a killer instinct, and not playing to win. Vince Lombardi said that winning is not everything—it is the only thing. The same goes for marketing. Marketing is not a hobby. It is put in place to win customers and business, and winning customers requires a winning marketing mindset.

So far we have discussed ways to develop the right mindset. Preventing a poor marketing mindset is just as important.

The following three actionable solutions will help you develop your marketing mindset:

1. Continuous learning and improvement, especially with all the new changes in marketing.

2. Competitive marketing analysis. Who is doing what marketing and what seems to be working in your marketplace?
3. Defining what business you are really in. Are you selling eyeglasses or are you selling vision? Are you selling drill bits or are you selling the holes? Are you selling circus tickets or are you selling thrills?

Another marketing mindset is the attitude that says each and every customer's visit is important to both them and you.

Delighting customers is your goal. Put them first. Every day think of several things you can do to amaze at least one customer. This is in addition to any other planned marketing initiatives and the 30 days of guerrilla marketing activities being mapped out here.

Guerrilla Marketing Mindset Tips

You can take two guerrilla marketing mindset tips to the bank:

1. Know where you're going to do business. You can't be everything to everyone. In marketing, knowing where not to play is as important as knowing where to play.
2. View marketing as an investment, not an expense. Talk with accountants, and they will show you the line item on an income statement listing marketing as an expense. But what is the marketing mindset of this accountant? Spending $2,000 on a postcard campaign that generates $3,000 in business doesn't cost you anything. Marketing that is done wrong and doesn't work is an expense.

Marketing that works is an investment; and when it works well, the return on your investment is high. The mindset is that the right investment provides the best returns possible.

Commitment to What Works

Marketing does not consist of mini-events that happen between orders. It's about always communicating, sharing information, and solving problems, all in the spirit of giving. Developing this mindset will ensure a constant marketing attack and a consistent approach to your markets and customers.

A marketing mindset combines motivation and passion to drive your business or organization's vision.

A marketing mindset means thinking, living, and breathing marketing. Many people know what to do, but they spend too much time getting into position to get into position or too much time getting started getting started. Starting and maintaining the right mindset ensures your success.

Maintaining the Marketing Mindset

- Continue to meet people to build a network.

- Keep track of who you meet.

- Constantly review, audit, and evaluate marketing activity in place, including every point of contact and the identity of the business.

- Have a plan and use it as a living, working document to guide activity.

Throughout the next 29 days you will learn ways to get your business noticed by the right people. The effectiveness of this program is based on the attitude toward marketing and the mindset in place of the learner—you. Congratulations on the beginning of your first 30 days and good luck!

DAY 1 SUMMARY

■ Marketing is everything you do or say that your prospects and customers see and hear.

■ The marketing mindset is dedicated to the idea that each person and every activity in a company or organization should be focused daily on the following question: How am I building awareness with my prospects and clients through our marketing?

- If you want to succeed, you will need to think about your marketing all the time.

- Think about your marketing in the same way you think about paying your bills. You pay them routinely every month without giving them much thought.

- The first step in learning marketing skills is to develop a sensible attitude toward marketing—an attitude based on your beliefs because what we believe determines how we behave.

- Your guerrilla marketing attitude combines optimism with energy so that marketing tasks are handled positively with enthusiasm and passion.

- Your marketing mindset is supported by your focus on the customer, focus on their needs and on satisfying those needs.

■ ■ ■

Action Steps

PART I

What do you really believe about your marketing? How would you describe your current mindset, attitude, and beliefs as they relate to marketing?

Complete these seven sentences:

1. I believe that the importance of marketing is _____.

2. This is what I think marketing will do for my business/organization:

   _____

3. How much time, effort, and thinking do I believe marketing requires?

4. How much time am I willing to devote to my marketing? Overall? Per week? Per day? Per project?

5. What will I do differently to make my marketing effective?

6. What will I do to make room for number 5 above?

7. What personal roadblocks might affect my marketing attitude, mindset, or effectiveness? Examples: money, time, knowledge, manpower, creativity.

After you complete these assessments, you will have a complete feel about your marketing beliefs, attitudes, and mindsets. You will know what to do more of, what to leave alone, and what to stop doing.

PART II

Start a marketing journal. Write down and keep track of your marketing journey. Label it something like "The first 30 days."

Write down your commitment to marketing. Example: "I know I get busy, but I need to raise my expectations about working on the marketing component of the business. I will read, write, send, call, or say something related to marketing everyday."

Read the Guerrilla Marketing Creed below every day, every other day, or as frequently as you feel comfortable.

GUERRILLA MARKETING CREED

- I am committed to marketing. I will think continually of my customers' needs and desires first and shape my business, products, and services around them.

- I will approach my thinking creatively, using my talents and the resources of others to develop the best solutions for clients and customers.

- I will always strive to improve my marketing knowledge, seeking new and innovative ways to develop products and services and ways to communicate with customers and prospects.

- I will give all my customers and prospects the proper attention all the time. This will be done in a proactive manner, not just reactive.

- I will continue to seek out new business opportunities. This includes strategic alliances, fusion marketing, joint ventures, cooperation, and other partnerships.

- I will think marketing all the time.

The Purpose of Your Marketing

THE MINNESOTA OFFICE OF TOURISM knows where it is going. Its employees have a purpose and goals for their marketing. Here are some real guerrillas in action at the state government level. They post their goals on their website (dted.state.mn.us/index.html). These simple goals, derived from their mission, are translated into marketing strategies. It's not rocket science:

- Sustain and grow travel-related sales.
- Increase nonresident travel.
- Stimulate in-state travel by Minnesota residents.

That's it. That's all there is to setting goals. Clarity, like these goals, increases the chance of goal completion. The Minnesota Office of Tourism is crystal clear about where it wants to go.

If you don't know where you're going, how do you know when you get there? The same question can be asked about any journey, vision, or goal. The same question can be asked about guerrilla marketing and, more specifically, your marketing. How do you know how effective your marketing is if you don't know what you want it to accomplish? A guerrilla marketer knows what and where point B is. On Day 2, you are at point A. You know what's next, getting from point A to point B.

On Day 1, you agreed to think marketing all the time. Now that your mind is set, it's time to think about where you're going with your marketing. At the end of Day 2, you will know. At the end of Day 2, you will be at point B.

Devoting time and energy at the beginning of your planning process, along with setting your sights and defining the results expected of your marketing, will give you a far greater chance to make frequent deposits at your favorite bank.

What are your marketing goals and what is your marketing vision? Your marketing goals are nothing more than a statement of what results you want to achieve with your marketing. What is the primary reason you are marketing?

Marketing goals should fit into and support your overall business goals. Just like any other goal, marketing goals should be measurable. Goals must be specific and realistic as well.

Forget about all the discussion of whether you need goals, objectives, strategies, tactics, or action steps. It doesn't matter what you call them. Purely and simply, you want to define your marketing goals in the most specific terms possible. You want to know where you are going. Nothing fancy here, we will just call them marketing goals.

Your goals are the building blocks of your marketing plan, the starting point of the plan. The first component of the guerrilla marketing attack is envisioning the goals—a crystal clear vision of what will be accomplished during the current year and each subsequent year, with great attention to detail. As an example, Disney's goal is to make people happy. This is the mission guiding all of its business and marketing activity. It is a clear vision, and it is measured along the way. When there is a question about the relevance of a particular activity, it is always reconciled to that crystal clear, overall goal of making people happy. Hopefully, a marketing goal-setting process will make you happy, even though Disney didn't participate in your planning!

Another line of thinking related to marketing goals is thinking about the true purpose of your marketing. Why do you do all the marketing that you do? Why do companies market all the time? What is the purpose of all of this marketing?

In creating your marketing plan, you force yourself to focus on the specific goals you want your marketing to achieve for you and on the outcome. The marketing plan also states actions to achieve those goals.

The paramount question at hand is: What specific actions do you want customers and prospects to take as a result of your marketing?

The paramount answer is the result of your "call to action" in all of your marketing communication.

Examples of Specific Results from Marketing Calls to Action

- Send for information.
- Call your toll-free 800 number.
- Visit your website.
- Sign up for your e-zine or special report.
- Place an order.
- Start a relationship.
- Capture customer and prospect data.
- Create top-of-mind awareness for your products and services.
- Visit your place of business, showroom, or store.
- Enter a contest.
- Refer a friend or associate.

Example: The purpose of this marketing campaign is to get prospects to send for information.

Do not leave it to chance that prospects know what to do as a result of your marketing. Tell them to do something. A simple ad that offers a phone number without a call to action is not effective marketing. The phone number needs to be accompanied with the simple commands, "Call Today!"

Every single item of your marketing ought to have that call to action stated. This applies to brochures, fliers, ads, radio commercials, television commercials, billboards, and any other marketing communication piece.

Al Bussman, Marketing Director for Perfect Lawns and Landworks of Austin, Texas, has a definite guerrilla approach in communicating the purpose of his marketing. He put his "call to action" on the license plate of his company vehicle. Al drives a Chevrolet HHR, a small retro-styled compact station wagon utility vehicle with his logo, company name and description painted all over the bright yellow body. If you look closely at his license plate you see his call to action: CALL US. Right above the license plate on the left fender, in plain sight, is the phone number of the business. There is no doubt what Al Bussman wants customers and prospects to do as a result of his vehicle marketing. When asked about the results of such a guerrilla technique, Al's reply is "People call us!" Guerrilla Marketing is designed to be simple yet effective. Al Bussman knows that and practices it in his landscaping business promotion and marketing.

It sounds simple, but without understanding guerrilla marketing goals or the purpose of your marketing, you might not get to where you want to be. You may remain stuck at point A.

A marketing goal can be a big number, such as a certain year-end revenue figure. It might be a smaller number over a shorter period of time, such as four new clients per month. Goals, although specific and measurable, can be a simple statement of a company's culture or attitude: To be number one in customer satisfaction in a particular industry.

Marketing goals can also be quantitative translations that fit with your company's financial objectives, stated in marketing terms such as to increase

- sales dollars.
- units sold.
- share of market.
- mix of products or services.
- ROI on advertising expenditures.

- awareness.
- public relations placements.
- number of new accounts/relationships.
- share of customer's business.
- sales conversion rates.

You might read this list and think that all of these goals apply to your marketing and your business and that they will all become your goals and part of your plan. Although this attitude is valiant, it may not be realistic.

A true guerrilla marketer knows that the selection and assortment of goals can be broad, but each individual goal must be specific, focused, and measurable. The more specific the goal, the easier it is to visualize and attain it.

Even though the assortment is broad, true guerrilla marketers also do not burden themselves with too many goals.

The right number of goals that you should undertake is the one that offers you a reasonably (with some stretch) high probability of success over a given period of time. "Reasonable," "period of time," and "success" all have to be defined by you and be consistent with your overall business goals and management commitment.

Not only must the number of goals be realistic, but so must the actual goals. Setting realistic marketing goals contributes to your marketing success.

Guerrilla marketers set goals that can be met by creating an unmistakable path to the goals and benchmarks along the way to measure progress. Operating under this credo will grease your path to profits.

Making goals too easy is not realistic. Easy goals require no stretch. Stretching yourself will produce the best results. Was John F. Kennedy's goal to put men on the moon a stretch goal? Did that stretch goal produce the best results and eventual success? The answer is obviously a resounding yes, and we now know the moon is not made of cheese.

Setting goals that are unreasonably high will cause you to become frustrated, discouraged, and defeated. Do you think a pole-vaulter sets his crossbar at 30 feet with the hopes of making it when the world record for men is just over 20 feet? A height of 30 feet is not realistic.

Here is a quick checklist of questions to give your goals a reality check:

- Can I really and truly do this?

- Have I come close before with similar efforts?
- Do the numbers, timeframe, and dollars seem somewhat practical?
- Has my competition or have other companies done similar things?
- Am I avoiding the attitude/mindset that says, "There is no way possible this can be accomplished"?

If you answered yes to the questions above, then your goals are realistic.

The biggest reality test is whether your goals are credible. Do you believe in your goals? Believability is what motivates you toward accomplishment. I'm not talking about whether others believe your goals are possible, but whether you do. You are the one who must believe because it's you that must be motivated to complete them and to fulfill the stated purpose. You are reading this book for your benefit, not someone else's.

Not all marketing goals need to be a stretch. Remember your purpose and the overall plan and business goals it's tied into. Some goals will be accomplished more easily than others. Gratification is important. This will keep you motivated to attack and accomplish your more challenging goals.

Your marketing goals should be recorded, either handwritten or logged into a computer. This allows for tracking, evaluating, measuring, and managing.

There's nothing better than scratching an item off a to-do list. That's the feeling you'll have when you accomplish your goals. Completion is a good habit. The completion of simpler goals is the foundation of loftier, more challenging goals. Challenge is good for growth. Inherently, your goal list will have a mix of the two goals.

Almost any goal, even the most challenging, can be made easier by breaking it down into smaller goals. The completion of the smaller goals builds confidence and momentum and eventually links to the completion of major goals and plans.

The statement at the beginning of the chapter pointed out that for each goal, you need to know where you're going so you know when it is accomplished. That is why the characteristics of being measurable and specific should be dripping off your goals.

Measurement is nothing fancy. It simply is what will tell you that your marketing is working and that your goal is accomplished. Establish goals that can be easily updated and tracked.

Prioritizing Goals

When people think of prioritization, they usually think of "What's most important?" or "What will give me the greatest return in the shortest amount of time?" While this is a good approach, you invariably run into situations where two goals are of equal importance. How do you prioritize these goals? Sometimes they are so close that you can work on them simultaneously. Which is more important, eating or breathing? They are equal and can still be treated as such.

Prioritization relates to focus. Which goal will you work on next? Which goal will get resources allocated to it? Just because you do one before the other doesn't always mean it is more important. Focus on completion as well as importance.

This does not imply working on goals one at a time. In today's fast-paced environment, multitasking is the name of the game. You will become the marketing octopus. Managing multiple goals and activities simultaneously can be done and will be done on earth as it is in guerrilla heaven, directing focus and resources as situations change and progress.

In today's world, you have more tools than ever to help you multitask. Cell phones, e-mail, instant messaging, voice mail, and PDAs allow you to be more efficient and effective than our forefathers who used single-tasked smoke signals or single telegraphs. This whole day could be spent discussing how best to multitask, but there is probably something else you should be doing.

Focus

We've used the word "focus" frequently when discussing goals. There is only one person that can make you focus, and that's you. You have to accept the responsibility to proceed down your path, to generate activity that will accomplish goals, and to hold yourself accountable. If you need help doing this, hire a guerrilla marketing coach. Ultimately, however, you are responsible. There will be distractions. They happen every day in our professional and personal lives. Accountability, attention, and action lead to goal focus.

Guerrilla marketing goals take into account the inevitability of change, changes that will occur in the market, in the economy, with technology, with customer demands, and with the guerrilla marketer personally.

When you set specific, measurable, believable goals and begin measuring your activity against them every day, your everyday activity is managed and focused in full support of these goals. This eventually starts to happen as a matter of course and becomes your marketing habit. Effort that is over and above set goals dramatically increases the speed and efficiency of the ensuing success. Faster success is better than slower success. Guerrilla success comes from focused guerrilla habits.

DAY 2 SUMMARY

- Devoting time and energy at the beginning of your planning process, along with setting your sights and defining the results expected of your marketing, will give you a far greater chance of success.

- Your marketing goals are nothing more than a statement of what results you want to achieve with your marketing.

- Marketing goals should fit into and support your overall business goals.

- A true guerrilla marketer knows that the selection and assortment of goals can be broad, but each individual goal must be specific, focused, and measurable.

- Guerrilla marketers set goals that can be met by creating an unmistakable path to the goals and benchmarks along the way to measure progress.

- Your marketing goals should be recorded, either written down or logged into a computer.

- You have to accept the responsibility to proceed down your path, generate activity that will accomplish goals, and hold yourself accountable.

■ ■ ■

Action Steps

1. Make a list of goals you have achieved lately. These could be big goals or smaller steps that led to lofty goals.

2. The place to begin envisioning the goal-setting process is looking at your starting point. Answer the following questions:

   - What does your company or organization have now?

   - Are you a startup company, a company under new management, or just in a situation where you need to renew your efforts?

   - Do you have current customers/prospects for current products/services?

   - Are you known by some prospects, or are you an unknown in your marketplace?

3. After answering these questions, you want an understanding of

   - What you strive to be, what your desired future is, and where you are going, both as a company and as a marketer. (Because this is guerrilla marketing in 30 days and not guerrilla management in 30 days, concentrate on answering this from a marketing perspective.)

   - Why you come to work every day.

   - How you intend to get where you want to be from where you are. Although this could be a thesis on business and marketing plans, that is not the intent here. It is a general question to put your mind in the perspective of getting from point A to point B. It is not the details that count here, but rather the general attitudinal scope of your thinking. Examples would be spending more time on the planning process, working as a planning group to brainstorm new product and service ideas, evaluating customer demands relative to what you deliver, or building an infrastructure of equipment and people to deliver products and services to your niche in the marketplace.

4. Brainstorm actual goals:

- Define the purpose of your marketing.

- Translate purpose into as many specific marketing goals as possible. Note: Don't confuse specific goals with detailed tactics.

- Write these goals down or record them in your computer.

- Roughly give some thought and identify what resources (time and money) are required to reach your goals.

- Review the goals with the reality checks described above.

- Announce your goals to an associate, coach, friend, or family member.

- Define what each goal will look like when accomplished.

5. You will hit roadblocks, so you will need to be flexible. To prepare yourself as much as possible for roadblocks, consider the following:

- Write out any concerns related to goal completion.

- Find someone to talk to about your stumbling blocks.

- Discover what might stop you.

- Identify what resources might be needed to overcome the hurdles.

- Commit to overcoming these roadblocks.

Sunday	Monday	Tuesday	Wednesday	Thursday	Friday	Saturday
	1	2	3 ✓	4	5	6
7	8	9	10	11	12	13
14	15	16	17	18	19	20
21	22	23	24	25	26	27
28	29	30				

Competition and Research

IKE IT OR NOT, COMPETITION is all around us, especially in a tough economy. Competitors are just as interested in surviving and thriving in a down economy as you are. Don't kid yourself, free enterprise still prevails, tough times or not.

In the spirit of free enterprise, competition is a good thing. In the spirit of a competitor eating your lunch, it is not so good. If the latter is the case, you must research your market and your competition more to see what problems they are solving that you are not, what benefits they are offering that you are not, and how the marketplace views them compared to you.

Customer Research

At the same time you research your marketing and competition, you must research your customers:

- What problems do they have that need to be solved?
- How do they want them solved?
- What is it worth to them to have their problems solved?

The answers to these questions are not only a basis for your marketing plan, they are also major components of your business model.

This last question related to the worth of your solution essentially takes "price" right out of any purchase decision. If you can prove the value of your solution, a customer will be willing to pay slightly less than that worth, no matter what the absolute price is. So many businesses are involved in "quotes" or "bid business." Proving the value of solutions can sometimes bypass traditional auction pricing.

You must really nail down what is important to your customers. If it's not important to them, it's not important to you. Any questions?

The perfect example of qualitative research is the age-old commercial for Miller Lite beer that claim it tastes great and is less filling. These are the two primary reasons people buy the product. Miller spent a lot of time and money to make sure these benefits were something its customers wanted, determined how much they wanted them, and then crafted its marketing around this research.

A guerrilla marketer knows everything going on in his marketplace, including information about leading prospects/customers and competitors. One of the first steps of a guerrilla marketing attack is gaining knowledge. There are many forces and factors behind how customers purchase products and services. Gaining this knowledge goes a long way toward earning your guerrilla designation.

Market research is a critical component in the overall business planning process. Many small businesses and entrepreneurs ignore this step. Guerrilla marketers do not. They realize that the return on the research investment will pay off in the long run many times over, but not in the short run.

As a guerrilla marketer, you are typically interested in two types of research. The first is quantitative, or how much of something. The other type is qualitative market research, which relates to why customers purchase.

A good example of quantitative research is to find out market share or how many in a certain group buy or do something. Radio and TV ratings are

Primary Components of Research

- What is being bought and where?

- Who is buying what from whom?

- Why do customers buy the way they do?

- How do these components predict future purchasing behavior?

- What influences customers to buy—marketing/promotion/advertising?

- What creates customer satisfaction?

- What brands are customers/prospects aware of?

- What media/advertising reaches customers best?

- What is the price that customers are willing to pay?

- What are the forecasted marketing trends?

quantitative market research. Preference studies are quantitative in nature (e.g., 76 percent of the tested group preferred sweetened iced tea over unsweetened). Based on this example, if you were introducing an unsweetened iced tea product, you would know that your market size is drastically less than the sweetened market. Without this knowledge you have no idea what size your market opportunity is, whether you should be shooting at this particular target, or whether you will even hit it.

There is little room for guesswork in business today. There is little room for guesswork in your marketing. Obtaining information that is to the point, objective, and thorough is essential to success. That happens only through research and testing.

Identifying the Competitor's Achilles Heel

A primary component of a research-based guerrilla marketing attack is insight into your competition. At some point you will develop a competitive advantage or unique selling point/proposition. The only way to know that you have an advantage is to know what the competition has and does not have.

In *Guerrilla Marketing* (3rd edition), you learn that your competitive advantage is a great marketing weapon. Your competitive advantage is the benefit you offer that your competitor does not. Research reveals this. Experience reveals this. Customers tell us this.

If you don't think you have a competitive advantage, it's time to put your thinking cap on. Some generic descriptions often heard are—"master brewed," "organically grown," "professionally tested." These are all competitive advantages. Marketers wearing thinking caps created these. They basically identify something that was already being done or a characteristic that already existed. Others might provide the same, but only if one talks about them and promotes them can they become competitive advantages. If only one company tells customers that a common feature is a unique benefit, that company then has a competitive advantage.

Mastering Guerrilla Marketing (Mariner Books) presents four criteria that a competitive advantage must meet:

1. It is a positive benefit—one of the ways people gain by doing business with you.
2. You are the only one that offers it—or so your customers think because you are the only one talking about it.
3. Your advantage can be communicated with a few, well-selected words.
4. People know it's you when they hear it or see it.

Opportunity Research

Market research and competitive intelligence anticipate emerging threats and uncover opportunities. There are many public sources, online and offline, where information on competition and the market environment can be focused.

A guerrilla marketer knows who the ideal customers are and what the competition is doing to go after them.

Your intensive research will uncover the potential market in which you will work and play, the customers within, and what is appealing to them now—appealing enough for them to pull out their wallets to spend money on your products and services. This could be classified as "top-of-wallet" appeal. Once you know these appealing factors, you can draft your strategies, tactics, and plan of attack. Be prepared, then, to put money in your wallet.

Today, we are blessed with the good fortune of technology to help with our research. Thank goodness for the internet, a tremendous research tool. Obviously, a competitor's website is a wide open door to peer through, almost an invitation to come visit. That didn't exist before. You can even buy something and understand the purchasing experience that you are up against, all under the disguise of an online browser/purchaser. Offline purchasing is also popular competitive research, but it can be awkward and uncomfortable if sleuthing is not your thing.

The internet allows a guerrilla marketer to carry out research in the following ways:

- Visit a competitor's website.
- Visit a customer's website.
- Visit a prospect's website.
- Participate or visit newsgroups and information forums.
- Mine sites for information.
- Extract and explore databases.
- Purchase competitive products and services.
- Find and contact strategic alliances.
- Communicate quicker than ever with customers, prospects, and employees.
- Conduct surveys.
- Test market products, surveys, headlines, and advertising.

The more information you gather, the better equipped you are to compete. This bears repeating and is the whole essence of research: The more information you gather, the better equipped you are to compete.

Research is most valuable if it is done regularly. Do your research before your competition does.

Guerrilla marketers are rarely taken by surprise. Plans and activities must be adjusted once important information is gathered, especially in reaction to what the research reveals about competition and customer demands.

The "Big Three"

Asking prospects and customers the Big Three questions is the first step in that potential repositioning:

1. What is your current supplier doing for you that you like?

2. What is your current supplier doing that you don't like?

3. If you could wave a magic wand and change things about your current supplier, what would you change?

When prospects start frequenting competitors, it may be a signal that you need to reposition yourself against the competition or at least research why prospects are moving to others.

Hiring a market research firm to help you with this research may be in order. However, nothing strengthens a relationship more than a one-on-one dialogue with a customer or prospect. Asking these questions helps you do this. On the other hand, prospects and customers may be more willing to speak honestly with an objective third party than with someone directly going after their business. Here, the process isn't as important as the answers to the Big Three.

When a guerrilla marketer researches the marketplace, it really means researching the market opportunity, products, services, media options, competition, industry, prospects, customers, technology, benefits, partnerships, external forces/threats, the economy, and more. The absence of this research is like taking off on your bike with no wheels. You will fall flat on your face and then realize you have a problem.

DAY 3 SUMMARY

■ At the same time you research your marketing and your competition, you must research your customers.

■ A guerrilla marketer knows everything going on in his marketplace, including information about leading prospects/customers and competitors.

■ Market research is a critical component in the overall business planning process.

■ The only way to know that you have a competitive advantage is to know what the competition has and does not have.

■ Market research and competitive intelligence anticipates emerging threats and uncovers opportunities.

■ A guerrilla marketer knows who the ideal customers are and what the competition is doing to go after them.

■ ■ ■

Action Steps

1. List your top three competitors that you want to research.

2. List the top three benefits of each competitor.

3. List your top three benefits.

4. Compare the competitor's benefit list with yours.

5. Describe your uniqueness compared to these competitors.

6. Write down every reason you can think of to do business with your company. Now do the same for your top competitors. Scratch off the common ones. Are the remaining reasons good enough to be your competitive advantage? Do you need more?

7. Visit three competitive websites and answer the following:

   • Does the company appear easy to do business with?

   • How does the company's identity compare with yours?

- What is appealing; what is not?
- How can you make your site better as a result of this review?

8. Survey five customers and five prospects by telephone with the Big Three questions.

9. Summarize what customers want that competitors aren't providing.

10. Summarize what customers are getting from competitors that they aren't getting from you.

11. Buy something from two competitors online or off. Document the pros and cons of the process.

12. Create a log for ongoing research and document your findings for the 30 days you read this book. Document anything you find that is on the list of research components at the beginning of this chapter. Concentrate on the benefits

- offered by you.
- offered by competitors.
- wanted by prospects and customers.
- wished for by prospects and customers.

Target Market

OCEAN CLUB RESORTS (oceanclubresorts.com) hired Cheryl Andrews Marketing Communications (cherylandrewsmarketing.com) to aim marketing communication at their newly defined target markets. The firm helped the resort focus its communication on the target markets of family vacationers, travelers in an upscale market, and a diving tourism. This was a clear case of putting publicity and marketing communication where the desired, potential buyers were located. Ocean Club Resort's communication clearly hits its target.

Sometimes marketing boils down to the point where it is easy to market if you know what to market and to whom to market. The last part of this statement is more than half of marketing. The right marketing with the right products to the wrong target is like a hunter shooting into the wind without hitting anything.

Imagine a duck hunter lying in a field early one damp morning surrounded by dozens of white flapping decoys. He's firing a shotgun into the air, aiming at a target that's flying in formation across the flyway. Now, imagine another hunter nearby, firing into the rising sun, and hoping, just hoping, that a trophy will fly by at the exact moment his spray of buckshot arrives.

The second hunter has little chance of ever needing a taxidermist. He has all the right equipment, but instead of setting his sights on a defined target, he's simply scatter shooting. Unfortunately, that is often the way businesses market their products and services. Sure, they put out ads, direct mail pieces, and other marketing materials, but then they sit back and hope that a buyer flies by just in time to need what they're selling. Everybody talks about target markets and taking aim. On Day 4, you will learn more than simply how to quack with a shrill duck call.

When it comes to target marketing, all activities need to be aimed as specifically as that successful duck hunter aims.

Think about how some businesses start out: They spend a lot of money identifying themselves to the marketplace, build a brand, then lose it all when they add services unrelated to their core purpose. Consider a long distance company that starts selling phone hardware or a gas station that begins serving fried chicken. What about commercial printers who add copy services? Sometimes shifts like these confuse customers, who end up transferring their allegiance to a business that better hits the target. They go where offers are more clearly defined, presented, and executed.

Targeting involves determining who buys what, why they buy it, and where they buy it. Identifying these factors is essential to your marketing and to using your resources in the most efficient way possible.

Narrowing Your Scope

You have to know to whom you want to sell your products and services before you can successfully zero in on them with your marketing efforts. Clearly identifying your target will help you create marketing materials that hit them squarely in the bull's eye.

For many years, savvy marketers have created strategies to sell to specific groups of buyers. The first known direct mail effort was when a certain

Regnault de Mouçon, Bishop of Chartres, sent fundraising requests to some high rollers in France and England. The objective: rebuilding his cathedral that had burned to the ground. The target: wealthy citizens with money to spare. The year: 1194. As you can see, target marketing was just as important 800 years ago as it is today!

To succeed in targeting does not mean you have to invest in specialty equipment or exotic service delivery. The important thing is to know what business you're in and what your typical customers want and need. Product and service offerings can then be planned around ideal clients. That's target marketing. Take aim.

Sometimes guerrillas ask, "How can I compete with large companies?" The best way to compete is to narrow your niche, then market and sell to it aggressively. If you want to soar with the big ducks, you have to find your piece of the sky and flap your wings.

That piece of sky might not be as obvious as the nose on your face; it may not be the most obvious niche, just waiting for someone to fly in and clean up. In reality, it's probably a smaller, less popular, and less worked niche that would thrive given the proper attention. The secret to cultivating a niche is that the more time you spend in it, the more expert you become, the more you expand your territory, and the more people you can expose to your expertise. People like to buy from experts. Being an expert is a tremendous positioning strategy. The one that bags the most ducks is usually an expert hunter.

Taking Dead Aim

Lying in that field, the experienced hunter listens intently for the sounds of the elusive ducks in the distance. He thinks ahead, so he's ready when he first sees the beaked heads of that small flock migrate across the early morning sky.

The key to targeting is planning ahead. Start by asking, "Who will benefit the most from my products and services?" The answer to this question is not the oft heard "everybody." If you think "everybody" is your target market, you have a high probability of running out of marketing money to market to this false mark. Begin building a detailed profile of your current customers.

Why do they do business with you? What do they have in common? How can you best service their current and future needs? Then, think about the "perfect customer." If you could magically create the ideal client, what would he or she look like?

Analyze the profiles of your most successful accounts and then devise a plan to reach potential customers who share their traits. Narrow your niche and sell it aggressively. Find your piece of the sky.

Part of the research that you did on Day 3 related to finding out as much as possible about your prospects. These are people with common characteristics, habits, desires, and activities that are different than the total group represented in a market or a niche. Each was uncovered in your prospect research. If this market is one that you feel you can sell to with success, it is a great candidate to be in your target market.

Target Market Considerations
Characteristics

Characteristics are sometimes defined as demographics when they relate to a market. Age, income, occupation, and ethnicity are demographic characteristics that can describe a market. Usually characteristics are measurable statistics. They are the questions the U.S. census taker asks.

Habits

Habits, or lifestyles, describe what your target market likes. Do they like less filling and more taste, or do they like vivid colors and loud music? Habits are also sometimes referred to as psychographics and relate to values, beliefs, and lifestyles.

Desires

Desires represent the demands or expectations a target market has. Do customers go first class in everything they buy or are they always looking for something on sale? Do they value delivery and availability or price and quality? What do they really want?

Activity

Activity describes typical practices of those in a target market. Do they buy books once a week and only socially drink at a dinner party? Do they always take a spring break vacation to the south or frequent a particular food store weekly? Do they do their own taxes and financial planning, or do they seek the help of a paid professional?

Geography

One more distinguishing factor about a target market is geography, the location of those that purchase from you. Geography is where your prospects do business and the area where you will sell your product. Are you global? Do you have a territory? Can you only serve a particular county, state, or region?

Here are examples of target market descriptions using the above considerations:

- Minority franchise business owners between the ages of 35 and 55 earning more than $50,000 annually.
- Families of three or more people who drive minivans because of their size and fuel efficiency.
- Teenagers who like rock 'n' roll music and buy CDs from shopping malls.
- Families who frequent Hawaii once per year during spring break.

Target markets are described and identified to make all strategies related to product and service design, pricing, distribution, packaging, and advertising more complete, comprehensive, cost effective, and efficient.

In the examples above, the marketing message and your marketing weapons are created to appeal to those prospects.

A targeted message particular to your market, rather than general mass communication you hope appeals to someone, can also be developed. Knowing who you are aiming at will allow you to create marketing strategies and communication that are direct hits, rather than shotgun sprays. Good guerrilla marketing is made up of direct hits.

Define your target market as tightly as you can. The tighter the definition, the higher the probability of hitting your target with your marketing. You can purchase or compile a list of target market members for any target market definition you can develop and define. Your list is your market.

Pulling the Trigger

You may not have realized it before, but by focusing on growing your business, you were actually targeting—finding customers who share defined ideal customer profiles. Now it's important to take the next step.

By identifying how you got your current customers, you can create more efficient marketing strategies that hit your target more accurately. By breaking down what you do best into smaller segments, you can capture niches that grow your business. You can capitalize on particular market opportunities by determining how to use your existing product and service offerings to make your customers more successful.

Your best prospect is a current customer. Your second best prospect is a past customer. These sets of target market members already know you, already like you, already trust you, and already have confidence in your products and services. It is much easier to sell to someone who already likes, knows, and trusts you than to go out and build this with those that do not know you. When putting on that marketing hat, you might think that you always have to go out and find new prospects. You really don't. All you have to do is to market to those that know, like, and trust you, over and over on a continuous, consistent basis. Sometimes this means that you have to make sure that your marketing is complete with each and every prospect. One thing you really don't want to hear from a potential purchaser is, "I didn't know you offered that!" This kind of statement indicates that the marketing to this target market member is incomplete. In this case the best prospect is the person that didn't know that you offered what they exclaimed about. It bears repeating: "Your best prospect is a current customer!"

This targeting concept also suggests that over half of your marketing dollars should be spent on current customers. That number surprises people all the time. Once again, when people think "marketing" they are usually thinking it means finding new people. Marketing to current customers has a higher degree of success than cold marketing.

Start focusing on your target today and you'll soon wake up one morning to more ducks on the pond than you ever thought possible.

DAY 4 SUMMARY

■ It is easy to market if you know what to market and to whom.

■ When it comes to target marketing, all activities need to be aimed as specificly as possible.

■ Targeting involves determining who buys what, why they buy it, and where they buy it.

■ You have to know to whom you want to sell your products and services before you can successfully zero in on them with your marketing efforts.

■ By identifying how you got your current customers, you can create more efficient marketing strategies that hit your target more accurately.

■ ■ ■

Action Steps

1. If you have customers now, describe each of the target market attributes for the majority of them:
   - Characteristics
   - Habits
   - Activities
   - Desires
   - Geography

2. Why do your customers do business with you?

3. What do they buy?

4. Can these target markets be broken down into even smaller segments?

5. Describe the perfect customer/ideal client using the criteria in step 1 for a target market.

6. What other prospects share this profile?

7. What characteristics, habits, activities, desires, or geography must you address to appeal to the prospects identified in step 6?

8. Do you see any trends or changes in your target market that you should address with your business, products, or services?

Positioning

GUERRILLA HINT: This is one of our favorite days because of the power behind positioning, in tough times and good times, and the related cost (no cost) of this marketing.

Consider HSR, an integrated marketing communications agency in Cincinnati, Ohio, (hsr.com). It has developed such a powerful positioning statement that it uses in advertisement copy. In a recent *Wall Street Journal* ad, big bold letters stated:

WE HELP INDUSTRY
LEADERS DEFEND
PREMIUM BRANDS
IN RAPIDLY
COMMODITIZING
BUSINESS MARKETS

It ends with a toll-free number, cites a prestigious award it won, and makes a website reference. That's it. This ad is its positioning statement. It represents clarity at its finest, and our guerrilla hats are off to CEO Rich Segal for the leadership and vision that led to this positioning.

During a recent World Series game, there were 12 pop flies and 6 singles. Batters hit to fielders in position to catch the pop flies for easy outs those 12 times. The 6 times the balls were struck for base hits, the batter hit where fielders weren't positioned to make a play. As Wee Willie Keeler said in 1897 in response to how a man of his size could hit so well, "It's simple. I keep my eyes clear and I hit 'em where they ain't." In Willie's case, he positioned his hits for success. In the fielders' case, they weren't in position for success.

Your marketing requires positioning for success. Positioning is considered one of the core elements of marketing strategy. Positioning is more than a catchy tag line or a heavily promoted feature or brand. It is more than being at the right place at the right time, and it is more than having a crackerjack sales team (although any of these can cause one-time windfall profits). Positioning is actually a base upon which all other marketing focused on the goal of building relationships with a target market develops.

A well thought-out positioning statement defines a company's vision and direction. It describes

- who you really are as a company.

- what business you are really in.

- who exactly buys your products and services.

- product and service demands by your market.

- competitive advantages and unique value you offered.

David Ogilvy, one of the best-known names in American advertising circles, stated that marketing results depend less on how advertising is written than on how the product or service is positioned.

Positioning is more than clever manipulation of a market's perception. It truly is a statement of your company or organization's true identity and true value to a target market. It is truly what your business will stand for in the minds of your prospects and customers.

Positioning involves planting these "seeds of perception" in the minds of prospects and customers. When and if a prospect or customer wants what you are offering you want them to think of you first and eventually buy from you. This will happen if you have planted enough of these seeds of perception. That's positioning. That's Guerrilla Marketing.

All of these define a company much more strategically than a catchy tag line or a repeat commercial during the Super Bowl. These form the foundation of the relationship that a company has with the markets it serves. And you know how important relationships are in the world of guerrilla marketing!

While the baseball example above describes a physical positioning, your marketing world requires a mental positioning. That mental positioning has to happen in an already crowded mind. With the daily communication barrage, being first, unique, and memorable becomes the underlying challenge of the best positioning. It requires targeting your message to a very narrow segment within your target market, directly to the minds of your potential customers.

Harry Beckwith, in his book, *Selling the Invisible* (Warner Books), says, "A position is a cold-hearted, no nonsense statement of how you are perceived in the minds of your prospects." He goes on further to explain, "It is the positioning statement that describes how you wish to be perceived. It is the core message you want to deliver every time you market."

According to Al Ries and Jack Trout in their marketing classic *Positioning, The Battle for Your Mind* (McGraw-Hill), "Positioning is not something you do with a product. Positioning is what you do in the mind of a prospect. That is, you put the product in the mind of the prospect." The same goes for services.

Positioning strategies must have amazing clarity. When stating positioning to clients or prospects either in writing or verbally, you want them to remember what you are positioning and motivate them to want more information about what you have. In most cases, you only have a very short time to do this. This positioning isn't always just rattling off a fancy tagline or revealing feature after feature. The positioning states what your prospects want so that they will bust your door down trying to get it.

In *The 22 Laws of Immutable Marketing* (HarperBusiness), Al Ries and Jack Trout clearly state, "All that exists in the world of marketing are perceptions in the minds of the customer or the prospect. The perception is reality."

It takes a visionary outlook to decide how you want the target marketplace to perceive you. Your positioning statement must also be visionary. You must have vision related to the value of your product and service and why it is unique or different than what the competitor is offering. This vision, coupled with all of your benefits, is the primary component of a positioning statement.

Answering the questions, Who is my target market? and What am I really selling? will provide the basis for your positioning. These two questions should be asked more often than just at the start of a new business. Markets change, customer demands change, and competition changes. The answers to these questions may direct you to more than one target, too. Once you identify all of your target markets, you are ready to take aim for their profit bull's-eyes with your positioning arrows.

Guerrilla Marketing says that when you have clearly focused on your markets, you can clarify a market position. This focus should measure the position against four criteria:

1. Does my position offer a benefit that my target market audience really wants?
2. Is it an honest to goodness benefit?
3. Does it truly separate me from my competition?
4. Is it unique or difficult to copy?

Unless the answers to these questions make you the positioning king or queen, keep refining. Customer input will help you refine further.

When you are satisfied with your answers, you will have a sensible position—a position that will lead to your marketing and company goals. No guerrilla marketer would think of doing any marketing without a proper marketing plan that includes strategic thinking and a statement related to positioning. Guerrillas must carve out a position where their company or organization stands tall for something. The ensuing marketing must reflect that carved-out position and that tall stance. This carved-out position is stated in the marketing plan and is apparent in every marketing weapon used. If it isn't, repeat this chapter.

Although positioning is more than a catchy tag line, there are associations that sound like tag lines that describe companies in terms of the perceptions in their customers' and prospects' minds. Consider the following:

- *Southwest Airlines* is the no frills, fun airline—definitely a perception and positioning.
- *7-Up is the Uncola.* We've all heard it and we all know exactly what its position is in the soft drink market.
- *United Airlines.* Friendly skies and friendly service, globally.
- *Federal Express.* Trust us to get it there overnight. This is a good example of a positioning with two components—overnight and trust, again putting a particular perception in the mind of the consumer.
- *Crest Toothpaste.* Fewer cavities.

In your guerrilla marketing mindset of time, energy, and imagination and focus on small business, you are probably thinking, "These are nice and these are brands I recognize. But I thought guerrilla marketing was geared toward small businesses like mine." You are correctamundo!

Some small business examples you probably have never heard of but will recognize as niche-oriented and well positioned are:

- *Expert Plumbing.* We never close—positioned as being open for your emergencies 24/7.
- *Inline Chiropractic.* Chiropractic for figure skaters, definitely a niche. Would you go there if you were a baseball player?
- *The Diabetic Chef.* Take-out meals for diabetics—again, niched and positioned in the mind of diabetics wanting take-out meals.

Other examples to consider are

- an appliance business that can provide the most affordable kitchen appliances to cost-conscious buyers.
- an education-oriented company that has the largest selection of educational tapes and books for parents of teenagers.
- the most cost-effective place for sports aficionados to purchase sporting goods online.
- the most complete source of health and fitness tips for people over the age of 50.
- the only company that combines online purchasing of French wine with in-home sampling.

Notice how crystal clear and narrowly targeted each of these are. Once you have a crystal clear positioning statement, communication to your target market becomes easier.

Upon a recent visit to Ann Arbor, Michigan, I completed my business at hand and ventured on to my hotel stay for the night. I had reservations at the local Holiday Inn. Upon arriving at the venue, I noticed a banner, prominently displayed at this hotel. The banner stated that the Holiday Inn that I was arriving at was changing its name. I certainly didn't remember any news of the Holiday Inn being acquired or merged with another company. As I approached, I noticed the proverbial small print at the bottom of the banner. The small print explained the name change: "We are changing our name to—The Holiday Inn, the Hotel Closest to the University of Michigan." I scoffed and moved inside to check in. As I was checking in, the hotel phone rang and the person checking me in answered it, "Hello, The Holiday Inn, The hotel closest to the University of Michigan, may I help you?" I then realized what was going on. The banner, the phone greeting, and their other marketing was planting seeds of perception that positioned this Holiday Inn location as the hotel closest to the University of Michigan. I have reason to return to Ann Arbor for business and pleasure. Upon my return I need a hotel close to the University of Michigan. I can't help but think of this Holiday Inn. They have positioned themselves and told me clearly that they are the hotel closest to the University of Michigan. Just by making a statement, they have positioned their business.

What did this bit of marketing cost? The answer is almost nothing—a banner modification is still low cost and/or no cost marketing. This is the essence of Guerrilla Marketing that will have an infinite return. Infinite returns on marketing investment are very guerrilla like.

When creating your own positioning statement, consider these factors:

- *Be unique.* What one thing can you say that positions you as the only company in the world that can do it? Think extremes—the fastest, best, largest, most convenient, etc.
- *Make it benefit-oriented.* You know your target audience. You know what they want and need. You know what will satisfy them the most and what will keep them coming back to you. What will always keep you

at the top of their mind from an awareness point of view? What will always keep you at the top of their wallet from a purchasing point of view?

Capitalize on Your Strengths and the Competition's Weaknesses

Your strengths must be promoted, communicated, and remembered the most. Your weaknesses—yes, we all have them—should be minimized in your communication and marketing. Aiming your strength right at the weakness of a competitor is a rifle shot to your target with your positioning ammo.

Position Benefits as Value-Oriented

Price is not always the number-one value that a consumer is looking for. Your analysis of your target market's wants and needs will determine what value is required. Unless you are the lowest cost producer or deliverer, don't let price lead your positioning. Added value is an over-used term from the '90s, but does apply here if value is truly offered and a part of the customer experience.

A final point of positioning involves planting that perception seed that you are an expert. Many reading this will immediately proclaim, "I don't think I'm an expert," or, "Can I really tell people I am an expert?"

Consider this:

I recently followed up with a contact that I had made at a networking event. During the course of the follow-up discussion I very pointedly asked the person what her job was. She indicated to me that she was a consultant. When I pursued this description, I found out she was a consultant who works with companies to put leadership programs and training in place. I immediately notified her that she was no longer to position herself as a consultant but as a "Leadership Expert."

She called me the day after our lunch meeting and exclaimed that she was just successful signing a contract for business with a prospect that she had been working on for many months. She positioned herself as an expert and she got business. People like to buy from experts, people trust experts, buyers have confidence in the work of experts. Use the title. It's OK to do.

Everyone reading this book, right now, is an expert in something. I am a Guerrilla Marketing expert and proclaim myself so. That is part of my positioning. Your positioning can be a similar proclamation of your expertise. What are you an expert at? I recently ran across a "transportation expert." This came from a taxi-cab driver in New York City.

Positioning is no-cost marketing and is very powerful. Many parts of Guerrilla Marketing can be highly leveraged marketing. That leverage is good when revenues skyrocket and marketing costs are low or non-existent. That leverage happens on this day with positioning.

Whereas positioning is the battle for your mind, your marketing is the battle for your prospect's wallet. If you don't position and battle for it, your competition will.

Market positioning can also be viewed as a promise from you to your target market. Delivering on that promise is done with all of the tactics discussed and planned during these 30 days of marketing. Positioning is a true guerrilla marketing component. Keeping your promise is a true guerrilla value.

DAY 5 SUMMARY

- ◼ Your marketing requires positioning for success.
- ◼ Positioning is more than a catchy tag line or a heavily promoted feature or brand.
- ◼ A position is how you are perceived in the minds of your prospects and customers.
- ◼ Positioning strategies must have amazing clarity.
- ◼ Once you have a crystal clear positioning statement, communication to your target market becomes easier.

■ Market positioning is a promise from you to your target market.

■   ■   ■

Action Steps

1. Complete the following:
   - Who do you offer benefits to?
   - What are the primary benefits?
   - What are any secondary benefits?
   - Who is your target market?
   - Who are you and what is your business all about?
   - What problems do you solve?
   - What are the most important benefits to your target market/segment?
   - What competitors offer the same benefits that you do?
   - Why can you offer these benefits better than competition? If this area is light, what increased value must you develop to achieve unique status?

2. Brainstorm tag lines in ten words or less. For example:
   - For an appliance store: "We cook it, chill it, clean it, and grill it"
   - For a financial planner: "Building Your Future Dreams"
   - For a health insurance agent: "Taking Care of You When You Need It Most"
   - For a local delivery service: "On their desk, out of your hands"
   - For a professional organizer: "Places, spaces, and peace of mind"

3. Do you know of any competitors that
   - were first to market?
   - have a great sales force?
   - just got lucky?

   Do these competitors have a real position or positioning strategy, or do they just rely on the above factors?

4. What is your perception and the market perception of the following, and how would you characterize the positioning of each:

- Sony

- Pepsi

- Ford Truck

- Your local chiropractor

- Your local florist

- Your favorite pizza delivery service

- Your local dry cleaner

- One of your favorite vendors

5. Why are they your favorite? Is that reason related to their positioning?

6. Fill in the blanks.

I represent a _____company and work with _____ who wants to improve/increase its _____ by _____.

7. What is the number-one thing you want your competitors to know and remember about you?

8. Write out your position statement.

Sunday	Monday	Tuesday	Wednesday	Thursday	Friday	Saturday
	1	2	3	4	5	6 ✓
7	8	9	10	11	12	13
14	15	16	17	18	19	20
21	22	23	24	25	26	27
28	29	30				

Niche Marketing

THERE IS A HIGH-END MENSWEAR label in New York City that has made a name for itself with masterfully tailored suits in fine woolens, top-notch shirts in the richest fabrics, such as cottons and fine-gauge knits, and neckwear.

Though classic in its roots, the label is thoroughly modern in its perspective and reflects the owners' love of dynamic color and texture combinations. Modernity is also suggested by edgy yet subtle details separating their clothes from those of other apparel makers and tailors and provides them with a sure niche in menswear. Their niche, which combines class with a hint of rogue, is why their products are attractive to high-style celebrities and well-known athletes. They target these people. They don't target everybody.

Everybody Is Not a Niche

One danger of entrepreneurial planning and execution, whether strategic or marketing, is trying to be everything to everybody. Just like "everybody" is not a target market, "everybody" is not a niche. No one company can effectively service everybody. It is for this reason that in the first week of your 30 days of guerrilla marketing, you will select and define your niche.

Concentrating your guerrilla marketing efforts on a specific segment of people in a target market will allow you to build a stellar reputation. Stellar reputations are magnets for prospective buyers.

A niche market is simply a very specific portion of a much larger target market. Niche marketing allows you to target a very specific audience and to give them exactly what they want and need (e.g., a target market niche that needs marketing consulting). Marketing consulting is a broad target market. Direct mail consulting, PR consulting, and strategic marketing planning are all niches within the broader target market.

Mark Victor Hansen, co-author of the *Chicken Soup for the Soul* series (HCI) and *The One Minute Millionaire* (Harmony), says "get rich in your niche." While neither guerrilla marketing nor Mark Victor Hansen are proponents of get-rich-quick programs, the point is to focus, serve what you serve best, and prosper accordingly, and prosper you will if you have found your niche. A target market that is too broad causes inefficiencies, higher costs, and underdeveloped customer service and attention. Narrowing a focus creates more of an environment for success. It is an opportunity to stand out, to be an expert, and be at the top of your customers' or prospects' minds for your targeted product or service area.

A niche market is a limited, crystal clear range of products or services sold to a tightly focused target group, all with particular wants and needs served by the niche products and services.

What's Different?

When considering the target markets that you operate in, you must consider what you offer that's different. You heard that when we discussed positioning. You'll hear it when we talk about benefits. You know by now that your differences are primary components of guerrilla marketing. The products and services you offer that are the same as everyone else's cannot be marketed or sold as effectively as those that are unique. The benefit you offer that the competition doesn't is a huge competitive advantage. Your differences and advantages can be sold and marketed.

If you don't have differences, you must find them, develop them, or create them. This is the basis of niche marketing.

Finding a niche is like finding a few select trees to camp under in a vast forest. You can't camp under the entire forest. You can only camp under one or two trees. The same goes for niche marketing. Select a few products, services, and targets to market to your customers.

The opposite of niche marketing is mass marketing. Take the marketing consultant example. The mass approach is that the marketing consultant serves small- to medium-size businesses. He might work with a chiropractor in the morning, a financial planner midday, and a small manufacturer in the afternoon. The niche marketer would consult only with chiropractors all day and not the other business types. A real niche-master would only work with one segment of the market and consult for one niche of that market. PR for chiropractors is a niched target market for a marketing consultant. Niche marketing is precision marketing, a rifle shot at a small target.

Niche marketing is well-developed in both the legal and medical fields. In each you see a high degree of specialization and tremendous focus on just one area. These specialists are usually the highest paid practitioners in their field. High pay is a good reason to niche market. Think of patent attorneys, criminal defense attorneys, and corporate attorneys in the legal field. In the medical field there are lawyers for heart surgeons, bone specialists, and brain surgeons. Guerrilla marketing is not like brain surgery, except in its high degree of focus.

Niche marketing is also present in the real estate market. Many times, real estate guerrillas who are working in a particular market will tie their specialty to their name; that is what they want their customers and prospects to remember about them. Dan O'Brien of Falls Church, Virginia, uses his name to niche market. He markets to other O'Brien's in his area. This might bring a chuckle, but it truly is a niche and is successful for him.

Other real estate professionals have worked niches according to where they market or what they market. Examples include the Condominium Queen, the Pool Home Expert, and the Green Realtor (homes in a golf course community).

Cheryl Andrews Marketing (cherylandrewsmarketing.com) puts her niche and positioning right in her tag line: Public Relations for Sun Destinations, Resorts, Hotels, and Cruise Lines.

Focusing on a single niche in the marketplace can distinguish a business and provide a competitive advantage.

Niche Strategies

Niche strategies are developed and evolve because a particular target market need or demand is not satisfied. Finding that need and satisfying it quickly elevates you to market leadership. Being a market leader can lead to your position as an expert. This translates into top-of-mind awareness with your customers and prospects. Your reputation within your niche will spread and strengthen as you continue to service, nurture, and market to it. Being a niche marketer earns you many guerrilla points. Guerrilla points can be traded in for bank deposits.

Finding your niche will give you an identity that a competitor doesn't have. If you can continue to supply this niche with benefits that the competition doesn't, then success and profits are yours for the taking. After all you've given, it's time to take.

Seek a niche that is big enough to serve, but not so big that it attracts large competitors. At that point, the niche becomes a flooded market. A flooded market is not a niche.

Market niches are defined by products and services sold. Take the whole pizza market. Domino's Pizza delivers hot pizza in 30 minutes. Little Caesar's offers two pizzas for the price of one. Pizza Hut sells the pizza with cheese in the crust. Each one of these companies has a following and a group of customers that buys from them because of the niche they serve.

Niches are present in any broad market or industry. Imagine how many niches there are in the computer industry. The niche not thought of yet represents a guerrilla opportunity.

The bottom line is not only uniqueness in your product or service, but uniqueness in the customer experience. The most successful marketers look for and strive for a more unique experience for the customer than the competition

Niche Rules

Consider the following five niche rules. These are questions and key points that will help you develop and find your niche. Without following these rules, competitors, large or small, take over. Without following them competitors capture, satisfy and retain your customers:

1. *Expertise.* Are you an expert resource leader in what you do, in what you offer, and in what solutions you offer to satisfy customer needs?

2. *Exclusivity.* Are you the only one in a particular geographical area offering what your customer needs? Anytime you can say that you are the only one doing something, you have a niche. The question then becomes, Is the niche large enough to sustain your business model, your guerrilla marketing goals, and your overall success goals.

3. *Efficiency.* Do you do things quicker than competitors, offer more convenience than competitors, or provide something that eliminates hassles or saves time for your customers? This includes distribution and availability of your product or service. What can you do to make your product or service more convenient for your customers? More convenience from you means more inconvenience for your competitors.

4. *Customer satisfaction.* Marketing an inferior product or service is like riding a bicycle with no wheels. Good products and services are the wheels of your marketing. Is your technical support the best in a market? Is it what your customers want? Are your guarantees better than those of your competition? Is your customer delighted by doing business with you? Delight and satisfaction can be a niche. What can you do to personalize or customize something?

5. *Loyalty.* Will customers return? Have you earned repeat business? Did you provide a specific reason or benefit so that the customer will only return to you?

Examples of Market Leader Uniqueness— Guerrilla Style

- Gourmet dog food bakery

- Left-handed scissors store

- Vegetarian Italian restaurant

- Snowboarding boot shop

- Magic book store

- Natural death fur salon

- Fishing Lure of the Month Club

offers. Just look at any market leader. Something is different. Something is unique. Something makes more people buy from them than their competitors. What is unique about you? Why do people buy from you over the competition?

Notice lowest price did not make the niche market list. Stay away from this niche unless you are the lowest cost producer or the best buyer. In the spirit of guerrilla marketing, lowest price too often affects profitability and does not build relationships. A true guerrilla measures successful marketing by profits and relationships.

Having a difference, especially for small businesses and the entrepreneur, is not only a matter of success, it is a matter of survival. No difference? No success.

I recently presented *Guerrilla Marketing in 30 Days* to the Promotional Products Association. These are the people that sell ad specialties, trinkets, promotional gadgets, etc. When discussing the concept of "niche" with this group, a number of examples within their industry immediately came to the surface. Here are a few that are represented within the general industry of promotional products:

- Pencil and Pen Market
- Recognition Market
- High End Premium Market
- Electronic Gadgets
- Golf Outing Marketing

Niche Positioning

Once you know your niche, you will know in what publications to run your ads, articles, and PR. You will know what online forums to participate in. You will know what to send to those with open wallets waiting for you. They will then know where to look for you, where to find you, and how to empty their wallets for you. That is the ultimate of niche marketing; that is the ultimate of guerrilla marketing.

Once you have your niche, you can position yourself as the expert by writing articles or offering valuable information in other ways. You will then be recognized as an authority in your niche. Being recognized as an authority attracts not only prospects, but also strategic alliance partners who have related products or services, which can be mutually beneficial.

These activities and strategies contribute to your goal of dominating a chosen niche. As you are tightly focused on your target market's needs and wants, you're consistently positioning yourself as an expert and offering products and services that solve your target market's problems. The more of this you do, the closer you get to being a niche-master. Niche-masters eventually become guerrilla marketing masters.

Niches are common to all successful businesses, products, and services. Creating a niche does not require great expense. It's right in line with guerrilla marketing values. It does require great focus and great imagination. Focus and imagination are free. Put that with the time and energy you are devoting to these 30 days, and you have just defined guerrilla marketing—again.

DAY 6 SUMMARY

■ Everybody is not a target market. Everybody is also not a niche.

■ A niche market is simply a very specific slice of a much larger target market.

■ Narrowing a focus creates more of an environment for success, an opportunity to stand out, and a chance to be an expert and at the top of your customers' or prospects' minds for your niche product or service area.

■ When considering the different target markets that you operate in, you must consider what you offer that's different.

■ If you don't have differences, you must find them, develop them, or create them.

■ Niche strategies develop and evolve because a particular target market need or demand is not satisfied.

■ Finding your niche will give you an identity that your competition doesn't have.

■ ■ ■

Action Steps

1. Pick three markets and list the leaders in that market. What product, service, or customer satisfactions are provided by these leaders?

2. What special things do you do that your competitors don't? For example:
   - Remembering names, kid's names, and birthdays
   - Smiling
   - Giving something away
   - Bailing out a customer in an emergency; going the extra mile
   - Saying thank you; offering a cordial greeting
   - Calling to follow up; calling for any reason
   - Sending a reminder and/or a thank-you note
   - Referring

- Finding a hard-to-get product or service for the customer

3. What are some of the publications, conferences, and trade shows for your niche?

4. Who are some of the top decision makers in your identified niche (by title or name, if you have them)?

5. Who are some of the key editors and reporters for publications serving your niche?

6. What problems, complaints, irritations, and hassles are you hearing from your target market that might identify a niche opportunity for you?

7. What are you doing that your customers like?

8. What are you doing that your customers don't like? (Fix these immediately.)

9. Could competitors do something better than you (such as those things in question 8 your customer didn't like about you)?

10. What can you add to your product or service that your competition doesn't have, doesn't do, or can't do?

11. Can you bundle products and services?

12. What can be done to make your product or service more convenient to your customers?

13. Can you make something on the edge and/or unconventional?

14. Can you make something last longer for your customer?

15. Can you offer something that will save time or money or be less hassle for your customers?

16. Can you give yourself or your company a niche-like moniker or tag line?

Marketing Plan and Strategy

HOW IMPORTANT IS MARKETING planning? Just ask Cheryl Spencer of Raspberry Ridge Farm in Newburgh, Ontario, owner of a working horse farm. During the course of her business startup, she researched her competition and potential market carefully. She deliberately chose to create a smaller, more intimate setting for her guests. Maintaining contact with her customers is a priority, and Cheryl keeps in touch with them on a regular basis through a direct-mail campaign. There is a Raspberry Ridge Farm website (raspberry ridge.com), and print advertisements are placed in two national equestrian magazines and various daily newspapers in her area and beyond. She is comfortable with spending money on advertising. Cheryl is never happy with the status quo and is always thinking of the next step for her business.

Cheryl attributes her startup success to a well-prepared business plan with a good marketing plan component. She notes that her plan is dynamic and has changed a great deal since it was first written, but is still a foundation for her business.

Brenda Scott launched her gift basket business, Bursta Baskets of Kingston, Ontario, with an open house, an event she still holds annually. To boost her profile, Brenda joined the local chamber of commerce. She also donated baskets to charities as raffle and auction items, satisfying her philanthropic nature and publicizing the business at the same time. Brenda had about 60 customers her first year.

The business has generated new and repeat customers based mainly on word of mouth. Most customers come from Kingston. Brenda also has a number of corporate clients. She attributes her focus and accomplishments to a well-defined business and marketing plan, prioritizing what she could do comfortably and not taking on too much. Only a plan would help her determine this.

Just like the business plans of Cheryl and Brenda, this book is your road map to your marketing journey of 30 days. It can be used to find your way and to get back on track if you're lost. It will show you the territory of what to cover and how to get there. It even shows you a starting point. At the end of this journey, you will have a marketing plan that will serve as the road map to your next destination. You will have a guidebook that emblazons your trail to your next level of success, a primer that will make you the king of the marketing jungle.

There are literally volumes written on marketing planning. Success boils down to developing your road map. What paths will you take, which turns will you make, and most important of all, where you are going? Unless you have an endpoint on your road map, how do you know which path to take? In the words of the immortal Yogi Berra, "You got to be very careful if you don't know where you're going because you might not get there."

Many companies devote departments, managers, and research to marketing planning. The guerrilla approach is quite simple. Once you understand your company to its fullest, the dynamics of the marketplace, and how to identify shifts, trends, and changes, you are ready to put pen to paper and finger to keyboard to document your road map.

20

All successful companies have been successful in their marketing planning. A good manager will view a marketing plan as important as a financial or management plan. Being the guerrilla that you are, you know that all other organization and company planning is driven by the marketing plan. Nothing happens until a customer hears of you. Nothing happens until something is sold.

This approach is real and present because attracting, obtaining, and retaining customers are your lifeline in business. The marketing plan keeps that lifeline secure. The correct application of the plan guarantees guerrilla success.

One good thing (and, believe me, there are many) about guerrilla marketing is its simplicity. That's why it's not called "Guerrilla Rocket Science" or "The Complexities of Guerrilla Marketing." In Guerrilla Marketing, you learned that a marketing plan is as simple as seven sentences although entire books, college marketing courses, and presentations are built around marketing plans. On this day, the simple approach will be the rule.

A plan, the ultimate result of this 30-day process, offers a simple strategy or set of strategies, a marketing calendar, an evaluation system, and a selection of weapons and tactics that give you complete control of your marketing.

A good plan conveys your company's vision to target markets, customers, and employees. As part of this vision, your plan should emphasize your company's long-term goals and the path to get there. Stops along the journey, in the form of initiatives and actions, are key landmarks on the road map to executing the plan.

Guerrilla Marketing Attack (Jay Levinson, Mariner Books) says, "Commit to your plan, and you'll get not miracles, but profits."

Planning is the first phase of guerrilla marketing, followed quickly by launching the marketing and then maintaining it.

After 30 days, you can put your *Guerrilla Marketing in 30 Days* book on the shelf. If you have methodically answered the questions and performed the actions described in this book, you will hold in your hand a set of notes, documents, and guidelines for your journey. The most important of these is the marketing plan.

To create a good marketing plan you need three basic things (besides the guerrilla marketing prerequisites of time, energy, and imagination). You need lots of information (see Day Three, Research). You need thinking time, analysis, ideas, creativity, and imagination, all wrapped up into brain power. Finally, you need initiative, the ability to want to do something and the ability to get it done.

Marketing plans range from those scribbled on the back of an envelope to those inside bound editions. The guerrilla rule of thumb is to lean toward the brief side, but with enough meat that it can be used for guidance along your marketing journey. A good guide will provide you with plenty of information to develop the initiatives, actions, follow-up, accountability, and measurement to run your business, and in this case your marketing, effectively.

The Seven-Sentence *Guerrilla Marketing in 30 Days* Marketing Plan

Guerrilla Marketing tells us how to develop a marketing plan in seven sentences, addressing each of the following components:

1. The purpose of your marketing (Day 2)

2. Target market (Day 4)

3. Niche (Day 6)

4. Benefits/competitive advantage (Day 8)

5. Identity (Day 9)

6. Weapons (various days)

7. Budget (Day 27)

Guerrilla Marketing in 30 Days adds one more component:

8. New market opportunities to be investigated in the coming year.

These eight components represent your marketing plan outline.

Before getting to the eight steps, there are a few other strategic considerations: Do you have a clear path? How can you make the plan the right size for you and your employees and still be understood by all necessary audiences? Does the plan lead to action by someone toward common goals and vision?

> Developing the eight steps is the easy part. The hard part is implementation, maintaining the journey, and understanding the future.

Marketing is not rocket science, and it's not the proverbial magic wand either. *Guerrilla Magic* has not been written yet.

One of the benefits of the marketing plan is it forces you to think and re-think your marketing. It causes you to ask questions such as, "What if?". If you are just revising last year's plan, you are not a guerrilla. Putting work, actions, and creativity together is the essence of the guerrilla marketing planning process.

"Build it and they will come" is not an effective marketing plan or strategy. A successful plan boils down to two essentials:

1. Knowing the market inside and out, including what customers want and expect
2. Knowing the way to satisfy customers by knowing competitors, barriers to entry, costs, outside influences, budgets, knowledge, etc.

Armed with this knowledge, you can develop the necessary marketing strategies that will allow you to attract, obtain, and keep customers. In addition, you will also be ready to react to any marketplace changes when they happen. A good guerrilla marketing plan must be flexible enough to respond to changes. Markets change, customers change, and company intentions and activity change. Flexibility is an inherent characteristic of a guerrilla marketer.

When you run the Boston Marathon, you make sure you are not stiff, tight, and inflexible, as those who are inflexible risk injury and do not finish the race. The same goes for your marketing marathon. Flexibility is necessary because you will be successful. Your business will grow. Something will change. Developing a plan and related strategies that will bend and not break brings you one step closer to the success for which you work so hard.

Sure, you have seen situations in which companies had a flash of success with the "Build it and they will come" strategy. Some have done one component of marketing and obtained customers quickly. Some have benefited from curiosity. These successes are driven by temporary situations and events. As we look at the process of business and marketing, think of the thousands of potential customers who will never hear your message if marketing strategies are not employed. An adequate marketing plan ensures communication to these groups of prospective buyers and reduces the reliance on luck and windfalls.

Attracting potential customers is job one. Job two is turning potential customers into paying customers. Job three is keeping those customers. A marketing plan is the job manual for each of these.

A lot of steps in the planning process have been reviewed here. Your outcome is a plan. As you complete all the steps necessary to the development of the plan, you will be immersed in your customers, your products and services, and all the related market dynamics. Once immersed, you are ready to launch your attack; you are ready to continue along that path of your marketing journey, a journey easily followed with a good road map.

DAY 7 SUMMARY

■ Once you understand your company to its fullest, the dynamics of the marketplace, and how to identify shifts, trends, and changes, you are ready to plan.

■ A good manager will see that a marketing plan is as important as a financial or management plan.

■ A plan, the ultimate result of this 30-day process, offers a simple strategy or set of strategies, a marketing calendar, an evaluation system, and a selection of weapons and tactics that give you complete control of your marketing.

■ A good plan conveys your company's vision to target markets, c̲ and employees.

■ Planning is the first phase of guerrilla marketing, followed quickly by the launching the marketing and then maintaining it.

■ A marketing plan can be developed with seven sentences addressing each of the following components:

- The purpose of your marketing (Day 2)

- Target market (Day 4)

- Niche (Day 6)

- Benefits/competitive advantage (Day 8)

- Identity (Day 9)

- Weapons (various days)

- Budget (Day 27)

■ One of the benefits of the marketing plan is it forces you to think and re-think your marketing.

■ A marketing plan is a job manual for attracting potential customers and turning them into paying customers.

■ ■ ■

Action Steps

Note: The outcome of this day will not be your total plan, but will be your total planning perspective. All components of the plan listed for this day are covered in separate days. Each day is as important as the others in creating your overall marketing plan. Your overall marketing plan development will take more than one day.

1. What portion of each day will you devote to reviewing your plan and any necessary revising?

2. Write a hypothetical outcome statement about the completion of your plan. Here is an example:

"After planning to increase leads and referrals for our sales staff to pursue and convert, many marketing weapons were employed. Utilizing the guerrilla marketing resources of time, energy, and imagination, we embarked on an aggressive PR campaign, issuing press releases for new services introduced, new information available demonstrating our expertise, and the announcement of events for our target market to sample the service. This was backed up with "meet and greet" programs at various networking events, ads in trade association directories, and telemarketing to trade shows attendees. The leads generated were focused, open to our follow-up, and ripe for conversion. We ended up getting more leads than our sales force could follow up on, so we implemented a telemarketing inside sales force. Conversion increased. Sales increased, and we made more trips to the bank to make deposits."

3. Outline your plan. Start with the eight components described on this day. Take the eight steps and develop plan subheadings, supplemental information, and new ideas.

4. What information (research) do you have relative to your planning outline?

5. What information (research) do you still need?

6. What market research methods will you use to obtain that information?

7. List and prioritize your marketing objectives. Examples include:
   - Product/service introduction
   - Position company, product, or service as a market leader
   - Counteraction to competitive strategy
   - Lead generation and referrals
   - Obtaining market share in a new geographical area
   - Renew, refresh, and communicate new identity

Sunday	Monday	Tuesday	Wednesday	Thursday	Friday	Saturday
	1	2	3	4	5	6
7	8 ✓	9	10	11	12	13
14	15	16	17	18	19	20
21	22	23	24	25	26	27
28	29	30				

Competitive Advantage and Benefits

DOMINO'S PIZZA never talked about the vehicles used to deliver hot pizzas quickly. You can be sure these vehicles ranged from wrecks to vans and everything in between—maybe even a Hummer. The type of vehicle didn't matter. Dominos could deliver hot pizza quickly in stretch limos, and the vehicle still wouldn't matter. Hot pizza quickly matters. Delivering hot pizza quickly is the benefit. You don't care about the delivery vehicle. What's in it for you, the pizza customer? Hot pizza that comes to your home quickly.

Today, on this eighth day, you will learn that prospects don't care about you. They care about themselves, and anything they have to read or listen to that is not related to them is of little or no interest. Period. End of conversation. No questions asked.

Wait, there might be one question asked by the prospect, "What's in it for me?" The mantra of the prospect is "How is whatever you are saying, doing, selling, or marketing a benefit to me?" The key word here is benefit. Notice the word feature was not used. Many marketers and sales people confuse features with benefits.

Features vs. Benefits

Features vs. benefits is not the name of the next boxing card at Caesar's Palace. It is, however, a boxing match in the minds of business owners, as evidenced by their confusion of the two. Today, we will eliminate that confusion and put you on the right guerrilla track.

A feature is a factual statement about a product or service. Factual statements aren't why customers buy. Benefits are the reason. Features are things that might be included in the "about us" section of a website.

Factual Statements Called Features

Many factual statements are called features.

- Self-cleaning oven
- 200 CD Jukebox
- One-click buying on Amazon
- Live operator on duty 24/7
- 125-page owners manual included
- In business since 1910
- We have the biggest widget maker
- Award-winning
- Made with 100 percent recycled product

Prospects and customers care very little about these statements. Sorry. Not one of these examples tells a prospect how their life or business will improve as a result of working with you and your company or buying your product or service.

The latest and greatest equipment means nothing to a prospective buyer unless that feature translates into lower costs, quicker delivery, or something else of value. Being established 100 years ago means nothing to a prospective buyer unless that feature can be translated into a benefit of reliability and a guarantee of being in business in the future.

Now let's look at those factual feature statements above and translate their value into benefits:

- Convenience
- Time savings
- Organization
- Easy access
- Immediacy
- Quicker answers
- Immediate access to information
- Fewer resources required
- Reliability

Benefits sell. Benefits clearly answer the customer questions, "What's in it for me?" or "What results will I get that will improve my current situation?" or "Will it make me healthier, wealthier, or wiser?" Ben Franklin was a benefits kind of guy.

The most compelling benefits are those that provide emotional or financial return. It's not the steak, it's the sizzle. It's not the gift, it's the thought. It's not the price, it's the overall value. Emotional returns are related to making the customer feel better in some way. Financial returns generally save money or make money for a customer.

How do you know if you are touting a benefit or a feature? It's actually easier than you think. If you can give an affirmative answer to the question, "Will this one thing improve the life, cost, health, or well-being of someone?" If the answer is yes, then you have a benefit that can be marketed to this someone who represents and is part of your target market. If the answer is

> *If you can answer the question, "So, what?" in a convincing manner, then chances are you have reached the benefit arena.*

no, chances are you have identified a feature. You must now find the benefit associated with that feature. If there is no benefit, forget about it, or for you easterners, fuggit-about-it.

Having the biggest machine producing a product for prospects does nothing to improve their life, cost of their health, and well-being. If having the biggest machine causes the product to arrive faster and cheaper at the prospect's doorstep, then their life is improved. The big machine is the feature.

Another way to get into the mindset of thinking about and defining your benefits is to answer the question, "What are you really selling?"

Those in the printing business are not selling ink on paper. They are selling communication of some sort. Those buying eyeglasses from their local optometrist are not buying glass and frames. They are buying clear vision and improved sight. If you go to your local hardware store to buy a drill bit, you probably don't care about how hard the steel in that bit is. You probably don't care what kind of package it's in. You probably don't even care about the price of that drill bit. What do you care about? You care most about the holes that drill bit will help you make. Based on that, all marketing and statements related to the benefits of that drill bit should focus on the quality of the holes, not the features of the products.

Charles Revson of the Revlon Corporation understands guerrilla marketing, especially from a benefits perspective. He states, **"In our factory, we make lipstick. In our advertising, we sell hope."** What are you really selling?

Now that you have this perspective on benefits, let's take it one step forward. How many benefits do you have that the competition has? How many companies now deliver hot pizza quickly? If several companies do it, what makes you select one over the other? You certainly select one for one reason or another. That reason represents a particular benefit and probably that benefit is not offered by others or at least not as well. Maybe it's the taste or texture of the pizza. Maybe it's because the pizza "tastes like mom used to make." Maybe you select one over the other because you get a free newspaper with every delivery. (Hey, I ought to share that with my pizza company friends.) Whatever the reason, the overriding benefit is unique to the company you choose. Are you getting the picture here, or would you rather have hot pizza now?

Once you have benefits defined clearly, you must market them. Put yourself in your customer's shoes and ask what results the benefits offer. When you use this approach, any marketing messages tied to results will be a guerrilla rifle shot right on target. You can't score if you don't hit the target.

Competitive Advantage

A benefit that you offer that the competition doesn't is a unique benefit and a competitive advantage.

The guerrilla marketing definition of the word advantage is a positive difference that makes for an obvious choice by your prospects/customers over the competition. Imitations are not a difference.

Creating an advantage that is difficult to duplicate is the ultimate competitive advantage.

A benefit is a competitive advantage when it

- gets the attention of prospects.
- sells your product or service.
- keeps customers coming back.
- causes prospects to talk about your product to other potential buyers.
- buries the competition.

You should be able to effectively communicate your competitive advantage to your target market, both verbally and in print.

Your competitive advantage becomes the basis of

- your message and communication to the marketplace.
- your headlines.
- your 30-second networking commercial.
- your positioning.
- your PR.
- all prospecting methods and communication.
- your overall marketing.

Communicating Benefits and Competitive Advantages

Chances are that when asked what they do, most companies would have trouble reciting something that flowed. Most would stumble and not have information explaining why they are different from their competitors. Typical responses are, for example, "We sell computers" or "We sell insurance" or "We are financial planners." Ask another company in the same business and you get the same response—no differences and no competitive advantage communication.

Finding and communicating unique competitive advantages will place you over and above the competition. That will lead to more orders in hand, continuing valuable relationships, and more guerrilla successes in your portfolio.

Those that do not know their competitive advantage or how to communicate it generally fall back on price, quality, and service pitches to customers. In today's world, competitive pricing, good quality, and service with attention are givens. In today's markets, you have to show service that is above and beyond. You have to set new standards with your quality and show that price includes more than numbers on an invoice. Doing business with you has to be advantageous to the customer. That's why they open their wallets for you and not the competition.

Pricing comes into play when customers and prospects can't tell the difference between your products and services and a competitor's. As guerrillas, though, you won't have any of that. On this day, you will differentiate your products and services to the point where customers view your company as a valuable partner, not just another vendor. That positive difference is your competitive advantage.

Guerrilla marketing does not focus on pricing. Sure, pricing is part of marketing, but you will be hard pressed to find a book in the Guerrilla Marketing series titled Guerrilla Pricing. Your customers want much more than a price on the invoice. You might be surprised to find out what they really value most. Maybe more useful a future book would be titled Guerrilla Value.

Now let's look at someone who has completed *Guerrilla Marketing in 30 Days*. Let's look at the Maximum Benefits Insurance Company:

My name is Lawrence from Maximum Benefits Insurance Company. We know there are many choices and much confusion when it comes to selecting health insurance. We've developed a menu of services based on five basic variables that cuts through the clutter and suggests the optimum plan for you instantly.

That sounds more like it. Advantageous statements are spilling out all over. The template is name, company, challenge at hand, and a unique solution that implies an advantage for the customer. Use this formula for your product, service, or company and you will not be misunderstood again when asked what you do and why someone should do business with you.

> Sometimes just being able to recite your advantage statement or business description is a competitive advantage.

"To survive is to prosper" is not always 100 percent accurate. Following guerrilla principles leads to prosperity. You just learned one of these principles, that is, that a small company must build a marketing presence upon a competitive advantage. The competitive advantage is not a one-time offering. It must be sustainable. Sustainability occurs through a continuous and ongoing analysis of your competitiveness.

Dig deep to find and best communicate the benefits you offer. For many years the Levinsons drove many miles to their favorite bookstore. In between that bookstore and their home, there were other bookstores that they could have easily visited. It was a true benefit and competitive advantage of that bookstore that caused them to visit the further location. That particular bookstore had the best carrot cake in their café. When that bookstore put together their list of benefits, carrot cake was not on that list. As they listened to their customers and prospects walking through the door, exclaiming that the bookstore had the best carrot cake in their café, they realized that they possessed a competitive advantage. The competition in the area did not have the best carrot cake. Offering the best carrot cake was a benefit that the competition didn't have therefore it was a competitive advantage that could be marketed over and over. They dug deep to find this benefit and advantage. The Levinsons dug deep in their pocketbooks to find the money to buy this uncovered benefit. What is the carrot cake in your business or organization?

If you find it difficult to find that real competitive advantage, try to focus on the things you do in excellent fashion, including your responsiveness and reliability, and try to find factors that differentiate you from your competition. Sometimes this is as simple as putting candy mints in the billing envelope to your customers, giving a gift to the receptionist, or sending news clippings about your customers' children to them. If you still are challenged, ask your customers why they do business with you. Perhaps you offer benefits that you don't know you're offering. Knowing why they do business with you will help you market to others like them and turn them into paying customers.

DAY 8 SUMMARY

■ The mantra of the prospect is, "How is whatever you are saying, doing, selling, and marketing a benefit to me?"

■ A feature is a factual statement about a product or service. Factual statements aren't why customers buy. Benefits are the reason.

■ Benefits sell. Benefits clearly answer the customer's question, "What's in it for me?"

■ The most compelling benefits are those that provide emotional or financial return.

■ A benefit will improve the life, cost, health, or well-being of someone.

■ A benefit you offer that the competition doesn't is a unique benefit and a competitive advantage.

■ Creating an advantage that is difficult to duplicate is the ultimate competitive advantage.

■ Asking your customers why they do business with you will provide you with your competitive advantages.

■ ■ ■

Action Steps

1. List five features of your product or service (e.g., what do you have that is the biggest, the quickest, the cheapest, the most up-to-date technologically, the friendliest, etc.).

2. For each of the features listed above, state what that feature can do for the customer (e.g., saves time, saves money, makes money, makes them healthier, keeps inventory low, tastes better, is less filling, etc.).

3. Create your benefits list (e.g., "parking spaces closer to the door so you don't have to walk as far" may be a benefit for a seniors-oriented medical supplies store that doesn't always show up on the benefits list).

4. Ask customers to identify your true benefits.

5. What does your typical customer profile tell you about your benefits?

6. Complaints and inquiries may uncover a need that the right benefit could satisfy. Are any of these within your company? Are there any benefits that could address these or be developed?

7. What can you do, what problem can you solve, or what can you offer for customers that no one else can?

8. What can you do that is faster, cheaper, or better than the competition?

9. What can your competitors solve, offer, or do that you can't?

10. From this benefits list, list prospects that might be interested in each (e.g., "Brubaker and Company would be interested in a quicker delivery time because they have too much inventory already").

11. Prepare a written description of your competitive advantage for all employees, salespeople, and customers.

12. Create a small display ad and classified ad using your benefit-based message and communication.

Sunday	Monday	Tuesday	Wednesday	Thursday	Friday	Saturday
	1	2	3	4	5	6
7	8	9 ✓	10	11	12	13
14	15	16	17	18	19	20
21	22	23	24	25	26	27
28	29	30				

Identity and Branding

PARADIGM PROACTIVE BUSINESS SERVICES of Houston, Texas, clarified its name and identity with a holiday card that played on the words of the company name. While paradigm is a popular and common word, it's still not always spelled, pronounced, or interpreted correctly. The holiday card featured two dimes glued to the front of the card, as ornaments. Inside the card read, "Hoping your holidays bring you a pair o' dimes and much more…" The company received numerous calls from people saying, "Finally, I understand and remember your name!" That is identity with clarity.

Another identity with clarity is the name your parents gave you when you were born. People know you by that name. When they see you, your name immediately registers in their mind, and they greet you by that name. They associate what they see, hear, and remember with the name they know you by. When they think of what you look like or what you sound like, they think of you and your name. If it's not you, you might hear, "Hey, that looks like Bob." The look and sound is just like Bob's. "Bob" has an identity. So do you. So should your business.

This describes the ultimate guerrilla identity. This is exactly what you want to happen with your product, service, company, and identity. On this day you will learn how to do this.

Who you are and what you do is the basis of all your marketing. Having your clients and prospects know who you are and remember what you do is the ultimate in guerrilla marketing communication.

Part of your identity is your primary marketing message—what you want people to remember and know you as. Your marketing message can take many forms. It can be a logo, a tagline, a 30-second synopsis, or a radio jingle. It can also be the look of your place of business, your signs, your brochure, your business card, or your on-hold message. Much like the definition of marketing, identity is everything a customer/prospect sees and hears about you and, most of all, what they remember about you.

Notice the word image was not used here. You read it in Guerrilla Marketing, (if you haven't, go purchase it now), and you will read it here. Identity is based on truth and honesty. Image is often phony and something that you are not. Customers and prospects are very good at knowing which is which. In the world of guerrilla marketing, integrity is at the top.

Guerrillas want an identity, not an image. Your identity is what you really are. If you screw up and that's what someone remembers, in that one person's mind, your screw-up is your identity. Positive PR, creative ads, and personal selling all create positive identities. That's why you see these in all guerrilla marketing portfolios. As marketing is made up of many, many, many things, chances are good that a client/prospect will remember the many, many, many good things rather than your one screw up. Your identity is saved, in this case, and is as true as you said in your marketing.

There are a few common characteristics of successful corporate identities. First, the identity needs to be clear and free of confusion. A confused customer is not a long-lasting customer. There should be no confusion as to who you are. A consistent identity is a successful identity, the same identity, everywhere, over and over. Change the identity and you change customer perceptions. Change perceptions and you collapse your marketing. The consistent use of your company's identity is critical to effective marketing communication and the eventual building of your company, product, service, or brand awareness. An identity plays a part in grabbing attention, getting interest, creating desire, and causing action, all goals of successful marketing and marketing communication programs.

Your brochure, presentation folders, ads, letterhead, and business cards, not to mention your products and services, all represent your identity. Your identity is valuable and one of the most controllable assets your company has.

Because it is so valuable, you should take the right amount of time to make sure that the identity is clear, consistent, and has the "personality" you want it to have.

Clear, Consistent, and Creative

Identity is not image. It bears repeating. Business identity and business image are clearly two different things. Image is usually a perception. Images can be accurate, inaccurate, or illusions. Magicians deal in images and illusions. Images can put a company in a good light or a bad light. Identity, on the other hand, is a visual reality. This visual reality may or may not enhance "image." There may be confusion with images. There is no confusion with identity.

Identity is the accumulation of all the visual elements of a company's communication to the outside world. Your identity clearly (if done right) states who you are, your beliefs and values, and your company's culture. A well-thought-out identity program can be a very powerful component in your company's marketing mix.

Whether a one-person entrepreneurial company or a ten-person service organization, every business needs a strong identity to be successful. Understanding and incorporating company goals and visions are as important to the development of identity as it is to strategies and planning.

Consistency in application is important for your identity. You want to make a lasting impression on your target market and help your prospects instantly recognize you. Just like your personal identity, you want those that have seen you before to recognize you. Just like Bob whom you met at the beginning of this day, those on whom you have left a lasting impression know you. A professional, up-to-date, appropriate identity makes that crucial first impression. Did you ever not recognize someone because they styled or cut their hair differently? They altered their identity. That was not a "consistent use."

Consistent use of your identity contributes toward building brand identity and the subsequent brand equity. Identities can also be developed and redeveloped to provide you with your desired market positioning.

Because your company's identity is one of its most valuable assets, periodic audits are recommended to ensure the asset remains relevant, and progressive and reinforces the brand positioning. This identity program then becomes the basis for a true, integrated strategic-marketing program and the related marketing communications to support it and the respective brands of your company.

Evaluation of this asset needs to be done periodically, just like the evaluation of every other asset. This evaluation needs to be done relative to positioning, relevance, message communication, and the look of your company. In some cases this evaluation will tell you that your identity needs revising. Maybe your company has added products or services or changed the product or service focus. Maybe you have acquired new companies, new assets, or opened a branch operation.

Identity closely relates to branding in that it is what is communicated and remembered. Branding is also the foundation of your marketing communication effort.

Just what is all this branding talk about and how does it apply to you?

Those questions come up from small business owners whether they are reading an article or book, hearing a tape, or attending a seminar related to marketing. Just what is all the hullabaloo?

Why does Coca-Cola spend millions of dollars on Super Bowl commercials when I already know Coke is my soft drink of preference? Isn't that wasted money on me and all the other people who already know what brand we prefer and what brand we will purchase?

The answer is no. You have to look at how that brand became your preference, how you grew up noticing, thinking, liking, and buying Coca-Cola. In fact, these four activities are the basis of brand building and awareness.

Branding creates an emotional bond to a product, company, service, or identity. Branding can almost be described as something that ties a relationship together when transacting business.

Branding considers things like the relationship your company, product, service, or identity has with a marketplace. Branding considers whether prospective buyers are aware of your brand, whether they prefer it, whether it is a benefit to them, or if they are loyal. Branding is how you are known in the marketplace.

As an accounting company, are you known as the 24-hour tax guy? As a florist, are you known as the lady who delivers in the Big Blue Bug delivery vehicle with daisies painted all over it? Regardless of how you brand yourself and your company, you want customers and prospects to think of you first when the need arises for your products and services. Coca-Cola will do that with big budgets and ad agencies. You will do that with guerrilla strategies and guerrilla tactics of time, energy and imagination.

Establishing Your Brand

Guerrilla marketing is made up of many, many things, all working together. The same can be said of branding. Branding is not only your logo, your identity, tagline, or mascot. Although these contribute to your brand, there is much more to it. Advertising is an important part of branding; however, you cannot build your brand solely through advertising.

Your goal in establishing your brand is to communicate to your target market what your brand stands for when people see it, use it, think of it, or refer it. PR introduces your brand to the marketplace over and over. Advertising and visual points of contact maintain your brand. Related to PR are word-of-mouth advertising, referrals, and recommendations. When you start hearing the "buzz" of your brand and start noticing it is preferred, you will know that you have established a true guerrilla brand.

Building the Brand

The only possible way to have a strong brand, whether starting one, building one, or maintaining one, is to have a quality product or service. In today's world, price, quality, and service are no longer differentiating qualities. Everybody has these attributes as part of their business offering. The absence of quality will deflate and/or dilute a brand very quickly. The emotional attachment becomes a negative attachment when poor quality is experienced. This kind of negativity is detrimental to any brand.

In your guerrilla world, the brand must be different. Remember, you can't say better quality, price, and service. What else are you the best at, the biggest of, or the quickest at doing? Whatever the distinction is, it will carry through to all you do and say regarding your product, service, identity, and brand. Guerrilla brands improve lives. This, too, can be a distinction associated with your brand. The strongest brands today stay strong because of their continual focus on these distinctions and benefits.

Your brand is as strong as the emotional response it evokes. People make purchasing decisions based on emotion first, logic second. The more your brand appeals to purchasers emotionally, the stronger it will be. Logic follows because purchasers will rationalize their purchase decision based on features and benefits. Once your purchasers are emotionally tied to your brand, they will refer it and recommend it perpetually. Guerrillas have these types of customers.

Guerrillas want more of these types of customers. The goal is to get more. They are sometimes referred to as raving fans. The more raving fans you have, the stronger your brand. Brands such as Apple, Harley-Davidson, Starbucks, and Krispy Kreme were all built on word-of-mouth referrals, not solely on large advertising budgets. Yes, they used guerrilla marketing strategies. Consumers who experienced the brand in a positive way and went on to tell others built this word-of-mouth reputation. The same goes for that well-known chiropractor you see everywhere or the delivery vehicle that stands out in your local guerrilla markets. Having customers share their experiences with a brand is one of the purest forms of guerrilla marketing.

When thinking brand, think identity. The working definition of marketing in this 30-day program is anything you do that your customers and prospects come in contact with. These points of contact should all communicate the points of distinction of your brand. This translates into your identity. The points could be the way you answer the phone, your appearance on a sales call, your signage, packaging, and website, or marketing materials, just to name a few. Points of contact also include all other employees, whether or not they have direct contact with prospects and customers on the job. Remember, they all talk to people, and many times their place of employment comes up in discussions. A strong guerrilla brand will evoke positive conversation that transmits positive feelings and that will keep the brand in high esteem.

The final point of your guerrilla brand building is making sure you deliver on what your brand promises. Coca-Cola better be "the real thing." Miller Lite Beer better be, "less filling and tastes great." Bounty paper towels better be the "quicker picker-upper." While these are consumer brand associations, the same applies to commercial brands. If you are a cleaner that guarantees dry cleaning in 24 hours, you better not be late. If HotPizzaNow.com promises hot pizza now, it better be. It's very important that you know what your

The Benefits of an Established Brand

Guerrilla brands that have been established and that are being maintained in the marketplace have many benefits:

- Customers are loyal, not just one-time purchasers.

- A strong brand helps to sell value.

- Top-of-mind awareness contributes to market share.

- A brand preference makes the purchasing decision a "no-brainer" for your customer.

- Many times a strong brand takes price out of the purchasing decision.

- An emotional attachment is price insensitive.

brand is suggesting and that the market knows that you really will provide the promise.

You will buy Coca-Cola if that is your preferred brand, if and when it is available to you. That brand is established with you.

Guerrilla brand building does not happen overnight. Branding, like much of marketing, is a process, not a marketing event. Some brands take a lot of time and money to build and even more to grow and maintain (i.e., Coca-Cola expenditures on Super Bowl commercials year after year).

The new trend in branding is association with more than just a product and service and promise. Customers and prospects are now looking for the most "positive experience."

Take Grant Hicks, co-author of *Guerrilla Marketing for Financial Advisors* (financialadvisormarketing.com) and a highly successful small business owner/financial advisor. He has created the "Island Lifestyle Investment Program." He lives on Vancouver Island and wants his retired clients to have a vision and identity in their mind about their retirement. He makes sure that the Island Lifestyle identity and brand is communicated enough so that they are at the top of mind awareness with his clients and prospects. This surely exerts tremendous guerrilla pressures on his competitors. He truly is the island lifestyle retirement planning guy! His identity and brand says so.

In an ideal world, if your brand is the most known and most associated with you, the marketing battle is won. Guerrillas like to win marketing

Brand Successes

- Creating a brand forces you to think through your points of distinction and differentiation.

- Brand building forces recognition in the marketplace.

- A strong guerrilla brand creates customer loyalty.

- A strong guerrilla brand improves relationships with customers.

- Increased brand awareness means increased market share.

battles. If you're in this ideal world, then maybe it's time for you to think about buying air time for the next Super Bowl.

DAY 9 SUMMARY

- Who you are and what you do is the basis of all your marketing.
- Part of your identity is your primary marketing message.
- Identity is everything a customer/prospect sees and hears about you and what they remember about you.
- Identity is based on truth and honesty. Image is often phoney and something that you are not.
- Identity needs to be clear and free of confusion.
- Identity is the accumulation of all visual elements of a company's communication to the outside world.
- Branding is also the foundation of your communication effort.
- Branding creates emotional bonding to a product, a company, a service, or an identity.
- The brand must be different.
- Your brand is a promise. Make sure you deliver on what your brand promises.

■ ■ ■

Action Steps

PART I

1. Write down ten adjectives, any adjectives. Now try and think of one company that comes to mind, local or national, business-to-business or consumer, for each adjective. Write down why you make this association or what made you remember it most: experience, advertisement, radio, referral, TV, delivery truck, billboard, sign, etc.

2. List five consumer products and five products or services that are business-to-business. What do you remember about each one? What made you remember each one (see association examples in number 1 above)?

3. How did you obtain the information that you remembered in number 2?

4. Now list one-word adjectives that describe you, your business and your products and services. Quantity is not the key, razor sharp adjectives are.

5. Which of the adjectives listed in number 4 do you want people to remember and know you for? Are there any not listed that you would like people to remember and know you for?

6. If you list new adjectives, how can you incorporate these into your identity?

One component of the audit is collecting marketing communication materials that feature the corporate identity, (brochures, business cards, letterheads, advertisements, signage, etc.). Once collected, it is all inspected (audited) to see how the identity is used. Typically, numerous variations of the identity will be found. This usually occurs because no one knows how the various components of the identity should be used (i.e., there is no standard).

PART II

1. Describe the look and feel of your identity.

2. List all the places where your identity is used.

3. Where is there inconsistent use of your identity in the items listed in number 2 above (e.g., letterhead, business cards, signage, website, delivery vehicle, logo apparel, etc.)?

4. What could be changed about your identity to update it?

5. Cite some standards for the use of your identity (e.g., color, size, fonts, application, design, etc.)?

PART III

1. What promise does your brand make? Are you keeping it?

2. Does your brand evoke an emotional response?

3. Does your brand represent or communicate a particular company or corporate culture?

Sunday	Monday	Tuesday	Wednesday	Thursday	Friday	Saturday
	1	2	3	4	5	6
7	8	9	10 ✓	11	12	13
14	15	16	17	18	19	20
21	22	23	24	25	26	27
28	29	30				

Marketing Communication and Creative Planning

I F A TREE FALLS IN A FOREST and no one is there to hear it, is there still sound? This age-old prophetic question has been the subject of debate by many. The same philosophical slant applies to marketing communications. If a company has a great product, service, or message and no one ever hears or knows about it, does the company really have a great product, service, or message? Can they even sell anything? Effective marketing communication and creative planning solves this marketing riddle. The riddle of the tree in the forest is still up to you and the debaters to solve.

The Importance of Communication

By this day you have identified your benefits and competitive advantages. You know who your target is and what it wants. Now these benefits and advantages have to be communicated to your prospects and customers. You have to make noise in the forest. Your advantages need to be communicated in a compelling and convincing way. Your message has to be articulated well and stated often. This is done by the many marketing avenues available for communication and falls under the heading of marketing communication. You have to get the word out.

Marketing communication takes all of these guerrilla marketing elements and blends them into a strategy that totally reflects the identity that you learned on Day 9. It also communicates product characteristics, benefits, and everything about your business and the people associated with it. This strategy then directs all of your communication and the subsequent development of your marketing communication materials.

Marketing communication is most often associated with advertising. Advertising is just a subset of marketing communications. In fact, with all the marketing messages bombarding you today, it's clear that stand-alone concepts such as advertising, PR, and direct mail are not enough to carry the whole marketing burden. The idea of "getting the word out" must combine all of these activities and more to create the cohesive whole of marketing communication.

We're all aware that communication is a necessary part of doing business, but are you aware of the tremendous impact that your ability to communicate has on your success? Communication is the key factor in determining whether a customer is retained, whether the customer spends more with you, and whether you outsell the competition.

Communication Essentials

Marketing communication includes such things as advertising, sales promotion, direct marketing, public relations, special events, signage, trade shows, and more. The messages associated with these and the vehicles used all seek to place information in the customer or prospect's mind that will influence future purchase decisions. Communication influences the purchase process. This communication can be verbal or visual.

Targeted marketing campaigns are an essential component of many overall communication strategies. The goal of these campaigns is to communicate your message and appeal in a systematic, recognizable, and persuasive manner.

People do read marketing materials, that is, people in your target market that are interested read them. People who are not prospects will not read your materials. The real reason you use marketing communication materials is to sell your prospective clients on your company, your products and services, and yourself in the clearest, most efficient way possible. Just the process of creating your materials will help you gain clarity about your offering so that you can communicate to your target market in the clearest of ways. Did someone say "clear message"?

Clarity is just one of the primary considerations when developing your marketing materials. Other considerations are:

- *Focus.* Focus your message and communication on what your prospect receives, not what you do, not who you are, and not how long you have been in business. The message should be about benefits, "What's in it for me, the prospect?"
- *Message.* Provide enough content and information to persuade. You want to grab the attention of your prospect, then lead them to action. That's guerrilla persuasion.
- *Design.* This includes layout and "the look." A good first impression goes a long way in getting attention and interest. Making things easy to read is a big consideration. Prospects do not like clutter or confusion.
- *Credibility.* Testimonials, case studies, correct grammar, and typo-free content all lead to instant credibility. Credibility is key in the relationship-building phase of marketing. Guerrilla marketers are credible.

Marketing materials typically are best used to inform, educate, and sell those who have already expressed an interest in your services. Designing marketing communication materials for mass mailing or distribution present other considerations because of the larger quantity of materials used. Be guerrillaesque in the management, especially from a cost point of view. Remember the cost isn't as important if you persuade enough people. The guerrilla marketing rule is that the only bad marketing investment is in marketing that doesn't work. Guerrillas market for profits.

The Use of Marketing Materials

There are as many uses of marketing materials as there are prospective preferences. These uses include information

1. sent in response to a prospect's inquiry.

2. mailed to a targeted group of prospects to keep in touch.

3. used on prospect appointments as a talking piece or a "leave behind" piece.

4. posted on a website or developed into a web page.

5. placed at your place of business for walk-in customers to pick up, i.e., "Take One."

6. enclosed with proposals for your products and services.

7. enclosed with your product packaging.

Creative Planning

The creative plan is what directs the marketing communication. The key components of this plan are used to develop all communication to prospects and customers.

Creative plan points to consider are:

1. Is the marketing communication directed to the right target market?
2. Are you communicating from the perspective of "What's in it for me, the prospect?"
3. Does the look and feel reflect who you really are, and are they consistent with other marketing communication?
4. Do you continually evaluate your marketing communications in response to changing customer demands, and competitive actions or for new products and services?
5. Are you thinking about how much money you are spending or how much you could get in return if your investment in marketing communication works?

6. Are you communicating frequently enough?

In the true definition of marketing, marketing communication is every potential contact with a prospect or customer. Marketing communications may include your company's name in an article based on a press release, in a news story on the radio, in a brochure left in a fusion partner's information rack, your company name on a billboard, or on the side of a delivery van (with your phone number). Much of this falls under a discussion on all the marketing weapons available. This book covers many of those weapons separately on the appropriate day. For now, the emphasis is on the creative marketing communication plan.

Creative Marketing Plan

Edward Albee, the famous 20th-century American playwright and dramatist, said, "The thing that makes a creative person is to be creative and that is all there is to it."

A creative strategy and its associated plan are similar to a marketing plan, but it is limited to the content of marketing materials and communication. Like the marketing plan, creative planning does not have to be fancy or complex. In the spirit of guerrilla marketing, simplicity is still king of the hill. You will see some similarities here to the marketing planning process reviewed on Day 7.

You should have a creative strategy for each component of your marketing communications plan. If you are using PR, direct mail, advertising, and signage, then each of these components will call for its own creative strategy.

The formula below applies to each and every component. Guerrillas love formulas. Formulas make things simple. Here is one for each of your creative strategies within your creative plan, with examples.

1. The first statement states your purpose. Wow, that sounds familiar already. If the creative strategy is advertising, state the purpose of the advertising. If the creative strategy is PR or direct mail, state the purpose of each.

   Long-term care insurance provider advertising

   The purpose of long-term health care insurance advertising is to convince the target market of 45- to 65-year-old people that now is the time to plan for long-term health care and that our package addresses each and every want and need of our potential clients.

Real estate professional

The purpose of Ajen Realty's direct-mail program is to convince the target audience of families who are relocating to the area and who want a suburban home in the range of $200,000 to $300,000 to contact us to find such a home.

2. The second statement of the creative plan explains how the purpose will be achieved.

Long-term care insurance provider

This will be accomplished by pointing out the financial advantages of purchasing the insurance at an earlier age and the resulting financial benefits to the beneficiaries.

Real estate professional

This will be accomplished by stating the level of expertise Ajen Realty has regarding the community, schools, and resale values and its success rate of matching prospective buyers with sellers.

3. Finally, sentence three of the creative strategy describes the look, mood, and tone of your product or service. This could also be described as the "personality" of your offering.

Long-term care insurance provider

The mood and tone of the advertising will be one of a close-knit family, warm environment, and emotional ties to aging parents.

Real estate professional

The mood and tone will be one of delight and happiness related to families finding their dream home, kids liking new schools and making new friends, and the overall friendliness of the new community and the Ajen real estate professional.

Using these three steps with each component of your creative campaign will provide thoroughness, clarity, and personality while assuring that your shot will hit your target.

Creative Ideas

Now that you have your creative strategies in place, you have to develop the actual creative spark and ideas that drive those strategies. Whether it's advertising, PR, direct mail, a website, or any other marketing component, these creative guidelines apply. The only thing missing here is your own creativity. Remember what Edward Albee said at the beginning of this section. Here are some guidelines to consider when developing your ideas:

1. *Get attention!* Grab attention and spark interest. You have studied your target market enough to know what they want and what true benefits you offer to satisfy them, so the only thing left to get their attention is being creative. This doesn't mean you have to know how to illustrate, draw, write, or even design. It just means that you need to generate the ideas and use your creative juices to fulfill your creative strategies.

2. *Believability and credibility.* State your benefit in such a way that it will be accepted beyond a doubt. Be careful of exaggerations and exclusivities. Don't lead with your chin like that vulnerable boxer. Make sure you can deliver on all of the promises you make.

3. *Motivate for action.* Audiences need to be told what to do. (Go tell six people to buy a copy of this book.) Actions include calling your toll-free number, visiting your website, or returning a business reply card. Part of motivating customers is by creating urgency. "Reply by Friday for your free special report!", "Limited time offer!", and "While supplies last!", are other ways to build the urgency and eventually motivate prospects to purchasing action.

These are all sparked by your creativity. Your ability to imagine new approaches is vital to your success as a marketer. Those that seek new ways to promote products and services have a higher probability for success. Guerrillas are creative all the way to the bank. You already have your creative strategies for each component. Now it's time for you to become the guerrilla idea man or woman.

Don't let creativity overshadow the job of selling and marketing. Make sure your audiences know what product or service you are offering and what you want them to do. Don't just dazzle them with bells and whistles, spark, and flair. How many times have you viewed a cool ad and walked away not knowing what was being advertised or by whom? Advertise and market your product, service, and brand, not your creative abilities (unless you sell creative services).

Here are two final thoughts for the close of this day:

1. Marketing demands more creativity than any other business activity, but marketing is not creative unless it sells.
2. Guerrilla marketers are up to both of these challenges.

DAY 10 SUMMARY

- Your advantages need to be communicated in a convincing and compelling way.

- Messages in your marketing communication need to be articulated well and stated often.

- Advertising is just a subset of marketing communications.

- Communication is the key factor in determining whether a customer is retained, whether the customer spends more with you, and whether you outsell the competition.

- Clarity is one of the primary considerations when developing your materials.

- Other considerations for marketing material are focus, message, design, and credibility.

- Marketing materials are best used to inform, educate, and sell those who have already expressed an interest in your product or service.

- The creative plan directs the marketing communication.

- You should have a creative strategy for each component of your marketing communications plan.

- One goal of your creative idea is to get attention.

- State your benefit in such a way that it will be accepted beyond doubt.

- Audiences need to be told what to do. Motivate for action.

- Don't let creativity overshadow the job of selling and marketing.

■ ■ ■

Action Plan

1. Pick five communication vehicles from the list below.

Letters	Signage	Brochures	Envelopes
Faxes	Billboards	Postcards	Letterhead
Website	Delivery vehicle	Newsletter	Packaging
Press kits	Speeches	Presentations	Videos
Trade show booths	Business cards	On-hold messages	Other

2. Write out the three components of the creative strategy for each.

3. Consider the six questions in the "Creative Plan Points to Consider" list on page 88.

4. Outline the various sections, (text, graphics, layout, design, etc.) of each of your marketing communication materials.

5. How will you evaluate the effectiveness of each of these: number of calls, returned cards, website hits, etc.?

6. How would you describe the look, feel, and spirit of your communication and of your identity?

7. Is it consistent throughout all of your communication?

8. What marketing communication piece do you use the most?

9. What marketing communication piece do you use the least?

10. What marketing communication do your prospects like/respond to?

11. If budget were not an issue, what marketing communication would you put in place?

12. If marketing budget is an issue, what one marketing communication piece will you put in place?

13. What different ways can you use your marketing communication pieces (e.g., direct mail, handouts, posted on a website, dropped from a helicopter, etc.)?

14. What ways can you economize on your marketing communication (e.g., different printing, paper, format, etc.)?

Sunday	Monday	Tuesday	Wednesday	Thursday	Friday	Saturday
	1	2	3	4	5	6
7	8	9	10	11 ✓	12	13
14	15	16	17	18	19	20
21	22	23	24	25	26	27
28	29	30				

Advertising and Media Plan

THE GUERRILLA MARKETING HANDBOOK (Levinson and Godin, Mariner Books) points out that Burger King had success against competitor McDonald's with guerrilla-like campaigns such as "Have it your way" and "grilled, not fried." BK's campaign had repetition, consistency, focus, and positioning. Soon after its success, BK focused on short-term promotional advertising instead of long-term positioning and brand building. It lost out going after quick hits. It interrupted its consistency. Lack of patience cost BK its profits—very un-guerrilla like, especially as it relates to advertising. We can all take a guerrilla lesson from this.

Mention advertising and the first thought that comes to mind for many is the plethora of television commercials we're exposed to. Others think of the lineup of billboards along an interstate highway, glossy magazines at local newsstands, and jingle-laden radio ads. These are advertising methods most often used by traditional mass marketers.

Advertising in the spirit of guerrilla marketing may or may not include these. Guerrillas use advertising that is more focused to a target market, less on the masses, and more personal, resulting in more sales conversions.

Advertising is the most visible form of marketing. It is also often referred to as the most elusive, seductive, and expensive branch of the marketing tree. Unfortunately, it is also the one small businesses misunderstand the most. It is just one of the many guerrilla marketing weapons.

Media exposure and advertising can build a business, but if not planned right and executed correctly, it will eat up a marketing budget faster than you can say mass market.

While advertising is actually at the heart of many guerrilla marketing plans, it shouldn't be intimidating. It may well be the best guerrilla marketing vehicle for your products or services, depending on your market and business. Well-designed advertising is effective advertising. Well-designed does not just mean a catchy slogan, an endorsing celebrity, or the ultimate in graphic design and animation.

David Ogilvy said in *Ogilvy on Advertising* (Vintage Books): "I do not regard advertising as entertainment or an art form, but as a medium of information. When I write an advertisement, I don't want you to tell me that you find it creative. I want you to find it so interesting that you buy the product."

This happens so many times. You see a great commercial, but you can't remember what was being advertised or who the advertiser was. Just watch TV any day and see if the ad is designed to be entertaining, or if there is a clear advertising objective present.

The most common form of advertising used by small businesses is in newspapers and magazines. Before advertising in these publications, a guerrilla must understand who and how many people read the publication and the geographical distribution (often referred to as demographics).

Notice nowhere on this day have we discussed Super Bowl commercials that cost $1.9 million for 30 seconds of airtime. Guerrilla marketers obtain more profits from advertising with less investment.

A characteristic of guerrilla advertising is that it is based on your real audience and their real needs, as well as real products and services against the real competition. Guerrilla advertising is not a lot of bells, whistles, and coins leaving your pockets.

There was once a Super Bowl commercial that advertised during the game at those exorbitant rates often discussed around the time of the game. The commercial was rated as a very creative commercial, in effect being a very good commercial. The commercial consisted of guys riding horses, out on the range, with lassos in their hands, herding . . . cats. Certainly herding cats was unusual and did get the attention of the viewer. But was there a proper marketing message communicated? Surveys just weeks later asked what the ad was about or what company was doing the advertising. A scant few, if any, retained who the advertiser was. A scant few, if any, retained what the message the business advertising was trying to portray. How good was this advertisement really, if the message was not communicated?

If you decide to jump into the advertising arena, make sure you have a message to communicate that your target market will hear. Make sure that marketing tree falling in the advertising forest makes marketing noise. Make sure you comply with David Ogilvy's point of being informative and interesting to the point of having your product or service bought.

Advertising is a potent weapon, but it is not the only weapon. To a guerrilla it is one of the many weapons in the arsenal. Advertising helps make the other weapons work more effectively and visa versa. Advertising works best and feels best when it is balanced with all other marketing.

There is a trend that is considered "guerrilla healthy." In 1983, 70 percent of retailer marketing budgets were invested in advertising. Ten years later that spending statistic was 25 percent of budgets. That trend continues today, especially as companies and organizations adopt guerrilla marketing strategies. The difference went into other guerrilla marketing weapons.

This trend is guerrilla healthy because advertising sometimes is overemphasized in many marketers' worlds. Most businesses advertise heavily at the outset. Guerrilla marketers advertise last. Because marketing is made up of many, many things (how many times is this going to be stated in this book?), there are many other areas where you should focus your resources before any advertising takes place, especially with a business startup.

Guerrillas use advertising to build share of mind. If you know exactly what you want to gain from your advertising, where to direct the message, and how to say what you want your audience to know in the most cost-effective manner possible, then your advertising will be effective.

So many times businesses confuse marketing with advertising. Marketing is not advertising. If you do not know it by now, you need to reread this chapter.

Advertising is a set of clear, creative messages with a guerrilla marketing budget of time, energy, and imagination.

If you choose mass advertising as one of your guerrilla marketing weapons, you will reach an audience much broader than your target market. You should still design your ad as if you're talking to your specific target market. In this way, you have a higher probability of getting the attention of those most interested in you and most likely to do business with you.

Brief, yet compelling messages rule. Think about "Got Milk?" That is one of the highest-rated and most compelling ads anywhere. Be original and creative. Don't design your ad the same (e.g., Got Guerrilla Marketing?).

Times change. Today's advertising is not like yesterday's advertising. The changes in demographics and customer demands have created alternative media marketing. Much of this alternative marketing has transformed the advertising industry. With the likes of the internet, cable TV, direct mail, e-mail, and desktop publishing, new industry opportunities and challenges exist for the guerrilla marketer compared to the marketer of yesterday. You will learn about these during the rest of your 30 days of guerrilla marketing.

Guerrillas are adaptive and responsive to change. In the following descriptions of "why to advertise," you will see how this responsiveness is applied to advertising:

1. *Getting your spot among the thousands of marketing messages heard and/or seen each day.* Your target market members hear competitive marketing messages, see ads of all kinds, hear broadcasts, and view other marketing messages by the thousands. They are constantly on the move. Advertising puts you in front of them as they pass by. Your ultimate goal with advertising is to get them to take notice again, stop, and make a purchase. That's guerrilla advertising.

2. *Relocation and turnover.* In some businesses, customer attrition is very high. People relocate, buyers change, companies get acquired,

purchasing becomes centralized, and companies go out of business. As new buyers and companies move in, your message needs to be reintroduced and communicated loudly. Advertising provides the continuous communication that addresses new audiences.

3. *Brain capacity.* It takes many times for a marketing message to be communicated before it sinks in (unless your target market niche is for those with photographic memories). It's not always forgetfulness that causes your message not to sink in, but sometimes prioritization. Does your prospect need or want what you have when you communicate it? Communicating and advertising helps them remember you when their need arises for what you are offering.

4. *Procrastination.* Sometimes people put off their purchasing decision so as to shop for deals or compare other product or service factors. Keeping your message at the top of their mind while they are shopping puts you at the top of their wallets when they are ready to purchase.

Consistency is not the same as repetition. If you place 12 ads with the same message versus 12 different ads with 12 different looks and 12 different messages, which one will your prospects remember when the time comes for them to make a purchase? Prospects don't have good memories, especially with thousands of marketing messages being thrown at them every day.

It's amazing how many individual components of marketing parallel overall marketing. Just like marketing, advertising works best through repetition. Just like marketing, advertising works best through repetition. Just like marketing, advertising works best through repetition. Get the point?

Repetition establishes contact and starts a relationship with the prospect

Four components of guerrilla advertising are

1. consistency
2. repetition
3. focus
4. positioning

or viewer. A high and frequent visibility achieves this. Repetition also provides constant reinforcement for your name, brand, and marketing message in the mind of your potential buyer. It keeps the awareness of your offering in their head so that when they need or want what you have, they replay the advertisement in their mind, eventually making a purchase from you. Advertising is reminding. Once is not enough. If you are planning just one advertisement, save your money. You will not be effective with a one-time placement of an ad unless you are darn lucky. Luck is not something guerrillas count on. If your budget is tight, run frequent, smaller ads.

Advertising Investment

Just like lack of frequency, spending too little on advertising is ineffective. Unlike too much frequency, spending too much on advertising is ineffective. How do you know what is too little or too much? Let's get through this day of marketing so you will know.

In many of the books in the guerrilla marketing series (and now you can add this one), a bad marketing expense is one that doesn't show a return on the investment. Likewise, a bad advertising expense is one that doesn't show a return. Spending $50 on an ad and getting nothing in return is a bad advertising expense. Spending $1,000 on an ad and getting $2,000 in return is a good advertising investment. Be careful of the "advertising bargain." You don't know that it is a bargain until the response measurements and sales conversion rates are known. Once the numbers are in, you can determine if you did get a bargain. Bargain shopping is not always spending the least amount of money possible, at least by guerrilla standards.

Creating a High-Quality Ad

By this day you have gone through some creative planning lessons. You have also witnessed the infamous Identity vs. Image duel. Advertising is another chance to show identity. *Guerrilla Marketing* said that "far more people see your ad than will see you, or your place of business, so their opinion will be shaped by your ad." Your identity will, too. Because of this, you want to be careful not to put your identity in the hands of an amateur designer. Make sure that your ad is professional, conveys the identity you want over and over, and is "you."

Where to Advertise

You want to be seen in those places where your target market is—where they hang out, what they read, where they view, or what they listen to.

Marketing can be a numbers game. So can advertising. Most advertising vehicles will tell you how many people they reach either by circulation, page views, or some other measurement. Your goal as a guerrilla advertiser is to pick the most frequent vehicle that fits your budget and that hits your target market. Advertising in places that are too wide for your focused target market is considered one of those bad marketing investments, or at least wasteful. You will be advertising sometimes where your target market is not. This has to do a lot with your geographical target market and local vs. national advertising, depending on where your target is.

We are bombarded by all kinds of advertisements during the course of the year and throughout our life. Statistics say that someone in your target market notices one out of nine advertisements. How many times an ad must be seen before it sinks in or creates action to make advertising effective, is a multiple of the "one out of nine" phenomena. If it takes three ads to affect a consumer, then the "effectiveness formula" becomes one out of 27 times. If you are not prepared to advertise 27 times to a target market, your whole program may be ineffective and your guerrilla marketing dollars will end up down the drain. There are, of course, exceptions to the rule, but winning in Las Vegas is also an exception to the rule.

> *Note: Just because an ad works in one place doesn't mean it works in another!*

If you don't know where your prospects go, ask them or revert back to your research experience from Day 3. Because creativity increases the effectiveness of your ad, be clear on the creativity planning discussed in Day 10. You now are getting your fill of the full 30 days of guerrilla marketing.

Different advertising media are associated with differing characteristics, which should be considered when planning your marketing:

- *Newspapers*. Marketing that is newsy, read by those interested in news.
- *Magazines*. Credibility. How does this sound: "As seen in *Time* magazine." Pretty credible, right?
- *Radio*. Wide-ranging and one-on-one. Do you ever feel that the radio is talking directly to you?
- *Direct mail*. Repetition and action oriented, sometimes with a sense of urgency—"for a limited time only" or "coupon expires tomorrow."
- *Television*. Even more wide-ranging and demonstrative.
- *Brochures*. Detail-oriented and long-lasting if used as a reference or filed.
- *Classified ads*. Short and to the point, filled with information.
- *Internet*. Interactivity and accessibility as more and more people get online.
- *Signs*. Motivator and reminder, taking advantage of impulse buyers.

What to Advertise

Now that you have learned why and where to advertise, let's concentrate on what to advertise.

Creating your copy for advertising can be less painful if you are like most guerrillas and develop a plan. The following components are the basis of your copy creative plan. This comes after developing the creative plan discussed for your advertising in Day 10.

Advertising Components

HEADLINE. Our guerrilla friend and advertising great, David Ogilvy said, "On the average, five times as many people read the headline as read the body copy. It follows that, unless your headline sells your product, you've wasted 80 percent of your money." Guerrillas don't waste. The headline markets your ad; it is the attention getter, designed to grab the reader or listener.

BODY. Who you are, what's special or different, where, when, and what are described in the body of your ad copy. Ad body copy is not like a school essay. It is short, succinct, and to the point, sometimes using incomplete sentences.

OFFER. This is why you are advertising; remember your purpose.

HOOK. See Day 19 for Marketing Hooks. This is an incentive for a response.

CALL TO ACTION. Tell the prospects what to do: make a decision for them so they don't have to.

AD GRAPHICS. Encapsulating all of these components are the ad graphics. There are books, courses, degrees, and businesses that solely concentrate on graphic design. The goal for good design is getting attention, creating interest and desire, in a visually appealing manner.

This is the first part of what is known as the AIDA formula. AIDA is an acronym for attention, interest, desire, and action. Do not let graphics override your message and purpose of advertising. In guerrilla fashion, simple is good; clean is good; to the point is good. Take the case of Corporron Acres, a cattle ranch located in Schulenburg, Texas. It advertises regularly in a magazine for its breeder's association. Most ranchers run full-color, graphically loud ads showing photographs of their cattle. To stand out, Corporron Acres runs a black and white humorous ad. It does this for every issue. Its readers look forward to the next month's ad because they stand out so much.

Also in guerrilla fashion, do what you do best and control your costs of design. If it increases your efficiency and effectiveness, consult a graphic professional. Guerrillas are efficient and effective with this day's information. On this day, you will be, too.

DAY 11 SUMMARY

- ■ Guerrillas use advertising that is more focused on a target market, less on the masses, and more personal, resulting in more sales conversions.

- ■ Advertising is the most visible form of marketing. It is also often referred to as the most elusive, seductive, and expensive branch of the marketing tree.

- ■ Advertising should not be intimidating.

- ■ The most common form of advertising used by small businesses is advertising in newspapers and magazines.

- ■ Advertising works best and feels best when it is balanced with all other marketing.

- ■ Guerrillas use advertising to build share of mind.

- ■ Advertising is a set of clear, creative messages with a guerrilla marketing budget of time, energy, and imagination.

- ■ Pick the most frequent advertising vehicle that fits your budget and that hits your target market.

■　■　■

Action Steps

1. Use the three-step creative formula from Day 10 to develop your ad.

2. What primary message do you want your advertising to convey?

3. Identify places to advertise based on what your target market sees and hears. Where do your prospects go when they need your product or service? Do they go online, to a directory, or to the Yellow Pages? Where your prospect goes is where you should advertise.

4. For each potential publication to advertise in, find out

   - the circulation, or reach, of the publication or broadcast.

   - the geography of the coverage.

- what target market it aims for.
- other demographics.
- what their advertising rates are.
- frequency of distribution and /or publication to the target market.

5. What is your break-even analysis if you have to run 27 ads?

6. What other marketing would support advertising: PR, reprints, website, etc.?

7. What action is suggested by your advertising?

8. What is the look and feel of your ad? Is it consistent with your identity and other marketing?

9. Sketch out a large ad and a small one based on the above component information. Concentrate on the message here and just note any graphic design implication. When you get time to implement your ad and purchase your space or time, hire a professional designer to create the final ad.

Sunday	Monday	Tuesday	Wednesday	Thursday	Friday	Saturday
	1	2	3	4	5	6
7	8	9	10	11	12 ✓	13
14	15	16	17	18	19	20
21	22	23	24	25	26	27
28	29	30				

Business Networking

WHEN TIMES ARE TOUGH, turn to marketing that you used to get your business started. Turn to things that require little or no monetary investment. It works.

In the business of networking, you have to stand out and you have to be remembered. Jeff Glaze of atlantaevent.com (justonebig idea.com) accomplishes both at the same time when he networks. Jeff uses pocket billboards. Pocket billboards are cards that are larger than a business card but smaller than a flier, containing more information than an average business card. Because of their uniqueness, people hang on to them. They really are hard to throw away. They usually end up on someone's desk and are easily remembered when the person wants to follow up. Because follow-up is one of the cornerstones of networking, along with differentiation, Jeff is a step ahead of all other networkers. Pocket Billboards scream for the recipient to take action and in many cases prompt them to contact you before you follow up with them, a perfect networking scenario.

By the time Day 12 rolls around, you are ready to try your hand at standing out in crowds and being remembered. You are ready to meet some important customers/prospects. It's time to meet the people that can or will do business directly with you or people that know others that can. These groups of people are the makings of a network. The act of working, communication, and interacting with this group is known as networking. The good news is that networking fits the spirit of guerrilla marketing because it has the potential for a high return while expending only time, energy, and imagination. No checks required here.

Networking should be an integral part of any guerrilla marketing plan and guerrilla effort. Understanding the dynamics, goals, and potential outcomes leverages this most important guerrilla activity to its fullest.

Simply stated, networking is making contact to establish relationships that can lead to business. Sometimes the path to business is direct; other times it is indirect with such things as referrals. The person you are acquainted with will know someone else who needs your products or services. This is the most important rule of networking. Many people go to a networking event hoping to do business. It doesn't work that way. Business is not done directly at a networking event. Your goal in attending a networking event is to meet two or three people, find a reason to follow up, and start a relationship. The business will most likely come from an indirect referral—they know someone who might need your products or services.

Networking Mindset

Before any networking starts, you must establish the proper mindset. First and foremost, people buy from people they like, know, and trust. Jeffrey Gitomer of gitomer.com says, "When all else is equal, people buy from people they like, know, and trust. When all things are not equal, they still buy from people they like, know, and trust."

Networking is a "touch" to a customer, a prospect, or someone of influence. We have gone from being a high-touch society/business world to high tech, and we are now creeping back to high-touch. We literally have gone full circle in this area. Understanding this "touching" is a critical part of establishing the networking mindset. It goes all the way to caring, showing interest, and trust. Guerrillas know that people don't care how much you know until they know how much you care.

Making Contact—It's Who You Know

Networking means making the necessary contacts and building upon them by talking with people about what you do and who you are. It also is listening to see how you might assist them in what they do. Giving as much or more than receiving is a recurring theme throughout any discussion on networking and throughout guerrilla marketing.

Knowing people who already believe in you and your company—people who will recommend you, refer to you, and open doors for you—can make the difference between marginal performance and guerrilla success.

The general notion is that you are already networking in one form or another. Networking is all around you, and the people to build your network are with you every day.

Believe it or not, you know at least 150–250 people. I tell people this all the time and many times get a funny, puzzled, skeptical look in response. People don't think they know that many people. To remove the skepticism I suggest to people that they make a list of people/business classifications like banker, neighbor, travel agent, realtor, insurance representative, etc. Beside each of these classifications place a name of someone you know who fits that classification. Once you do this and compile your list you will quickly see more people in your network than you originally thought of. You will see that this list can quickly approach the 150–250 people that I mentioned. This list represents a great pool of networking prospects that already probably know you, like you and trust you; all the basis for doing business directly with you or referring likely prospects for you to cash in on.

Networking Is Relationship Building

Contacts to establish relationships that can lead to business only happen when the relationship is mutually beneficial. Networking is giving and receiving, with the giving usually happening first. If one party does all the giving, then the relationship will not last and the networking truly ends. Networking relationships take work and cooperation by all parties involved. Guerrilla networking relationships are not one-night-stands.

The Networking Process

Networking doesn't just happen. It has to be part of your marketing plan with activity and initiatives associated with it. A timetable must be established and responsibility assigned. It is a learned skill. Everyone is not born with the required networking skills. The skills need to be learned because they are part of a total process, not a one-time event (as is often said about all of marketing).

The key components of the networking process are

- planning which networking events to attend.
- setting networking goals in total and for each event.
- knowing who to target in the process of networking.
- relationship building.
- establishing trust as well as showing interest.
- follow-up.
- continuing the relationship.

Planning Networking Events

Not every event where there are people to meet is the right event to network. Networking takes a plan. The plan is developed for efficiency and to leverage and manage time. Strategically choosing networking events assures that.

Choose networking events that allow you to meet your networking goals. If you rely on decision makers, attend a networking function that decision makers will be present at. If you work in the educational markets, choose an event where educators will be present. On the other hand, if you have an aggressive networking plan with aggressive goals, attending a social event will not meet your goals. The question to ask for each event is, "Is attending this event the best use of my time, relative to my networking goals?"

How do you know whether the event is business or socially oriented? Events such as an after-hours affair of the chamber of commerce are many times a social event. The event has no clear agenda; people spend time net-eating, net-drinking, and net-sitting.

Another way to evaluate whether the event will be right for you is to determine how many people you know who are going to the event. If the function is attended by people you already know, chances are the event will be non-productive for you from a networking point of view. If your goal is to continue a relationship, then this event might be appropriate.

Ask yourself how you heard about the particular networking event. Was there marketing done to promote it? What did the promotional material communicate? Did it give you enough information about the sponsoring organization? The answers to these questions are good indicators about the worth of a particular networking event.

It's best to list your events every 30 days to further optimize your networking plan. I know you will do this during our 30 days together.

Some websites in cities or regions do this. A good example is atlantaevent.com. A quick glance at this site shows all the networking events, seminars, and professional group meetings in and around the city of Atlanta. This site makes planning which events to attend much easier.

Setting Networking Goals

Showing up at a networking event without networking goals almost guarantees that the event will be social for you. Knowing whether the event or function is right for you depends on whether your networking goals are met.

Most people go to a networking event armed with a massive stack of business cards ready to pounce on anyone breathing. The goal of networking is not to pass out business cards. One goal is to receive them. This goal is part of the plan to obtain information. The goal of networking is to make contacts and get information that lead to relationships that lead to increased business.

Finding a reason for a follow-up visit and meeting one-on-one with your new contact will mean that you met one of your networking goals.

Receiving business cards puts the follow-up initiative in your court instead of relying on someone else to contact you.

A typical set of networking goals breaks down like this:

- Meet ten new people.
- Receive eight business cards.
- Note something of interest on each card.
- Write a follow-up note to five of these people (or all).
- Call and set up an appointment after writing to three contacts.
- Continue the relationship with two of these.

Notice that nowhere did I mention a goal for how many business cards to pass around. If you attend two networking events a month, you will add four or more people to your network with which you will have ongoing, continual relationships.

Knowing Who to Target in Your Networking

How do you know who to contact? How do you know your time won't be wasted with a particular person or, more specifically, that your networking goals won't be accomplished?

The real answer is that you don't always know. We have all been to a networking meeting where we start talking with someone only to find out there are no mutual interests, goals are different, and there are no reasons to establish a relationship. What do you do in that situation? Here is where the importance of networking goals can really help you or, in some cases, rescue you.

You can state very cordially and professionally,

> *It's very nice to meet you. I am doing well to meet my networking goals for this event and want to make sure that I accomplish all of my goals. I don't want to keep you from meeting your networking goals as well, so I will be*

moving on. I hope you don't mind, and I hope the event works out well for you. It's nice to meet you, and good luck.

State also that you would like to continue the conversation as soon as you hit your goal or soon thereafter. This is professional, cordial, and usually works as a good "out."

Firms that have the same types of prospects and the same common interests as you are usually good for making contact. Firms or businesses that compliment your products and services are good networking targets. An estate-planning attorney compliments a life insurance sales representative. A graphic designer compliments a printing company. A photographer compliments a wedding planner or caterer.

Knowing who could best assist you with referrals and building relationships in similar industries is your best networking target. The mindset here is networking for the indirect referrals. Very little actual business is done at a networking event. Most true business is done in the follow-up phase, after relationships are nurtured.

Accomplishing direct business with networking contacts means they fit the profile of your ideal client that buys your product or service.

Relationship Building as It Relates to Networking

People like to do business with those they like and trust. This can be done even at a price premium. Can this trust and confidence be established at one networking event with one introduction? No, it can't. It takes follow-up, getting to know each other, and finding common ground, interests, and compatibility.

Part of relationship-building, especially at the start, is being interested and showing that interest in the other person—his or her business, family, hobbies, goals and aspirations, etc.

In addition to interest, an integral part of networking and relationship-building is listening. Hearing what the other person has to say is more important than delivering your sales pitch instantly. Many times while listening, you can pick up signals about business potential, direct and indirect. The contact might state a particular problem that needs solving or might mention some one else who might need your product or service. You might hear of a problem that can be solved with the referral of someone else's business. You build a relationship for helping your contact and you also build a relationship with the business you referred. In this case, three different networks benefit.

In the spirit of guerrilla marketing, the number of orders does not always measure business. Many times the number of relationships is a good measure of a successful business.

The All Important Follow-Up and Continuing the Relationship

The key to lead success is follow-up. Just like any other form of marketing, it sometimes takes a number of times before a lead can be converted to interest and from there to eventual closing of the sale.

Follow up with your new contact with an invitation to coffee, lunch, or an after-hours meeting. Send a card or a note to those of interest immediately. Follow up and schedule a true business meeting.

Contact and follow up with information that may be helpful to your contact or something of interest to them. This can be the start and continuance of a great relationship builder.

Remember key points from your initial contact and mention them in your follow-up. The more personal you can make your follow-up, the better. It also can help to get past a gatekeeper. "I'd like to speak to Mr./Ms. _____ about the information I sent him/her about his/her daughter's soccer team."

Now Is the Time to Dance

You're at a networking function and you've made that all important contact. You want help but know it takes a relationship. Now what?

The hardest thing for people to understand about networking functions is that very little real business gets done the first time you meet someone. If you attend a function or meeting without expecting to get order after order or any business at all, the function will be more of a success for you. Your real goal is to make contacts for potential follow-up.

Ongoing Networking Tips and Techniques

- Set goals before arriving.
- Arrive early.
- Review the attendees.
- Help at the registration desk.
- Determine prospecting vs. suspecting.
- Target a few "power partners."
- Maintain eye contact.
- Show enthusiasm.
- Ask questions.
- Be nonthreatening.
- Don't come on too strong.
- Gather information.
- Act interested.
- Learn about their profession.
- Find out about their personal lives.
- Find out what they really need/want.
- Don't be in a rush to leave a meeting; some of the best networking takes place at the end, after the event.
- Act like a host, not a guest. Guests wait to be introduced. A host introduces him- or herself.

DAY 12 SUMMARY

■ The act of working, communicating, and interacting with groups is what is known as networking.

■ Networking should be an integral part of any guerrilla marketing plan.

■ Networking is making contact to establish relationships that can lead to business.

■ Your goal in attending a networking event is to meet people to follow up with and start a relationship.

■ Every event where people meet is not always the right event to network.

■ Choose networking events that allow you to meet your networking goals.

■ The goal of networking is to make contacts and get information that leads to relationships that lead to increased business.

■ Those who could best assist you with referrals and building relationships in similar industries are your best networking targets.

■ The number of relationships is a good measure of a successful business.

■ The key to lead success is follow-up.

■ ■ ■

Action Steps

1. The people you need to know and the people that can help might be right under your nose. To help build that list, answer the following:

   • Who has taken an interest in you lately or in the past?

   • Who have you been good friends with?

   • Who do you always talk business with when you get together?

   • Who has helped or offered you encouragement or advice in your business?

   • Who do you go to when you have a challenge or particular need?

- Who comes to you for help?
- Who do you respect?

2. Research available and appropriate networking events that you could attend that are occurring in the next 30 days.

3. Schedule these events. Plan to attend four events for each 30-day period.

4. Plan your personal networking agenda and goals for each event.

5. After attending the events, call five people to schedule a lunch, coffee, or get-together just to get to know them more.

6. Send a handwritten note or card to people with whom you want to start or continue a networking relationship. This might be as a result of one meeting or a result of a subsequent follow-up meeting.

7. Call, e-mail, or write to three people in your network just to say "hello." You never can tell who knows which person and how that might benefit both of your businesses.

8. Find one new place to network. This could be an association, civic or business meeting, presentation, or luncheon. Add this to your networking schedule if you think it is worthwhile attending again.

Sunday	Monday	Tuesday	Wednesday	Thursday	Friday	Saturday
	1	2	3	4	5	6
7	8	9	10	11	12	13 ✓
14	15	16	17	18	19	20
21	22	23	24	25	26	27
28	29	30				

Strategic Alliances and Fusion Marketing

IMAGINE THE SURPRISE on people's faces when three weeks after they move they get a coupon in the mail from Lowe's home building supplies stores says, "Congratulations on your move! Here's a house-warming gift for you—10 percent off special savings, compliments of Lowe's."

No one ever sends a change of address notice to Lowes. How does the company know? Do you think they have a fusion marketing arrangement with the U.S. Post Office? Coincidentally, the same day the coupon goes out, a confirming change of address letter arrives from the USPS. Is this a coincidence? Lowe's and the Post Office know all about fusion marketing. Now, you will too.

Mention fusion marketing and non-guerrillas react with a questioned look on their faces. Mention strategic alliances, and they get it.

On this day we will fix your face if you don't get it. Fusion marketing is nothing more than a strategic alliance with another business. Part of *Webster's* definition fits, even as it relates to guerrilla marketing: "a merging of diverse, distinct, or separate elements into a unified whole." Doing this under the guise of a business partnership is fusion marketing.

There are several ways you can partner with other businesses to get more business. One is for them to be a customer! That's a great partnership and one all guerrillas strive for. On this day, though, we will discuss noncustomer partnerships.

One of the cardinal rules for all entrepreneurs is that you can't do it alone. Michael Gerber speaks about it in *The E-Myth Revisited* (HarperBusiness) when describing the concept of working in the business vs. working on the business. Many entrepreneurs work in the business because they try to do too much alone. The plumbing company owner fits pipes. The florist owner arranges flowers. The bookstore owner stocks shelves. All do their own bookkeeping and marketing as well. Sometimes what they do, they do best. Sometimes they don't. Guerrillas do what they do best and get the help of others in areas where they are not at their best. Getting the help of others builds your foundation many times better than the proverbial bricks and mortar.

Business connections (noncustomers) with other businesses are often referred to as strategic alliances, affinity marketing, joint venturing, affiliate relationships, or fusion marketing. In guerrilla language, we will use the term fusion marketing. To add to what Mr. Webster stated, fusion marketing is combining the efforts of two entities to "explode" their joint marketing efforts.

Lorraine Segal, author of *Intelligent Business Alliances* (Times Business), has observed that 30 percent of most U.S. companies' revenue comes from alliances of one type or another. She also notes that one trend becoming the norm is small-business-to-large-business collaboration. Smaller, guerrilla-type companies can help meet the need for speed, responsiveness, and attention that challenge some larger companies. In this case the alliance is mutually beneficial and synergistic. Michael Gerber would be proud. So will you.

Fusion marketing makes sense when two companies have similar target markets, prospects, and values. Take, for example, the whole world of online marketing, a commonplace area for fusion marketing. Here companies work together to display one another's information. It can be as simple as a link to each other's sites or links to articles, order forms, applications, case studies, etc. Each participant gains more exposure while adding to the content and quality of each other's marketing.

An estate-planning attorney might supply a "Top Ten Tips to Avoid Probate" article to a life insurance company's site, and the insurance site would have a "free consultation for will preparation" link back to the attorney's site. The guerrilla factor here is that the cost to put these links on the sites is next to nothing. That, along with the energy and imagination involved, equals coins in your guerrilla piggy bank.

In the networking discussion on Day 12, we discussed power partners. Power partners are an example of fusion marketing: two companies working with like customers and like prospects in synergistic fashion.

Examples of fusion marketing partners in the power partner sense include

- a printing company and a graphic designer.
- a professional organizer and a moving and storage company.
- a construction firm and an architect.
- a hotel/resort and travel agency.
- a real estate professional and a mortgage broker.

This list of examples is endless, bound only by your guerrilla imagination and the ability to work together. Who was that guerrilla who said two heads are better than one?

I visited my local dry cleaners recently to drop off a batch of cleaning. I approached the counter, deposited my clothing, obtained my receipt, and turned to leave. As I did, I looked down on the counter and there in plain view was a coupon. The coupon was for the pizza store, two doors down from the dry cleaners, in a concentrated strip mall. I walked in to the recommended pizza vendor and cashed in my coupon. I was proud of my savings. When I turned to leave, I noticed a coupon on their countertop. Their coupon was for a discount off of dry cleaning at the dry cleaners that I just left. That's fusion marketing. That's guerrilla fusion marketing. These two businesses were driving traffic and buyers to each other simply by referring each other. There was no cost associated with this, only profits to enjoy as traffic increased. We as entrepreneurs do not always have to act alone. We can join forces with others to synergize our marketing efforts. Doing this with time, energy, and imagination without writing checks is the essence of Guerrilla Marketing. Doing it in 30 Days is the essence of *Guerrilla Marketing in 30 Days*.

Each fusion partnership offers the opportunity to market to an audience that's interested in what you offer and one that you want to ultimately purchase from you. Without fusion marketing, new audiences aren't reached and new wallets aren't found.

Fusion marketing is one of the most underused, inexpensive, and effective methods of guerrilla marketing. Anytime you can tie in your marketing efforts with those of others, you stand to gain more.

Consistent with all guerrilla marketing thinking, fusion marketing doesn't have to be complex. Power partners aren't complex. A joint mailing is not complex. Referring others with a coupon exchange is not complex. Including your partner's fact sheet with your next delivery and vice versa is not complex. Fusion marketing can be as simple as putting a stack of your business cards on a partner's counter in their place of business and their cards on your counter.

Partnering and fusing reduces marketing costs. The overall investment is not less. It's just shared, reducing the cost per partner. As guerrillas, we like that because it turns more profits.

A favorite example of fusion marketing and one that has turned into quite a separate business is the display of brands and products in movies and television shows. Advertisers spend an estimated $360 million a year to squeeze brands into your favorite movie. Now there is a growing trend to do the same in television shows. That alliance between Madison Avenue and Hollywood is no accident. It is no accident that your favorite actor in the latest thriller was drinking a Coca-Cola. Actors don't have preferences until the movie companies create one for them. It is no accident that the copier being operated in the latest television drama was manufactured, branded, and displayed as a Xerox machine. These companies paid the movie and television production companies big money to show their products. Spending this big money was an efficient means to show their respective products to the masses that attend movies and to supplement other advertising and marketing of the products that moviegoers see.

Although these are larger business examples, this type of placement is happening more and more with both small and large businesses.

Call it leverage. Guerrillas call it fusion marketing. *Webster* might join in on the fusion vote as well.

Most of our examples have been single company alliances. Guerrillas also align themselves with a wide assortment of fusion marketing partners. If partners share similar values, ambitions, and prospects, then the visibility and awareness for each partner goes sky high at less cost, with a fusion arrangement. What a guerrilla combination!

Fusion marketing partners don't just show up on your doorstep one morning. Using the time component of the time, energy, and imagination, the guerrilla marketing formula comes into play to develop the partnership. Guerrillas have to search for the right partner. When looking for partners, consider the following:

- A company with similar values
- A company with similar business goals
- A company with a similar marketing attitude and mindset
- Online marketing possibilities
- A willingness to share and give

Finding companies like this to share your fusion is the ultimate in cooperation and the ultimate in profits.

Two forms of fusion marketing that aren't necessarily labeled as such are co-op advertising funds and sponsorships.

A sponsorship is nothing more than a mention of a company in advertising in exchange for money, favors, services, or other benefits. Just look at the nonprofit and charitable worlds you participate in. Sponsorships are heavy in that area.

Co-op advertising funds are marketing monies made available to businesses by manufacturers of products or their distributors. If a manufacturer, distributor, or other supplier doesn't have a cooperative ad program, ask them to establish one. Use some of that guerrilla imagination and energy on them. Don't hold back. Guerrillas don't hold back.

When the *Guerrilla Marketing in 30 Days* seminar toured the United States, mention of companies in ads and at the seminar was given in exchange for the use of a seminar room. Simple sponsorships. Simple fusion marketing.

The same goes for establishing fusion marketing partners of all kinds. If you don't have enough partners now, just ask. Just ask businesses to cooperate, market more together, and double the impact of their marketing expenditures.

In the online world, fusion marketing is ever present and growing at a fast rate. Most relationships are in the form of "affiliates." Affiliate marketing programs are simple partnerships between a seller and another seller or distributor that reaches beyond selling their own products and services. Each gives an incentive or commission for products and services sold by the other. Another way to look at it is that it is as an online distributorship. Distributors are affiliates as well as fusion marketing partners. Hopefully they all can be guerrillas, too.

During the course of presenting *Guerrilla Marketing in 30 Days* to businesses and associations around the country, I travel to remote locations. Once, after an event, I arrived at my reserved hotel in a downstate Illinois location. It was late and I was craving a pizza to be delivered to my room. The hotel room service was not available. As I pondered who to call for my next pizza delivery, I looked down at my hotel room key, the kind of key of the credit card type that is swiped in the door lock, and lo and behold, printed on the plastic room key was the number of the local pizza delivery company. I called, received my pizza, and enjoyed it thoroughly, all while thinking about this wonderful example of fusion marketing; of one company working with the other to target similar prospects while not competing. (Note: not all fusion marketing involves pizza! I just happen to be a great collector of pizza so these examples are always fresh in my experience base.)

There are many different ways to create alliances, affiliates, and fusion marketing partnerships. Two marketers are better than one, especially if the two share one cost. Fusion marketing will enhance your bottom line.

DAY 13 SUMMARY

■ Fusion marketing is nothing more than a strategic alliance with another business.

■ Fusion marketing makes sense when two companies have similar target markets and similar values.

■ Fusion marketing is one of the most underused, inexpensive, and effective methods of guerrilla marketing.

■ Guerrillas align themselves with a wide assortment of fusion marketing partners.

■ Two forms of fusion marketing that aren't necessarily labeled as such are co-op advertising funds and sponsorships.

■ Affiliate marketing programs are simple partnerships between a seller and another seller or distributor that reaches beyond selling their own products and services. Affiliate marketing is another form of fusion marketing.

■ Two marketers are better than one, especially if the two share one cost.

■ ■ ■

Action Steps

1. List the type of company that would be a good power partner with you.

2. List specific companies that fit this type.

3. What could you offer a fusion marketing partner?

   • Website link

   • Article to post online or handout

   • Sign exchange

   • Coupon or flier exchange

4. How will both companies benefit from a fusion marketing arrangement?

5. Discuss with them other fusion marketing ideas, especially the online marketing-related ones.

6. Agree to test some fusion marketing together and expand as both of you get comfortable with the arrangement.

7. Who would benefit by sponsoring something that you do (e.g., a seminar, a website page, another type of event, a contribution to a nonprofit organization, etc.).

8. What suppliers have co-operative advertising funds available?

9. For the suppliers that don't have co-op funds, ask them about the possibility of creating a program.

Sunday	Monday	Tuesday	Wednesday	Thursday	Friday	Saturday
	1	2	3	4	5	6
7	8	9	10	11	12	13
14 ✓	15	16	17	18	19	20
21	22	23	24	25	26	27
28	29	30				

Direct Selling

GUERRILLAS KNOW TO be proactive when it comes to direct selling. Waiting for a client to specify a desired solution and playing the competitive bid game is unguerrilla like. Direct sales overcome this. Kevin Nations, while selling for a well-recognized Fortune 100 telecommunications company and currently the "Six Figure Sales Coach" (kevinnations.com), found that even when he represented an industry leader, he and his company were always being edged out of a large local school district primarily because of price. With several equipment manufacturers and by asking all the right questions, they designed a complete communications solution that answered the district's long-term needs.

This combined strategy placed Kevin and his partners in a position of competitive advantage. No other company had asked the same questions or could offer the complete solution Kevin had developed. The client would never have known of the benefits, advantages, and complete solution had it not been for a well-planned direct sales approach. The client also wouldn't have had such a positive relationship had it not been for Kevin's aggressive sales attitude and approach. The result: Kevin and his company won a $30 million plus contract. Kevin Nations is a guerrilla seller.

Guerrilla marketers say nothing happens in a company until something is marketed. Guerrilla sellers say nothing happens until something is sold. All guerrillas know that both are right, and they work together.

Selling has often been called the distribution arm of marketing. Getting your marketing message out face-to-face to a prospect always wins out. One-on-one interaction allows for dialogue. A postcard can't answer a question on the spot. A radio commercial can't overcome an objection by a prospect. A sign can't supply additional information when requested. Personal selling can.

When the early caveman was asked about his wheel for sale, he could answer back. When asked, "What is that round thing that you are selling used for?" he could demonstrate. He could collect cave bucks once he answered, once he sold.

Personal selling, whether you are a caveman or a guerrilla, allows you to develop and adjust a message to satisfy a prospect's need for information or to answer a question. Developing and adjusting messages is marketing. Satisfying prospects' needs is guerrilla marketing.

Dialogue happens when you are face-to-face with a prospect. Personal selling is dialogue between you and your prospects with the objective of getting them to open their wallets in exchange for your products and services, even if those wallets contain cave bucks.

According to the U.S. Department of Labor, more than 14 million people are employed in sales positions. Sales positions that first come to mind are real estate professionals, retail clerks, stockbrokers, representatives selling a manufactured product, automobile sales people, and door-to-door selling.

Personal selling also allows for targeting the most promising leads. A newsletter, advertisement, or TV commercial can't always be as selective because they communicate to the masses.

The guerrilla drawback to personal selling is the cost. Typically, a business will spend a great deal more on personal selling than on any other form of marketing. High costs don't contribute well to guerrilla profits, unless guerrilla selling provides guerrilla revenues higher than these costs.

Nothing develops a personal relationship better than personal contact. Direct selling is personal contact. The telephone comes close, but did you ever try to read body language over the phone?

There is a lot more to personal selling than personally delivering a message to a prospect face-to-face.

First you have to identify whom to deliver your message to. You already know from Day 4 that "everybody" is not a target market. Knowing those most interested in your product or service increases the probability of exchanging goods and services for cash. These people are candidates for your message delivery. These are the candidates for your one-on-one, face-to-face dialogue. These are your best personal selling targets and those most likely to be relationship-bound.

Preparation is part of personal selling. What to say and when to say it come with training and experience. Knowledge is powerful in all selling situations. Knowledge about the company, the person, the need, the problems to be solved, and the objections all prepare a personal salesperson to win the victory trophy of the selling contest.

Armed with knowledge, you are ready to deliver your message. This happens in the form of a conversation or presentation. Presentations could be demonstrations, explanations, testimonials, or fact-finding. All deliver information. Guerrillas know that presentations can be exchanged for checks. All are designed to transact business upon completion.

Transacting business is the ultimate goal of personal selling. This happens when prospects have decided you can solve their problems or enhance their business, quality of work life, or profits. This also happens when you establish a high degree of trust with prospects. Trust leads to confidence. Combining the two leads to business transactions, the fruit produced by guerrilla marketing seeds.

You might not know the prospect's mind is made up until you ask. This is what is known as a close. Identifying the next mutually agreed upon action is a close. Not doing so lengthens the selling process, leaves things to chance, and makes this already high-cost form of marketing even more costly. This is not part of the guerrilla success formula. Prospects need to utter the words "I'll take it" at some point. The focus here is one customer at a time. This follows all of the persuading and information provided by marketing and selling. It is a one-on-one personal selling effort that gets to these words.

Follow-up and relationship building round out direct personal selling efforts. Customers and prospects want attention before, after, and during their purchasing experience. Reinforcement and encouragement go a long way in providing this attention and building these relationships. Guerrilla Marketing points out that guerrilla marketers concentrate on how many relationships are made each month, not just the amount of sales receipts received.

Half the cars sold in Japan are sold door to door. These guerrillas meet the right prospects to start, develop relationships, supply information, and act as a resource. Business transactions increase significantly when you and the buyer know and trust each other. This is exactly what happens in the world of Japanese car sales.

Loyalty

Building and maintaining relationships keeps the customer coming back. Traditional marketing focuses on always getting new customers. Guerrilla marketing focuses on getting more from existing customers. Personal selling relationships ensure this will happen. Your best prospect is still a current customer.

Listening

Guerrillas excel at listening. Guerrillas are active listeners. Learn how to listen well. It's very difficult for someone trained to present a message to keep quiet. Guerrilla sales people are disciplined to do so. Listening shows intent. How do you know what problems need to be solved unless a prospect tells you? If you start in on a pitch to solve a problem that the prospect doesn't have, you will not sell anything. Guaranteed. Listening is a key skill in all sales calls.

Customers and prospects love to talk about their favorite subjects: themselves. Listening to them shows that you care more about them than yourself. Showing interest and caring leads to more completed order forms. Are you listening?

Asking Questions

Some of the best selling happens when you listen. Understanding what a prospect wants and needs and hearing it from them personally tells you what to target, what to sell, what problems to solve, and what challenges to overcome. This understanding comes from the dialogue in a personal selling situation. The dialogue involves asking questions.

Questions uncover needs, problems, pains, concerns, and objections. Questions move to create prospect commitment as a result of the information uncovered.

There are many benefits to asking the right questions. Questions not only qualify the buyer, but also establish rapport, identify the real needs and challenges, and find the prospect's hot buttons. Questions give you an understanding in most sales situations. The answers to all of these questions are important when establishing relationships to develop into the proper sales dialogue.

Questions that will reveal the best information and make the dialogue flow best are in general categories:

- Opening
- Motivation/vision
- Concerns
- Current situation
- Current supply
- Relationships
- Perceptions
- Product usage
- Communication
- Referrals
- Purchasing process
- Final thoughts

Asking questions is nothing more than a form of interviewing. The result is that you gain knowledge, build relationships, gather referrals, and ultimately generate new business. All of these are right up on that championship medal platform along with all the other guerrilla marketing values and principles.

Relationships

Just think of all the relationships you have in your life aside from your family and friends. You probably go to the same store regularly for groceries. Everyone has a favorite place to get his or her hair cut or styled. We all have our favorite restaurants. Businesses only buy from certain suppliers for a myriad of reasons. A good relationship is one of the most important. Marketing enhances all of these relationships: signs, mailings, radio ads, appearance, product and service delivery, and so on. All of these support the personal contact that occurs in the course of business transactions with relationship partners. The marketing supports the personal contact involved in selling, which ultimately leads to the exchange of dollars for products and services. Ongoing communication keeps customers returning and loyal. Returning customers provide lifetime value to you. Understanding the lifetime value of those returning customers gives you the high return on your marketing and sales investment that guerrillas expect.

Selling isn't always having every prospecting, presentation, and closing technique down pat. It mostly is establishing trust, being credible, and making sure you are offering and communicating value to your prospective buyer.

Selling is a very important part of the marketing process, but it is not a replacement for it.

A sales rep or the selling process is part of your company's promotional and marketing communications mix. Conveying information about benefits to prospects and keeping them informed of new products, services, or ways to solve new problems all lead to customer satisfaction. Customer satisfaction generates revenue. Without satisfied customers you have no business.

Many consumer businesses rely on advertising and promotion. B2B organizations rely more on the personal selling arm of marketing. Much of this is related to the nature of the customer's buying process and the buyer-seller relationship.

Because communication is a two-way process, being face to face with a prospect in a sales situation also allows for prospect feedback. The salesperson can then communicate back to the selling organization in an effort to respond, solve, improve, or communicate more effectively.

Marketing will get you to the dance. Once you're at the dance, you have to do your own dancing. Marketing generates leads, makes the phone ring, causes people to ask for your product. Selling (dancing) convinces prospects to take money from their bank account and put it in yours in exchange for something.

Great dance lessons, looking sharp, and following the etiquette doesn't always make you the best dancer. Great marketing doesn't always make the sale. Marketing, advertising, PR, and promotions lay the groundwork, but the sale actually happens after all this marketing informs, persuades, and motivates prospects to visit with you, request more information, or try a test run.

Marketing communication materials and print collateral are often referred to as sales collateral. Sales collateral is as much a part of the marketing process as a sales person is.

Many guerrilla businesses don't have large numbers of salespeople, if any. As the owner, principle, or manager of the business, you are thrown to the prospect wolves in the form of a sales rep. Knowing and exerting the selling fundamentals will lead you to make more business transactions.

Guerrillas like to maximize their trips to the bank with deposits. Up-selling is one of these fundamentals. Guerrillas up-sell by being prepared—prepared even when the customer says, "Yes, I'll take it." Kevin Nations, the Six-Figure Sales Coach, says that customers who have just bought are in the most receptive state possible to make a buying decision (they've just proved it). Once in this state up-selling can be done. His success and his coaching client's successes are due primarily to three direct up-sells. These up-sells will increase profits:

- Offer a premium version of the service your customer has just purchased at a reduced rate.

- Offer a subscription version of the services. (i.e., If you are a carpet cleaner and someone buys cleaning, offer him or her a subscription cleaning service where you deliver and they pay many times per year.)
- Ask for many referrals. Narrow your customer's universe to get your referrals. "Who do you know who has small children at home, pets, the cleanest home, or the dirtiest?" Also go overboard thanking them when a referral turns into new business for you.

Figuring out how to win a customer's time, consideration, and money is the key to successful selling. Even with complexities related to products and services, there still are many times when subtle differences between your offering and the competitor's make a difference. The closer products in the marketplace are to parity, the better the salesperson has to be if the company is to succeed.

We are not in business because it's a hobby. We are in business to earn a living or provide a living for others. We can only do this if there are profits. We can only have profits if there is revenue and revenue comes as a result of selling. How's that for a crash course in business? Marketing supports and aids in generating a sale.

Sales is not marketing, and marketing is not sales. In fact, the word sales is not even listed in the Guerrilla Marketing index, but it is an important part of the marketing formula.

Marketing can't exist without sales, and sales cannot exist without marketing. Though they have the same objective, the two require different strategies and tactics. These different strategies and tactics must be integrated to be effective. These integrated actions are the tools for finding the right prospects who are then converted to paying clients, with the final part of the process leading to returning customers and growing the resulting customer. That's sales. That's marketing. That's guerrilla revenue and eventual guerrilla profitability.

DAY 14 SUMMARY

■ Selling has often been called the distribution arm of marketing.

■ Personal selling allows you to develop and adjust a message to satisfy a prospect's need for information or to answer a question.

■ Nothing develops a personal relationship better than personal contact. Direct selling is personal contact.

■ Preparation is part of personal selling.

■ Business will be transacted when prospects determine you can solve their problems or enhance their business, quality of work life, or profits.

■ Identifying the next mutually agreed upon action is a close.

■ Understanding what a prospect wants and needs and hearing it from them personally tells you what to target, what to sell, and what problems to solve.

■ Selling is a very important part of the marketing process, but it is not a replacement for it.

■ Figuring out how to win a customer's time, consideration, and money is the key to successful selling.

■ Marketing can't exist without sales, and sales cannot exist without marketing.

■ ■ ■

Action Steps

1. Describe your selling process. Is listening a part of your process?

2. Do you have sales goals? How many prospects do you call a day? How many appointments do you get from those calls? How many sales do you get from those appointments? Understand these numbers and how they work for you and your business, and set selling goals accordingly.

3. What question will you ask your prospect to understand their

    - interest?
    - challenges?
    - objections?
    - likelihood to buy?

4. What uses of your product or service can you demonstrate for a prospect?

5. List 25 points from your sales presentation. Now condense these 25 points into the five most important.

6. When was the last time you were on the purchasing side of a sales presentation? What do you remember about it? What was good about it? What didn't you like about it? Did you buy? Why or why not? Adapt your sales process/plan accordingly.

7. List all the potential objections that a prospect will state when being sold to. Now write out the script for the way to overcome each of these objections.

8. How often will you call on a prospect or customer?

    - before you stop trying to get them to buy
    - after the initial sale is made

9. Scan newspapers and magazines and pick out advertising and marketing communication that supports personal selling efforts.

10. In what other ways can your marketing and advertising support selling efforts?

11. How could you adapt your website to be more of a sales support mechanism? How could you adapt your other marketing to do the same?

12. What relationship-building action can you do after a sale is made?

Telephone Selling and Marketing

VERY TIME A NEW COMMUNICATION device is invented, a new marketing vehicle emerges. The Pony Express was the beginning of direct mail. The telegraph has often been referred to as the Victorian internet, and you see what is happening in the whole world of e-mail marketing. Little did we think that the telephone would ever be referred to as "the old fashioned" way of communicating. But regardless of this moniker, it still is a very effective marketing tool. Companies have emerged that only offer telemarketing services, and now we see new laws governing their use—a sure sign of progress!

On this day you will add this weapon to your guerrilla marketing arsenal and learn how to do it right, ethically, and effectively. Right up your guerrilla road.

There are many ways for you to approach your customers and a like number for approaching your prospects. Some companies and individuals will be successful with direct mail over and over and with nothing else. Others will establish a position or niche and garner business from just using the internet. Still others will rely on one-to-one direct, face-to-face selling. To take full advantage of the guerrilla marketing credos of time, efficiency, optimum energy expended, and creativity and imagination to the max, marketing and selling need to take place when you're not present in person with the prospect/customer.

Teleselling, telemarketing, or selling and marketing by phone all happen without you being physically present with the prospect or customer. Sometimes people buy over the phone and sometimes they don't. Be prepared to rate the effectiveness of this weapon. Measure the number of calls, the time involved, and the resulting sales and profits. If the profits are there and are worth the number of calls made, then selling by telephone is a worthwhile weapon in your arsenal. If you are making too many calls without enough results, either revise your approach or put this weapon in the guerrilla recycling bin.

Our "territories" are expanding minute by minute, with some even going global. With the way travel costs are increasing and the amount of time sellers travel, the cost of sales is escalating. On Day 14 you were cautioned that the great disadvantage of personal selling is high costs. We have almost become a world of travelers selling instead of sellers traveling. Selling by telephone overcomes some of these high costs of true selling.

Telephone sales are one of the fastest growing segments of the sales profession. This does not refer to solely traditional telemarketing so much in the legislative headlines today.

With the pace of today's business, some of your customers don't want to wait for you or your salesperson to visit. Your prospects and customers want solutions now. They want information now. They want product now. They want service now. You want something sold now.

In the book *Guerrilla Teleselling* (John Wiley), the authors talk about a telepresence in the same sense that a business has an identity. This presence or identity is the combination of all the "telerelated" marketing weapons in your arsenal: FedEx, voice mail, the telephone, e-mail, audio, and videotape, the internet, and today, wireless communication. All this extends to what your customers and prospects think of you when you're not around in person.

Teleselling is more than just making phone calls to a decision maker. If only sales and marketing could be so easy.

The bottom line (and that's what we like talking about in guerrilla marketing) is you have to take care of your customers somehow, someway, right now, all the time. Teleselling will do that.

Selling closes the business (gets the order in hand). Teleselling closes the business (gets the order in hand) when you can't be there.

Most sales begin with a telephone call. "Doing good phone" is critical to sales success. Part of doing good phone is transmitting a high degree of trust and building confidence to the point of transaction. Part of it is uncovering a prospect's needs and wants and then offering no-brainer reasons to buy from you.

The Teleselling Process

The teleselling process is much like a direct selling process. The steps still need to be planned out. Your process should include a definite form.

Pre-Call Planning

Before that attempt at good phone, a little planning is in order. You know by now guerrillas are planners. In this case, planning what you want to accomplish by the phone call sounds like common sense. Planning sometimes is common sense, but not always common practice. What do you want the people you call to do as a result of your call? Do you want them to place an order, supply you with information, offer a referral. or take another action?

Prepare Questions

One of the ways to accomplish your objective is to ask questions. The answers to your questions are the keys that unlock your guerrilla treasure. The right questions provide the right keys. Many of the questions covered in Day 14, Direct Selling, can be applied to your telephone questioning strategy.

Your Opening Statement

Picking up the phone and making that phone call starts with the opening greeting and opening statement. Your opening statement is the make or break point of your call. Getting past the opening leads to a conversation. Not getting past this generally leads to hearing a dial tone on the other end. Your opening statement must be positive and interesting. It must get attention and be relevant. The goal is to make it so interesting that the conversation moves to the subsequent stage of questioning. Attention, interest, desire, and action. Here we go again. AIDA applies to just about every guerrilla marketing weapon.

Questions

Just like selling, how can you make a presentation, address problems, and suggest solutions for challenges if you don't know what problems or challenges your prospect has? These are all uncovered by asking questions—questions related to needs, wants, pains, challenges, goals, and objectives. This is the information gathering stage. It is only at this point that you will ever be in a position to give information. Giving the right information for a challenge that your prospect doesn't have is a futile telephone sales experience. With the questions and the associated answers, you can then direct your benefits to a potential solution.

Don't make your line of questioning complex. You can bet the answers won't be complex. One question at a time is a good pace. Remember some of the best sales calls occur when the salesperson is silent most of the time. The same thing applies to telephone selling. Give your prospect a chance to answer, reveal, uncover, and cite needs before you start in on your presentation. Answering with additional questions is OK, especially if you need to quantify or clarify something that your prospect mentioned or commented on. Quantification uncovers many needs and challenges: how often something happens, how much it costs, what time is involved, what resources are expended, etc.

Presentations

Just like in direct selling (see Day 14) you have to have a presentation, develop a trusting relationship, ask a lot of questions, and eventually close the sale.

Many of the personal selling techniques discussed on Day 14 are transferable to this day: building relationships, understanding needs, listening, and offering solutions of value.

Without the other tools you normally have in your arsenal, it's tough to demonstrate effectively over the phone. However, you can provide plenty of information to persuade a prospect and obtain an order.

Telemarketing/teleselling calls aren't long sales presentations. You want to communicate quickly and effectively that you have something of value for prospects as soon as you have learned more about them. Your solution should address those challenges or problems that were uncovered in the line of questioning earlier in the call. Only discuss how your solution will solve their problem, address their need, or create what they want.

Quality phone calls will sell more than quantity. Making sure that you are calling a targeted prospect that has the need for your product or solution is key. Otherwise, you are an interruption. People don't sit in their office or at home hoping and waiting for someone to call them to sell something. They are, however, hoping and wishing for a solution to their problem.

Just like personal selling, telephone communication is used to build and maintain relationships. It's not always a direct, hard-hitting sales call. Following up on orders, questions, and providing additional information is all part of customer attention. The number-one reason customers leave to use your competition is lack of attention. Making a follow-up call lets your customers and prospects know that you don't take them for granted.

Sometimes your follow-up call will be a call asking for an order. Your goal is to move prospects to the next level of commitment, with the ultimate level being the placing of an order. If you have developed the proper relationship, earned trust, and built confidence, your telephone contact will be successful. Failing to do any of these steps will cause your target prospect to think of every excuse in the book (not this book) not to take your call.

Because you are not physically present when using your telephone as a marketing weapon, there are a few things necessary for "safe marketing."

- *Don't talk in a monotone.* Feel free to be a bit more animated, putting emphasis where emphasis is needed. It's even OK to "talk with your hands" on the phone.

- *Don't think you have to have absolute privacy to make your call.* Shyness will come across even on the telephone. Practice talking on the phone in public. This will increase your presentation and your confidence.
- *Take into account that you are an interruption.* If you sense this, ask when it would be a better time to call back.
- *Continue to be positive.* Body language can't be read (and this includes yours) back to the customer. Positive tones lead to positive results.
- *Smile when talking on the phone.* It is unbelievable how this works. This can be detected in the mood and tone.
- *Use visual examples, touch the prospect's senses, and be a bit more graphic.* You have to overcome the sense of not being there.
- *Close.* Be decisive. Get the order. Get the information. Get the business. Complete the job. Don't make your telemarketing or teleselling call a casual conversation. Save that for your personal time.

Telephone marketing will not be the only weapon in your campaigns or attacks. Sending out a letter of introduction stating who you are, when you might be calling, and why you will be calling is a good punch to put with telemarketing. This one-two punch many times helps with relationship building and eventual sales.

Just one comment on voice mail: Voice mail has emerged as rapidly as telephone selling. Leaving a voice mail message for a targeted prospect is still an opportunity to market and sell if done right.

The successful telesales call follows this path:

- First, establish the value of the conversation—the reason for the call.
- Be sensitive to time and the fact that your phone call is probably an interruption—is this a good time to talk?
- Get to the point—what you want and how they benefit.
- Ask, ask, ask; don't tell.
- Listen, listen, listen, listen. Don't present until your time.
- Learn continuously; don't oversell.
- Have a benefits orientation in all of your solutions.
- Close; move the call to the next level of commitment or an order.

Prospects want phone calls that focus on them not you. Your messages need to state a care in response to what they want. Your solutions must be actionable and doable. The telephone experience must complement your other marketing and what your prospect sees, hears, and knows about you, including your personal visits. The success of selling by telephone varies from company to company and person to person. Having the right message, reaching the right target, and responding either with the right question or right presentation will determine most outcomes.

Someone is going to do business over the telephone on this day. It might as well be you.

DAY 15 SUMMARY

- Selling and marketing by phone happen without you being physically present with the prospect or customer.

- Selling by telephone overcomes some of the high costs of selling.

- Some of your customers don't want to wait for you or your salesperson to visit. That's where teleselling comes in.

- Your telepresence or identity is the combination of all the "telerelated" marketing weapons in your arsenal.

- Teleselling closes the business when you can't be there.

- "Good phone" uncovers a prospect's needs and wants and then offers convincing reasons to buy from you.

- Presenting on the telephone quickly and effectively communicates that you have something of value for prospects as soon as you have learned more about them.

- Telephone communication is used to build and maintain relationships.

- Prospects want phone calls that focus on them.

- Having the right message, reaching the right target, and responding with the right question or presentation will determine the outcome of a teleselling effort.

■ ■ ■

Action Steps

1. Review the action steps from Direct Sales, Day 14, and see which ones adapt directly to selling over the telephone.

2. Decide what the purpose of your call is.

3. Write down your best opening statement for your teleselling phone call.

4. Script out your offering of value for prospects (e.g., "My name is ____ with _____. We specialize in ____for_____. Could this solve any of your current challenges?").

5. Script out your follow-up statement for a follow-up call (e.g., "Hi, this is _____. On ____we spoke about _____. I'm calling to see if _____.").

6. Practice your opening statement so it doesn't sound like you're reading from a script.

7. Check your list to confirm the name, position, and pronunciation of the decision maker's name. Script out what you will say on this call (e.g., "I need to send information to ___. Can you verify the spelling of their name and the address and position?"). If you use a title in this query, get the name (e.g., " . . . and what is the name of your purchasing agent?").

8. If your list is in alphabetical order, start in the middle or the end of the list, not the beginning.

Printed Collateral, Brochures, and Sales Sheets

ICHAEL SHARP, A MINNEAPOLIS-BASED real estate agent, knows the value of the details in his brochure. Using a consistent barrage of mailings anchored by his award-winning, full-color personal brochure, he infiltrated a market that had previously been dominated by two long-time agents. In his downtown marketplace, customers and prospects describe a "new environment" because of Michael's entry and dominance of the market. Another phenomenon resulted from his campaign. People recognized him before actually meeting him. This accelerated the development of new relationships, created more listings with Michael, and eventually led to more trips to the deposit line at the bank—just what printed collateral should do.

In 1828, Noah Webster was considered just a humorless, arrogant old man. Almost 200 years later, he is praised as a militant patriot and

Christian stalwart. Most people think all he did was bother people about the English language and write a mediocre dictionary. The real fact is that he was one of the early guerrillas. Just look at two of the components of the word collateral according to him:

1. serving to support or corroborate: collateral evidence
2. of, relating to, or guaranteed by a security pledged against the performance of an obligation: a collateral loan

Look at the guerrilla implication of these two definitions. Collateral is sometimes called sales collateral, marketing collateral, print collateral, or just collateral. When used in this sense, it supports sales, marketing, and guerrilla efforts. Part one of the definition refers to this support in the form of serving and corroboration. The second part pledges something against the performance of an obligation. This is the part of the definition that people often associate with loans. Forget loans for the moment, and let's look at marketing. The obligation in our marketing is providing benefits or solutions for a customer's or prospect's problem or challenge. Anything we provide that guarantees this is considered by Guerrilla Noah to be collateral. You now are set to think like Noah Webster on Day 16. You make a promise supported by your print collateral, your sales collateral, or your marketing collateral.

In the 15th century, another guerrilla by the name of Johann Gutenberg invented a way to produce moveable metal type along with ink and a paper medium that led the way to the mass production of books. The first one was the Bible. Printing has been evolving ever since, including the printing of marketing collateral.

Gutenberg's genius was in his ability to put various existing technologies together to create something infinitely better, a true clinic in synergism. The combination of moveable type, ink, paper, and his newly devised press around 1450 created a revolution in the printing industry and led to what soon became known as the Information Age.

It was during that information explosion that print collateral got its birth. You can bet there was selling going on during Gutenberg's time. His invention led to the support of sales then and sales now. Little did we know that his invention would be a vital component of guerrilla marketing in the modern world! Well, here we are, and hats off to our early guerrilla, Johann Gutenberg.

Now that you are part of the modern world, you have to consider print collateral to support your own marketing and sales. When considering all the different print collateral options, you only have to go as far as looking at your overall marketing plan developed on Day 7. In that plan, you discuss

- communicating the benefits of your products and services to the marketplace.
- keeping in touch with clients about your company, people, products, services, and special offers.
- packaging.
- your identity.
- new product development and introductions.
- your selling process and presentation.
- awareness and PR campaigns.
- informing, persuading, and answering questions about anything to do with your company or organization.

If these are in your plan from Day 7, then you have a great starting point for developing your print collateral. Each one of these takes one or more different print collateral pieces. If they are not in your plan, revisit and revise accordingly.

Many of these plan components require an investment in supporting collateral, and all guerrillas want to make the right investment. A good investment is one that returns profits to your bottom line. The only bad marketing investment is the one that doesn't work. Making sure that it works from start to finish is good "investment" management. You are exposed to more than 3,000 marketing messages in one day. A large percentage are made up of brochures, mailers, newsletters, and fliers. Just look at your daily mail. The daily mail is a commercial printing company's prospect treasure.

These pieces are someone's marketing. As in all marketing, they must communicate an identity, an offering, what's in it for the customer/prospect, and what action needs to be taken. All that must happen with lightning speed to be effective. Collateral support can make that happen. Collateral marketing is not marketing by thesis; the briefer, the better for message communication.

A printed piece offers readers their unique brand experience to hold, touch, feel, fold, and reread. They all connect readers with the printed piece and leave a lasting impression that many times is the beginning of a long-term relationship.

What makes good print collateral? A high-gloss brochure sprinkled with testimonials and loud graphics? A sales sheet with bullet after bullet of features and benefits? Your annual report citing your challenges and accomplishments?

The answer is all three if each contains information your customers and prospects need to make purchasing decisions.

Pictures are worth a thousand words, but your marketing communication and related collateral must go beyond pictures to be effective. Purchasing discussions rely heavily on product or service information, specifications, features, benefits, and performance information, including capabilities and all information related to reliability.

Graphics are key, but the content must interest, intrigue, inspire, and initiate a purchase. When properly executed, printed collateral will accomplish this.

Print collateral is a vital component for establishing your brand and identity in the marketplace. Design and visual look and feel reflect your company's personality and solidifies the perception of your product and service in the mind of your prospects. Whether it is in the form of a direct-mail postcard or a seasonal catalog, the collateral contributes to this identity.

Print collateral is a tool that every sales person should use to enhance the presentation of goods and services and to develop prospects. Strategically designed and professionally produced printed literature gets you noticed and enhances the whole sales process.

Printed collateral is your "in absentia" sales force. When you are not around to personally represent your company, your marketing communication, printed collateral, and literature represent you. The objective here is to shape the beliefs and feelings of your target market on your products or services. Beliefs lead to action or no action. Guerrillas want action. The last page of *Guerrilla Marketing* says that the purpose of guerrilla marketing is action. Print collateral upholds that purpose.

Collateral is used for many purposes. It is used to provide information related to your capabilities and your product or service features and benefits.

Collateral can also be used to introduce your business to prospects. The key is to provide information that will induce prospects to purchase or supply information that will answer their questions along the way of the sales process, to the point of purchasing. Remember, your prospects will love your information and carefully read it.

You learned on Day 10, when discussing marketing communications, that the chosen marketing vehicle to communicate your marketing message should be in the format that best reaches your target market. In the guerrilla marketing world, this collateral is in the form of brochures, fliers, circulars, business cards, fact sheets, and other printed items that carry your identity, reputation, and information into the marketplace.

On this day, we focus on brochures, sales sheets, and company identity material. They include:

- *Brochures*. The highlights of a product, a service, or an overall company in an easy-to-read, graphically appealing format that informs customers and prospects.
- *Sales sheets/fact sheets*. A high-level, detail-oriented overview of products and services that educates customers and prospects about benefits.
- *Company identity*. Letterhead, envelopes, and business cards are designed to present your identity and tie all parts together in a uniformed design, look, and feel. Many times the first impression you make on a customer or prospect is via these identity materials.

Brochures

One of the main pieces of your company's collateral collection is the brochure. Before saying you need a brochure, make sure you can answer the question of why you need one. Some of those reasons are: your prospect is difficult to contact, your product or service information borders on being complex, graphics tell your story of benefits, and collateral warms up a prospect before a sales call, acts as a leave-behind after a sales call, or is used as a follow-up mechanism after a sales call. Many companies have a story that does not translate well in display advertising, but becomes brilliantly clear when the details are communicated in a brochure. This communication can be verbal or graphic. Combining the two, your brochure becomes a tool to

- get the attention and interest of prospects to the point of requesting more information and more contact or to the point of a purchase.
- provide information and answer questions that help prospects in their purchase decision. This includes plenty of detailed descriptions.
- communicate in a way that is consistent with your company identity.
- use as a handout on sales calls, a direct mail piece, a response mechanism for more information or inquiry, or a part of a press kit.

A brochure alone is insufficient to fulfill your total marketing plan; however, it can bring you closer to a goal of cost-effective communication with your target market. Brochures should be created for your high probability prospects and filled with the information they most crave. Brochures should be distributed only to those that request them or have a high probability of using the information disseminated. Who cares about the details communicated in a brochure? Your real prospects do.

You have seen many brochures in your business life. Some you liked, some you didn't. Those that you liked and those that worked were designed to tell potential clients exactly what they want to hear in just a few seconds. If it doesn't, it's on its way to the proverbial recycling bin.

The key to effective collateral is to find the happy medium between a bestselling novel about your company or organization and a one-page resume. That happy medium makes use of the following brochure guidelines and tips:

- *What's in it for the prospect?* This essentially makes sure that you are talking about benefits and not overloading the copy with feature after feature. When your prospects read your brochure, they want to know how your products or services will help them. They don't care about a litany of features and facts about who you are.
- *What's short and sweet is what's read.* Brochures aren't designed to be a thesis for a graduate degree. You don't need a large number of pages to convince a prospect of your company's size. Long, lengthy, and wordy doesn't work. Your goal is to convey key messages. Get your

point across quick and concisely. Don't clutter your brochure with words and overused text. Many times a picture can tell a story much more efficiently than a cluster of words.

- *Remember why you are producing and using a brochure.* You want your prospect to do something. Prospects have to be told what to do. In the guerrilla marketing world, that is a call to action. Sales collateral isn't going to close a deal by itself. Remember what Mr. Webster told you. It is support for your sales and marketing effort.

Done right, your collateral materials should pique prospects' interest, give them all the information necessary to make a decision, and offer them a way to move directly to a purchase or request for more information, whether you are present or not. A collateral brochure should act as a tour guide for your company, products, or services, delivering only the information you choose. Complementing your sales copy and messages with attention-getting graphics will leave prospects with everything they need to pique their interest even more and help turn their ultimate purchasing decision in your favor.

Sales Sheets

Another popular form of sales and marketing collateral is the sales sheet, sometimes referred to as a one sheet, fact sheet, sales flier, spec sheet, or product data sheet.

Sales sheets are often used when you have one or more products or services to offer a prospect. They allow you to give prospects only the product/service information that is relevant to solving their problems or helping them with their particular challenge.

Sales sheets are important during presentations because they help you communicate the value and benefits of your product and service.

A great deal of selling actually takes place behind the scenes when you can't be present. Sales-ready documents put your messages in front of the prospects, helping them understand your features and benefits, while communicating the value of your product or service specifically for them. Sales sheets are most effective when they are based on a foundation of the customer's requirements and when presented in the form that best answers the question, What's in it for me, the prospect?

Sales sheets provide a written and pictorial confirmation of the sales presentation and illustrate to prospects the benefits they can expect to receive from purchasing your product or service. Sales sheets will improve the interactions you have with prospects and will help you spend less time trying to piece together complex sales messages.

Sales-ready collateral increases sales productivity and effectiveness for you or your sales rep. Preparing sales sheets ahead of time allows you to spend more time selling.

These selling documents help improve prospect interactions while increasing overall sales force effectiveness and consistency. Sales sheets won't make the sale by themselves. Just ask Mr. Webster. I'm sure he used them to support his efforts when selling dictionaries.

Printed Materials in the Age of the Internet

With the growth of the internet, isn't there less use for printed collateral?

Despite the growth of electronic marketing collateral, communication by print collateral remains vital to an organization's marketing communication strategy and success.

A great online communication effort can become even greater with corresponding print materials to reinforce the electronic message.

Lauron Sonnier McCulloch of Sonnier Marketing Communications Inc., (sonniermarketing.com) advises her clients that any time they launch a website, they should be aggressive in telling their own clients and prospects about it with offline marketing communication. The firm produces a look, tone, and message that is carried out in a direct mail piece, statement stuffer, fax cover sheet, and flier that can be inserted with other company marketing materials such as brochures and sales sheets. All of these pieces give potential customers many benefits and reasons to visit the company's new or updated website.

The use of all sales collateral brochures, folders, catalog sheets, annual reports, sales sheets, etc., should remain strong. They still are the marketing tools that offer the ultimate in targeting. With today's print-on-demand technology, they can be produced in smaller quantities. You can target only prime prospects and at the specific time that you want to target them.

Print communication still has some advantages over electronic media. Hard copy and print collateral stays around more than a casual, online browse. While the trend is shifting, print communication is still preferred by many purchasers/prospects.

Print communication is more conducive to the complex presentation in which study and comprehension take time. Pieces can be read and reread, used for reference and comparisons, and referred to others more easily.

Print, on the other hand, offers no interaction and is difficult and costly to continuously update. Regardless, it is still "comfortable" and preferred by the masses.

This day only touched on a small portion of the many forms of print collateral. With so many forms, the key is to plan them, plan your budget accordingly, be consistent with their use, and use them as support vehicles. I highly suggest consulting with your local printing expert who often is a mailing and marketing expert. If you are at a loss finding such a company, visit 1-800-inkwell.com. Do all this and you will be right up there with fellow guerrillas Gutenberg and Webster.

DAY 16 SUMMARY

■ Collateral is sometimes called sales collateral, marketing collateral, print collateral, or just collateral. It supports both sales and marketing.

■ Collateral offers the reader a unique brand experience to hold, touch, feel, fold, and reread. It connects the reader with the printed piece and leaves a lasting impression that starts a relationship.

■ Good print collateral contains information your customers and prospects need to make purchasing decisions.

■ Print collateral is your "absentia" sales force.

■ One key to collateral is to provide information that will induce the prospect to purchase or provide information that will answer questions leading to a purchase.

■ The best collateral formats to reach your target market are brochures, fliers, circulars, business cards, fact sheets, and other print material. All carry your identity, reputation, and information into the marketplace.

■ One of the main pieces in your company's collateral collection is the brochure.

■ Another popular form of collateral is the sales sheet. It is sometimes referred to as a one sheet, fact sheet, sales flier, spec sheet, or product data sheet.

■ The key to collateral is to plan the pieces, plan the budget accordingly, be consistent with their use, and use them as support vehicles.

■ ■ ■

Action Steps

1. Which pieces of mail have you thrown away in the last few days or weeks? Why did you throw them away? Jot down the reasons: wasn't interested in product, didn't need it, didn't like it, looked like a shoddy offering, etc.

2. Which piece of mail did you keep? Why did you keep it?

3. Collect brochures that you like.

4. What are some ideas for brochure headlines, pictures, bullet points, and FAQs?

5. What is your objective with other print collateral?

6. What costs are involved with each piece of collateral?

7. How will you distribute each piece of collateral to the marketplace?

8. What budget do you need to produce a brochure that looks professional, does the right job, is as timeless as possible, and is appealing to your prospects? Can you afford this?

9. What identity items do you want included in your collateral?

10. How will you use the various pieces of your marketing collateral? How will you get them to your prospects?

11. How many different ways can you use each individual collateral piece?

    - Direct mail piece
    - Web site posting
    - Handout flyer
    - Packaging enclosure
    - Other

12. What other printed marketing material have you noticed? Where did you see it? What made you notice it? Did it influence your purchasing decision?

Sunday	Monday	Tuesday	Wednesday	Thursday	Friday	Saturday
	1	2	3	4	5	6
7	8	9	10	11	12	13
14	15	16	17 ✓	18	19	20
21	22	23	24	25	26	27
28	29	30				

Direct Mail

JAY CANNONE, A REAL ESTATE AGENT in the northeastern United States, learned not only about consistency and frequency in his direct mail campaign, but also about patience. Hobbs Herder, a real estate marketing advisory firm, put a plan in place for Jay. After about ten months he told his advisors that nothing was working, even though he had followed the recommended plan exactly. Don Hobbs told Jay to just stick with it. Jay did. About two months after this sage advice, Jay reported that business started flowing like a faucet was turned on. He learned that in marketing, repetition pays. Patience pays. Perseverance pays. He knew then that most of his competitors didn't have these same qualities. They wanted instant gratification, so after a few months they would redirect their marketing dollars and jump from marketing plan to marketing plan. The quick fix approach didn't work. The patient approach paid off for Jay. He almost classifies direct mail as a career commitment, not a three- or six-month commitment. So add commitment to consistent, persistent, and patient not only for direct mail but also for all your marketing. Targeting and consistency made the difference between "love" mail and "junk" mail for Jay Cannone.

How much junk mail do you receive each day? If you respond to it, notice it, or buy something as a result of it, is it still junk mail? Many commercial printing and mailing companies don't use the term junk mail. Their preferred term is "love" mail because they love to print and process it. Prospects that act upon it also love it. You will love it, too, if they are your prospects.

Junk mail is slang for direct mail. The term was applied because incoming mailboxes were starting to overflow with mail that was ineffective in marketing products or services. Ineffective messages started piling up; effective messages were set aside and not classified as junk.

We get it every day. Junk mail. Is it really junk? Over 65 percent of what is mailed is direct mail marketing. Can more than half of the mailing public be participating in a junk war? What about all the printing and mailing companies and the U.S. Post Office? I'm sure if you ask these people, whose income depends on all of this junk, they will have a different opinion. Direct mail is only junk when it is of no interest to the receiver. When targeted to those with an interest, this direct form of marketing is no longer junk. If the messages communicated offer value to the receiver, direct mail is no longer junk. The guerrilla code here is to target your mailing to those interested and curious about what you have to offer. The bottom line, and guerrillas love bottom lines, is that direct mail is one of the most efficient and cost-effective ways to get a message to a target audience.

Why is direct mail called direct mail? Why isn't it called indirect mail or just mail? Other forms of marketing and advertising communicate to the masses. You're never really sure who is receiving your message in mass communication. With direct mail, you communicate one-on-one directly to your intended audience. It is more of a rifle shot to your target market. You control who receives your message. You control how often they see it and how many people are reached. These are all direct effects of direct mail. Direct mail is simply direct communication to targeted prospects and customers. This form of one-to-one marketing is the opposite of mass marketing.

Direct mail is one of the most efficient and cost-effective ways to get a message to a target audience. Because one of your top priorities as a guerrilla business is reaching your target audience, these qualities make direct mail the marketing medium of choice for you and many other guerrilla marketers. Direct mail informs, persuades, and educates prospects that are inaccessible by other means. Direct mail helps to level the playing field for small companies going against larger companies. The fight is for the mindshare of one targeted person.

In the spirit of guerrilla marketing, direct mail translates into one of the more profitable ways to touch existing and potential clients. It is also an effective way to get your prospects to open their wallets.

Direct mail uses a wide variety of marketing communication pieces. Catalogs, brochures, postcards, fliers, newsletters, and letters make up the majority of mailings in direct mail programs.

These marketing vehicles, when mailed, can be targeted to exactly the people most interested in your product or service. They also arrive in less of a communication clutter than other interruptive marketing that your prospects and customers are bombarded with daily. Many times direct mail is welcomed by the prospect, especially if you have done your homework on your target list and they are part of the target researched.

Advantages of Direct Mail

In addition to the fact that direct mail is so direct, there are other unique characteristics of this marketing weapon that are true strengths. Direct mail is efficient and cost-effective because of these strengths and the many advantages associated with them:

- *Personalization.* Communication and messages can truly be one-on-one. People like to see their name and personal information in print or in writing. Using personalization extends the potential relationship further and faster.
- *Targeted and focused.* Direct mail allows you to target according to your own specifications: demographically, geographically, by prospects or customers, and a combination of all of these along with your desired quantity. Other marketing does not offer this same "targetability." Your

message goes right to the person, company, or organization that is interested in you.

- *Call to action.* Direct mail inspires action and is sales oriented. Direct mail has a purpose. That purpose is to inform, educate, or persuade a prospect. Designed and distributed correctly, direct mail can be nonintrusive compared to the other 3,500 marketing messages a prospect receives each day. Prospects read it at their own pace and, if targeted right, will be interested in the information. Direct mail can be reread, studied, and thought about as the prospect goes through the purchasing decision process. Action is requested by the sender. The receiver taking the appropriate action fulfills one objective of direct mail.

- *Sales oriented.* Direct mail breaks the ice for sales people. It may announce an upcoming visit or a follow-up or gently and cordially introduce the sales person. This warms up the prospect for the subsequent sales call. Direct mail can be a "direct-sales" mechanism related to response, reminder, and fulfillment, with the ultimate goal being a purchase from you again and again.

- *Measurable.* Direct mail is one of the easier marketing methods to measure. You always know how many pieces you send, how often you send them, the cost of each printed piece, and the associated postage. When a prospect comes to you as a result of the mailing and is converted into a paying client, you get a return on your direct mail investment. Get enough responses and paying clients as a result and you reach guerrilla

Key Components

An effective direct mail campaign includes four key components. These are also key components of most guerrilla marketing, but they related here to direct mail:

1. Message
2. Vehicle
3. Target
4. Frequency

standards of return on investment. That's very good news. The other good news related to your direct-mail investment is that you are spending your guerrilla dollars on those most likely to be interested in your products and services—thus the definition of target market and the direct part of direct mail.

The Target

If a tree falls in a forest and no one is there to hear it, is there still sound? This age-old question, mentioned earlier, can apply to mailing when it comes to your target audience. You could have the best marketing message and vehicle ever. If the right potential buyer doesn't receive your message, nothing gets marketed; no one acts. Putting yourself in front of a potential buyer is the key to marketing and selling. No potential buyers? No selling. The right target audience might be the right segment, the right niche within a segment, or the right people within a niche. If you are mailing to banks, are you mailing to the bank president or the branch manager? If you are mailing to manufacturers are you mailing to the operations department or the purchasing department? Success is determined by having the right target audience for your mailing. Don't forget about current customers as part of your target audience. Even breaking up current customer segments into different targets may be more effective for your mailing. Find the people to populate the forest and let the direct-mail trees fall.

More than half the success of your mailing campaign is a function of how well you have identified your audience. The more you know about them the more you can target. How old are they? What do they like or dislike? What are their aspirations and challenges? Do they have a lot of money or operate on a strict budget? The answers to all of these questions go into defining a laser-focused target list to attack. The more focused the attack, the more victorious you will be.

Are you targeting young or old? Male or female? A particular industry or general consumers? These are the types of questions that best determine your target audience and the list that you ultimately develop and send to. Knowing your ideal clients and what they want, need, and prefer will further refine your target market definition to the point where direct mailings will hit a guerrilla bull's-eye, instead of a non-guerrilla trash can. Knowing your prospects' thoughts, dreams, goals, and pain also helps you define where you want your guerrilla dart to hit.

It's OK to buy lists from list suppliers. Just specify as best you can what you want. There is a difference between a good quality list and a poor quality list. Your response and results will show you how good your target list is. You can also compile all the contacts you have for your own list development. This includes customers, people you have met during your networking, referrals, and other acquaintances.

The Message

Although sometimes subjective, the marketing message in a mailing must be clear, concise, and attention-getting. Does the message create interest and desire and is there a call to action? Does the message relate to you, your company, product, or service, or does it relate to the challenge that you are offering a solution for? Sometimes more than one message can be ideal for a mailing situation. It is still OK to test messages. If the message you have is working now and is effective for your target market, leave it unchanged. Testing and measuring will determine this.

The message in a mailing is sometimes referred to as your offer. This is the other significant component of direct mail. Are you making a special offer? A sale? Free information? A consultation? A contest? Be bold with your offering and don't beat around the bush. This will lead to what you want your prospects to do when they get your mailing. Do you want them to call, send for information, visit your place of business, visit your website, or refer someone?

Messages must be creative. You need to stand out from the pile of mail received. Capturing attention and creating interest leads to the desire and action that you want. Don't make your direct mail look like all the rest you get. Be different. Creative headlines and interesting opening statements are essential to a good message. Copy sells. Make the copy appropriate for your audience. Be appealing. Good design will lead the reader through the piece. Don't let design dominate your mailing piece. Too many designers design mail pieces where the prospect remembers the design and not the product or service being offered. Guerrillas avoid this trap.

Capturing attention and interest, while creating desire and action are the jobs of your direct-mail message. Headlines, bullet points, diagrams, or creative design do this. Be careful not to draw attention to your marketing and vehicle to the point where the product or service is not noticed. Concentrate on marketing and communicating information about the product and service.

In marketing, copy is king. Yes, design is important and will certainly aid in gaining attention and interest, but the copy is still what does the selling. Your message does the work in the form of information, persuasion, humor, convincing statements, facts, risk relievers, and motivation.

A good message also includes a direct call to action. Many customers like to be told what to do, so the decision is not left up to them to make. This is one of the advantages of direct mail and why it is on the guerrilla marketers preferred list.

The Vehicle

The definition of a vehicle is something that takes you somewhere. If it is not taking you where you want to go, you need to change vehicles. The same thing applies to mailing. The U.S. Post Office says that anything can be mailed as long as it has the proper postage and can pass through mail processing (I wonder if the postage to mail a person is less than airfare?). Most direct mailings consist of postcards and letters although the use of catalogs is growing rapidly. Different target markets react to different vehicles. Different product or service focuses require different vehicles. Use what your target audience will respond to and what you can afford.

You may be using a nice letter in an envelope that appears promotional in nature and is automatically discarded by the receiver when a postcard would do the job more effectively. If you know you have the right message for the right audience but it's not getting communicated, change the vehicle. Test its effectiveness and make the necessary corrections to optimize your mailing.

The Frequency

Getting one response from a mailing of 10,000 is not as good as getting four responses from four mailings of 2,500. The latter is more likely to happen because of an increased frequency of communicating your message. The direct cost of doing four mailings of 2,500 and one mailing of 10,000 is the same. The expense is higher in the mailing that only generates one response.

At the risk of repetition (although you're learning that repetition is good in marketing), direct mail works better when complemented with all other marketing and not as a single marketing strategy.

How frequently a message gets to a target market can make or break a mailing campaign. Someone once said, "I tried direct mail once and didn't get any business." There are all kinds of statistics on how many times someone must be exposed to you or your message before they take action. Once is certainly not ideal. Most will say six to eight times while others have said even more. This being the case, have you given your message a chance before you stop or change it? Usually the people who tire of the message first are the marketers themselves. Usually the target audience doesn't remember as well as the sender and still can be motivated when receiving the message.

Does this mean you communicate your marketing message once a day? Usually not, but sometimes you see or hear something related to consumer brands daily (e.g., Coca-Cola). This must be measured against audiences tiring of your contacts and effectiveness. In the case of direct mail, once per month is optimal. Different audiences will require different frequencies of messages. Each must be evaluated for optimum effectiveness. If it's not enough (measured by response rates), change it. If it's too much (measured by costs and return on investment), change it. Consistency and frequency are just two more components to be evaluated when planning your mailing.

The general rule of thumb related to the frequency of mailing is to mail whatever you can afford to mail on a monthly basis, over and over, consistently. If you can afford to mail a quantity of 1,000 pieces for six months, consider cutting the quantity in half and mail twice as long (500 pieces, once a month, consistently for 12 months).

Direct mail is a numbers game. The typical response rate is about 1 to 2 percent. There are ways to increase this and ways to guarantee no response. I recently was speaking to a group of about 100 business owners about direct mail usage and gave the example of a large credit card company that continues to bombard us all with direct mail. Everyone I know discards this well-known, branded mail as junk mail. When I made that statement to this group a gentleman in the back of the room raised his hand and politely disagreed with me. He said he was interested in that mail and would probably take action. One person in a room of 100 represents 1 percent, that typical response rate. That one person's action will pay for the junk mail that was discarded by the other 99 people. The company in reference here plays that numbers game all the time and so should you with your target market of customers and prospects.

Put the right offers in the hands of the right prospect and sales will grow. Put the wrong offer in the hands of the wrong prospect and the only thing that will grow is mailing costs.

Other Considerations

The direct mailer also needs to think about:

- *Proper timing of the mailing*. You need to reach prospects when it is convenient for them and when they will read your message. The week between Christmas and New Year's Day is, believe it or not, a quiet mail time and a good time for your mailing to stand out.
- *Budget*. Cutting too many corners and saving pennies may cost you dollars on the return. Get the biggest bang for your buck with all the budgetary components involved in a mailing campaign. Be prudent and conservative, not cheap.
- *Testing*. Split a mailing into two different mailings and test offers, headlines, designs, and frequency. Make sure you have a good evaluation process in place and repeat what works. Revise what doesn't or eliminate it.
- *Personalization*. We are living in a one-on-one world or at least one moving fast in that direction. Personalization will return a higher response rate. As Robert DeNiro said in Taxi Driver, "You talking to me?" If your prospects feel you are talking one-on-one to them, you have made strides towards starting a good relationship, which will eventually help you sell. Personalized mailings always outpull mailings that are not personalized.

Direct Mail Guidelines

The following guerrilla guidelines will help you be more effective in your direct-mail campaigns and benefit the receiver of your "love" mail:

- Make it easy for the recipient to take action.
- Testimonials improve response rates.
- Color sells.
- Headlines sell.
- Benefits sell.
- Success comes with the cumulative effect of repeat mailings.
- Success is due 60 percent to the target list, 30 percent to the offer, and 10 percent to the creativity of your mailing.
- Direct mail that looks like junk mail will not get opened or read.
- Writing letters still works as a direct mail vehicle.
- Creating a sense of urgency and special offers increase response rates.
- Postcards don't have to be opened, and you save the cost of the envelopes, insertion, and sealing.
- Use direct mail to promote your website and to invite people there.

- *Benefits orientation.* This orientation exists if you don't overload your copy with features and useless verbiage. Readers care about how you can help them or improve their lives, not about you. Benefits sell. Repeat them over and over in your direct mail campaigns.

Direct-mail marketing may be changed by the popularity of the internet, but it won't eliminate it. As long as the U.S. Post Office is in existence, direct mail marketing will be, too. People still like to get mail from their friendly postal worker. Let direct mail work for you, and you will mail more checks to your bank.

DAY 17 SUMMARY

■ Direct mail is junk when it is of no interest to the receiver. Targeted to those with interest, this direct form of marketing is no longer junk.

■ Direct mail is one of the most efficient and cost-effective ways to get a message to a target audience.

■ With direct mail, you control who receives your message.

■ Direct mail uses a wide variety of marketing communication pieces.

■ Direct mail is efficient and cost effective because of the strengths and advantages associated with it:

- Personalization
- Targeted and focused
- Call to action
- Sales oriented
- Measurable

■ Key components of direct mail are message, vehicle, target, and frequency.

■ As long as the U.S. Post Office is in existence, direct-mail marketing will be strong.

■ ■ ■

Action Steps

1. Calculate the total costs of your mailing campaign and calculate what your break-even point will have to be for sales of your product or service. Don't forget to include printing, design, mail prep, and postage costs in your calculations. Cost of mailing/customer value = break-even point (number of responses/sales needed). Customer value = total profits (short-term and long-term) derived from the lifetime of the customer.

2. Investigate outsource vendors for

- printing.

- bulk mail processing, addressing (often referred to as a mail house or a letter shop).
- list supplier.
- graphic designer.

All may be under one roof at one business (e.g., typically printing companies employ graphic designers to help with the design of mail pieces).

3. What do you want prospects to do when they receive your mailing:
   - Buy a product or service?
   - Request more information?
   - Request personal contact?
   - Enter a contest?
   - Call your toll-free number?
   - Visit your website?
   - A combination of the above?

4. Will you mail according to a geographical area, a set of demographics, or a combination of the two? Describe each.

5. What is the format of your mailing campaign: letter, postcard, self-mailer, and reply mechanism? What are the associated costs of each?

6. How often will you mail to your target?

7. What main points do you want to communicate in your mailing?

8. What other marketing will direct mail support?

9. What other marketing will support direct mail?

10. What other ways can you use your direct-mail pieces?

Radio/Television/Cable TV

HIS JUST IN: YOUR PROSPECTS and customers are tuned into the broadcast world. With TV sets in more than 99 percent of our homes and radios in 95 percent of cars, your target market is reachable by the airwaves. Venturing into this advertising arena can seem at first to be unguerrilla-like. By Day 18 you know enough about guerrilla marketing to realize that using these weapons in the right way, with the right plan, and with a profit orientation can be the difference between a marginal or successful guerrilla marketing attack.

Joe Marble, a real estate agent in Minneapolis, had a lifelong love for and connection to the Minnesota Twins. He made an agreement with the Twins to shoot his cable TV commercial inside their stadium, the Metrodome, while the team took batting practice. Joe assembled his family and friends to pose as real fans watching the game behind him. When he yelled "Action," it was like he was standing on the field during a live game talking to his audience. The impact on his small business was astounding. It gave him a lot of recognition and a lot of listings for his real estate business. He measured the results and ended up realizing that he used to throw away money in magazine ads that reached 30,000 homes with little or no results. His commercials were seen by 170,000 people at $25 per spot, making the exposure and dollar per exposure much cheaper and more effective. Joe Marble has found the guerrilla benefit of TV advertising.

Whether you use radio, television, or cable TV, the airwaves will reach your clients. Deciding whether it is good for your business will depend on your target, product, and guerrilla attack.

Many businesses and organizations don't consider advertising on the radio or TV because they think it is too expensive. While this might be true for advertising on prime time network television or once a year Super Bowl commercials, there are other affordable, guerrilla-friendly on-air alternatives and strategies to consider. We will look at each part of the broadcast world separately.

Radio

Ninety percent of men, women, and teens listen to radio, which is a good medium for a very mobile society. Consumers have less and less time for fixed attention media. Your radio ad can be heard while people are driving, jogging, walking in the park, dining, or in their own backyard.

Consider this question as you decide whether radio is right for your business: How can I sell, promote, brand, and continue to make targeted prospects aware of my product/service in 60 seconds? That's the standard length of a radio commercial slot. Crafting your marketing message to fit that slot is the challenge of using radio.

Radio marketing strategies should accomplish the following:

- Increase customer traffic to your location
- Identify building and positioning
- Promote special events (e.g., clearance sales, celebrity appearances, or open houses)
- Generate leads from a wide target audience

- Forge a closer relationship with prospects/customers/listeners
- Help to communicate emotions (emotions sell)
- Reach prospects and customers you otherwise might not be able to reach
- Act as a direct response mechanism for the purchase of your products and services

Radio can be very targeted. Not every radio station has the same format. Stations target certain demographical groups with different programming. Each radio station's format and programming is designed to meet the needs, wants, tastes, and preferences of specific listening audiences. The mere turn of a dial can present your message to listeners who prefer talk radio, rock 'n' roll, or easy listening. You need to pick the right station. What programming do your prospects like? If these demographics and genre targets match up with your targeting, then radio advertising will be a guerrilla win for you.

Radio advertising clearly must address the first A (attention) of the AIDA formula. Grabbing attention in radio is like writing an attention-grabbing headline for a print ad or newspaper story. Use the same headline in a radio commercial. You only have a few seconds to snag the listener. After that, it's just like all the other fundamental marketing that you do. Tell the listener what's in it for them, the true benefits. Make sure your identity comes through, even if it's just the name of your business. Make a call to action; tell the listener what to do. And do all of this over and over and over. And do all of this over and over and over. And do all of this over and over and over. You can sprinkle spice and variety throughout the ad with phrases and words that create a sense of urgency and motivation: "Hurry, only a few left," "For today only . . .," etc. That's Radio 101 in a nutshell. It's not rocket science. Guerrilla marketing is not rocket science. Building the radio is.

Let's look at actual ad copy for radio. The who, what, where, when, and why formula applies here as it does to most marketing communication.

Books-a-Go-Go, the bookstore with more variety, is clearing out its old inventory this weekend only. Visit the large warehouse at the end of the Main Street Strip, next to the Pearlman Building in Todd's Corner.

This brief paragraph is either a 15-second ad or a 15-second introduction to a longer ad. Try it. Time it. You'll then get a good feel for radio ad writing.

Let's say you understand headlines and you can write succinct copy that sells. What's next? The next part is getting your commercial on the air. In the spirit of guerrilla marketing, you don't necessarily have to hire an ad agency. Call your radio salesperson. They are experts. They know the ins and outs of putting an ad together and getting it on the air. They will think of the details that you don't.

Radio salespeople want your radio marketing to be successful. They have an incentive for repeat business and referrals because of the ad's success, two main ingredients in any guerrilla marketing pie. They can make it easy for you. You are the expert in guerrilla marketing. Guerrillas do what they do best and leave the rest to experts in their field.

Here we go again with that guerrilla mantra of repetition. Repetition on the radio builds awareness. The frequency you need can be affordable, but it must fit into your overall marketing budget. Evaluation of the audience and its response to your ad must be done to determine whether radio is a worthwhile investment. If radio marketing delivers a higher percentage of a demographic group you are targeting more than other marketing, it may be your best marketing vehicle.

The size and quality of the listening audience has to be evaluated. How many listeners does the station reach? Are the listeners made up of business owners and managers, or do they consist of mostly working women and teens? How many times can you reach the specified audience (frequency)? Reach creates awareness. Frequency causes more guerrilla order forms to be completed. These factors will determine your marketing effectiveness with radio.

Using a station rate card, you can calculate your cost per message per person for this type of marketing (i.e., how many advertising impressions). Measuring response rates and the associated sales conversions will provide you with the return on your marketing investment. As with any guerrilla program, constant planning, measuring, and evaluating will determine how long radio stays a part of your guerrilla marketing mix.

Radio is effective when used in combination with your other marketing; it represents another touch to the prospect with your message and your identity. With enough repetition, you will eventually achieve a higher awareness for your product or service.

Guerrilla Hint Number 1: All published rate cards are very negotiable. You don't receive if you don't ask. Ask your radio salesperson for guerrilla rates.

Guerrilla Hint Number 2: Ask about advertising rates for different times of day. Make sure your target audience listens when you advertise.

Guerrilla Secret (bigger than a guerrilla hint):
It is important for your commercial to be played first in a series of commercials. Ask your radio sales rep how this order is determined. In the world of radio-speak, this is referred to as how commercials are "stacked." Finding out how commercials are stacked will help you determine how to produce your commercial. Some stations stack commercials with jingles first. Stations might play 60-second commercials before 30-second ones. Other stations may stack in the opposite manner.

Using these secrets will keep you ahead of your competition. You guerrilla, you!

Radio advertising is one marketing weapon. It is not a complete marketing program. It may be the only weapon, but you still have to develop your benefits-oriented message in such a way that it hits your target audience squarely between the eyes. These are all guerrilla marketing components of your total marketing attack. Radio might be one of those for you.

Television

You might be thinking, "I'll skip this section because I'm too small for TV advertising, or it costs too much, or TV advertising is for the other guys." If these things were true, then this chapter would end here. As you can see, though, there is writing on these pages and more for you to read, learn, and implement successfully in guerrilla marketing style.

Mention television and immediately people think big-company advertising. With the growth of cable and regional TV, however, a small business can benefit from advertising, just like the big guys. Look how cable stations have popped up everywhere over the past few years. All these channels need advertising revenue to remain on the air. Because of the increased competitiveness in this arena, many stations are offering very affordable rate packages, within easy reach for small guerrilla businesses and organizations.

TV advertising is powerful. Used incorrectly, this power becomes negative power. A bad ad will cause you to lose customers. A bad plan or execution of the plan will cause you to lose money. Both are "guerrilla-nots." A great ad executed well will result in many guerrilla celebrations paid for by the newly-found profits.

People pay attention to marketing in the following order: graphics, headlines, bullets, and text. Television uses headlines, too. You only have a few seconds to grab a viewer's attention. The headline must be the strong opening along with a simple and clear message that stresses benefits. This all has to be done visually. Show rather than tell, and don't forget that call to action. Television has made the term "Call today!" a very popular call to action in all advertising. You just learned the importance of headlines in radio advertising. Television advertising is nothing more than using the same headlines and the same marketing message while adding on television graphics and visuals. That's what skyrocketed MTV to success. They added visuals to songs. Your marketing message is your song. The dancing video represents the graphics that tell your story.

Read each line of your radio ad (or print ad) and think of an image that portrays that message. Another way is to tell your story with pictures. That's what television programming and advertising is all about.

Television is a perfect medium for introducing a new product or showing a comparison. It is a visual advertising medium. A good way to test a successful ad is to see if you can tell what is being advertised with the sound turned down. The script is a support to the visuals. You have a good script if you can close your eyes and tell what product or service is being advertised. Utilizing both will effectively hit your target with this weapon of mass marketing.

Because television advertising is so visual, viewers will remember more how they felt watching the ad than every detail of the ad. You want them to feel good, but also feel informed, persuaded, and motivated enough to buy your product or service.

Speaking with a clear message to your target audience is key in any advertising but especially television. For instance, women purchase 60 to 70 percent of legal services for accident injuries. TV advertising in this case has to speak directly to a female audience with a very clear message. Typically, this message should be relationship-oriented and communicate a high degree of trust. These are elements this target audience wants and that will cause them to buy these services when needed.

The key to television advertising is repetition. No surprise here. It's much like all other advertising, whether print or on-air. Direct mail requires frequency as well, but sometimes with two or three different mailers in a campaign. In the spirit of guerrilla marketing, only one television ad is needed because repetition wins out over more ads. Doing more than one is a waste of your hard-earned guerrilla marketing dollars.

Products, services, and businesses gain instant credibility if they advertise on television. "As seen on TV" puts you in the big leagues in the eyes of your prospects and customers. This may or may not be big league enough to generate big league profits, but big league credibility will be there.

A television target audience will call you if you tell them what you do, what's in it for them, and how they can reach you easily. They will also want to know your location and your toll-free phone number if you have one. If your commercial is memorable enough, the viewer might even refer others as a result of your ad. That would be a guerrilla bonus.

Television advertising can be expensive. Make sure you evaluate the ad budget needed to generate your expected profit level. Return on television ads take time. Factor that into your budget. The time required to break even in television advertising may be longer than a year. Television ad people may not tell you that if they are looking for a quick-hit sales commission.

Television advertising works, shouldn't be intimidating, and could be just what the guerrilla doctor ordered for marketing your products and services. Heed guerrilla caution in this arena. You don't want to end up with a small (or no) fortune from a big fortune because of TV advertising that is done wrong or that is too costly.

Cable TV

Look at all the cable TV stations that have emerged over the past several years. Tune into your satellite dish and the choice of channels is virtually endless. These stations are supported by advertising just like network television stations. With the increased number of television stations, cable television advertising has become a lot less expensive than traditional television advertising, making it affordable for guerrilla marketers. Just ask Joe Marble whose example of success led off this day. What will your success story be?

DAY 18 SUMMARY

- There are on-air alternatives and strategies that are very affordable for small businesses.
- The best way to think about radio is by asking how can you sell, promote, brand, and continue to make targeted prospects aware of your product/service in 60 seconds?
- Repetition on radio builds awareness.
- Radio is effective in combination with your other marketing; it represents another touch to the prospect with your message and your identity.
- Television advertising is nothing more than using the same headlines and using the same marketing message that was used in radio and adding television graphics and visuals to it.
- Viewers will remember more how they felt watching an ad than the details of the ad. You want viewers to feel good but also feel informed, persuaded, and motivated enough to buy your product or service.
- The key to TV advertising is also repetition.
- Products, services, and businesses gain instant credibility if they advertise on television.
- A television target audience will call you if you tell them what to do, what's in it for them, and how they can reach you easily.

■ With the increased number of television stations due to the rise of cable television, TV advertising has become a lot less expensive for marketers making it affordable.

■ ■ ■

Action Steps

1. What type of radio programming do members of your target market listen to?

2. Listen to the radio for the next five commercial ads. Visualize how you would tell these ad stories with visuals. Write out or roughly draw each theme or action moment block by block, kind of like a newspaper comic strip. In the video business, this is called storyboarding.

3. Now take your own marketing message/radio or print ad and do the same storyboarding exercise.

4. Write a 15-second ad like Books-a-Go-Go using your product, service, and company. Time it. Record it. Try different voice inflections. Expand it to a 30-second commercial. Let others hear it and see what they think of it.

5. What are the television viewing habits of your target audience?

6. Are your competitors advertising on TV?

7. What message will you want to get across to your audience in your radio and TV advertising?

8. What is the break-even volume you must attain to pay for the cost of your product sold and the airtime bought for radio? For TV?

9. What is your reason for advertising on television?

Marketing Hooks

I
N CHICAGOLAND, EVERYONE KNOWS the phone number for Empire Carpet. It is obnoxiously repeated over and over in their one commercial. It is featured and held out as their bait. People bite on it because they can't get the ad jingle out of their head. Their mind is totally hooked.

Budweiser used the greeting "Whassup?" as a hook in their commercials in early 2000. How many people did you use this greeting with? If you used it at least once, you were hooked. You remember the one person who used it on you. They were hooked.

How to Obtain More Customers and Increase Profits One Day at a Time. Did that get your attention? I know that it did because that was one of the subtitles considered for this book. A subtitle of a book hooks you. I'm glad this one did.

Seth Godin in *Permission Marketing* (Simon & Schuster) said that we get bombarded with more than 3,000 marketing messages per day. It's no wonder that response rates for direct mail, radio, and TV commercials, telemarketing, and other marketing are at a few percent or less.

You've read it here and you've read in all other guerrilla marketing books: You have to be different to be heard. You have to stand out for your marketing to be noticed. Mr. Godin would say that all of the above is true and you must do it "with permission."

Regardless of the differentiation and of the permission, the prospect must be hooked.

When you go fishing and use your favorite lure, the intention is not just to hope that the fish notices the bait (even if the lure stands out from all the others) but that the fish takes the bait!

Your goal is to hook the fish in your pond. Just like fishing, you want your marketing to hook that prospect in your marketing pond (i.e., your target audience).

To hook customers you must have interesting bait. This is where understanding your markets needs, wants, characteristics, habits, and preferences becomes very important. Researching to get this information must be done before you develop or design your hook (see Day 3, Research).

Information Is Good Bait

A hook is not the whole offering. It is a tease, a sample, and a mental appetizer. The hook should give you just enough taste to leave you wanting more. Information does this. Information is an ideal hook because the costs of developing this type of hook are relatively low or nonexistent. Let's look at some examples:

FOR A PR/MARKETING COMPANY
Call us today for a free list of fax numbers of editors to send your press release to.

FOR A CHOCOLATE CANDY COMPANY
Contact us today for a free recipe booklet using our candy bars to create outrageous desserts.

FOR A HEALTH PRODUCTS COMPANY

E-mail us today for your free height/weight/blood pressure and cholesterol chart.

These hooks are related to the products or services of the companies offering the hook. The whole marketing concept of AIDA (Attention, Interest, Desire, and Attention) is included in these hooks. Response rates increase, feedback increases, and general contact increases with use of a successful hook.

Free consultations are average hooks. Customers and consumers are savvy enough today to know that a free consultation is nothing more than an attempt to obtain an appointment. If I call you for an appointment, you're going to come see me regardless of whether you've offered a free consultation or not. This is like inviting the fish into your boat to see what other lures you have to offer. If the fish wants that, they will let you know.

Taking the hook is permission to follow up and market more to the hooked prospect—just like the fish that took the bait is giving you permission to do something further (throw back or pull it in). The fish might not agree 100 percent with this statement.

Hooks attract attention to you and your business. They are also used in your one-on-one interaction with others. In the world of networking, you are often asked to give your 30-second commercial. How many commercials do you remember from networking events you have attended? Why don't you remember them? More importantly, why do you remember the few that you do? Whatever it is, something hooked you. As a prospect, you bit the bait. You asked more questions. These are all characteristics of a good marketing hook.

A memorable hook attracts attention to you, your message, and your business. There are things that can make your hook more memorable:

- Hooks can announce new information.
- Hooks should be surprising. Catching a prospect off guard gets attention.
- Hooks can be emotional or exclamatory.
- Hooks can promise a benefit or a solution.

Here are hooking techniques for one-on-one interactions:

- Be upbeat, enthusiastic, and full of energy.
- When presenting your 30-second commercial and hook, be sincere and caring.
- Look people right in the eye when speaking to them.
- Make your hook positive.
- Humor works. People remember humor and like to be around it.
- Ask questions. Let your prospects know that you have the answer to the question or the solution to their challenge.
- Offer something for free, such as a referral or an idea. This is a great hook.
- Save your name, company, and title for last. These aren't necessarily hooks.
- State early in conversation what problems you solve.

Hooks also come in the form of jingles, tag lines, and memorable ad content. If you remembered one of these from a company or advertiser, you were hooked. If you told someone about one of these, you were hooked.

You probably can list five to ten tag lines with no problem. A tag line can be a hook. It is usually memorable and sometimes remembered more than the product itself. Look what "Just Do It" did for Nike.

Nike is a big business. Let's "guerrillaize" this concept and look at how some small businesses hook prospective purchasers:

- *Dentist*: Just relax. We know the drill.
- *Bakery*: A fresh approach to your morning.
- *Plumber*: We are your security plumber. No leaks anywhere.
- *Financial planner*: Your peace of mind is a piece of our mind.
- *Caterer*: We'll make you the guest, not the host, at your own party.
- *Body shop*: We're the one for you when you run into old friends or strangers.
- *Appliance store*: We cook it, we clean it, we chill it.
- *Car wash/detailer*: Leave the details to us.
- *Orthodontist*: We'll give you the straight talk.
- *Cleaning service*: We do the dirty work.
- *Sub sandwich shop*: Made with nice warm buns.

Hooks are just as important for online marketing. The hook on a website is the difference between a brochure online and your site actually doing marketing. Some of the more popular hooks online include a coupon, contests, free downloads, free consultations, and free e-zine subscriptions. Once you get a prospect or, in this case, a browser to take one of those hooks, your probability of converting them to a paying client increases significantly.

These hook guidelines also apply to using hooks in stories, articles, and press releases. Hooking a reader is one more step in landing a prospect as a paying client.

Hooks can also be something you do differently in your business that is noticeable. That's what was in the mind of the first hotel that offered free newspapers at the doorstep of every room each morning. Now most do it. Think of the restaurant that offers free coffee with every dessert purchase. People remember that one. That's a hook.

Most of these would surprise you, and you would probably tell someone about your experience. You would be hooked.

A hook is something that delights. That's why it's not always something you do. It can be something you heard, that appeals to the senses, or that

Other hooks of note:

- The florist that gives each grandmother that visits the store a rose.

- The dentist that plays your favorite CD music over headphones to drown out the sound of the drill.

- The barber with internet-ready laptop computers available for clients to surf on instead of tattered magazines.

- The plumber that delivers a case of bottled water (with his label on each bottle) on every service call.

- The bank that gives biscuits to dogs accompanying drive-through customers makes you feel really good or special. A hook says to a prospect, "STOP—Look at me!"

Hype is not a hook. Even though you want to appeal to the basic instincts of curiosity, desire, and convenience, overexaggeration is a turnoff. On the other hand, excitement, encouragement, impulse, and value are all things that make a hook work.

Making a website "sticky," increasing the response of a direct mailing, or causing more visitors to visit your place of business all are enhanced by hooks. Effective use of marketing hooks will fill your boat with more interested fish.

Evan Geiselhart, president of Home Trust Mortgage in Schaumburg, Illinois (hometrustmortgage.com), offers to pay one month's mortgage payment for the visitors to his website in exchange for their e-mail and permission to communicate with them on an ongoing basis. People are hooked by this offer, generally sign up, and usually appreciate staying in touch with Home Trust.

A hook can also be an offer of something of value to customers and prospects. Many times this takes the shape of information: special report, top ten list, checklist, article, white paper, etc. Catching the attention of the prospect increases the chance that the hook will do its job. Here are the titles of some examples of a special report that you can craft for your audience:

- 7 Mistakes People Make When Choosing a *(insert your business here)*__
- Before You Purchase *(insert your product or service here)*__ You Should Read this Report
- This Is What Our Competition Won't Tell You about *(insert your industry or product or service here)*__

Lastly, the placement of the offer of a marketing hook within your marketing can take many forms:

- On or offline
- Brochures or other marketing communication material
- Point-of-purchase displays
- Packaging materials
- Bounce-back offers

A marketing hook is a start. It holds your bait. It's a taste of more to come. "Leave them begging for more" was never truer than it is with a marketing hook. The best part is the cost. A marketing hook costs you nothing. This is guerrilla marketing, isn't it? Imagination is your cost. You've got plenty of that. Just put your mind to it, think out of the box, and let your mind wander. Still challenged? Ask for help. Sometimes an objective viewpoint can open up your mind. Two guerrilla minds are better than one, especially when imagination is the job at hand.

DAY 19 SUMMARY

- You have to be different to be heard; the prospect must be hooked by you.

- Response rates increase, feedback increases, and general contact increases with use of a hook.

- Prospects that take the hook are giving you permission to follow up and market more to them.

- A memorable hook attracts attention to you, what you are saying, and your business.

- A tag line can be a hook.

- The hook on a website makes it interactive.

- Hype is not a hook. Even though you want to appeal to the basic instincts of curiosity, desire, and convenience, overexaggeration is a turnoff.

■ ■ ■

Action Steps

1. What reports, lists, studies, articles, or survey information do you have now that prospects might be interested in receiving?

2. What article or white paper titles are appealing to your target market?

3. Would your hooks be best offered with direct mail, in ads, in commercials, or on websites?

4. What hooks from other companies have you noticed in direct mail, ads, commercials, or on websites?

5. Do you have a way to fulfill requests for what is offered by your hook? If not, what simple steps can be put in place?

Sunday	Monday	Tuesday	Wednesday	Thursday	Friday	Saturday
	1	2	3	4	5	6
7	8	9	10	11	12	13
14	15	16	17	18	19	20 ✓
21	22	23	24	25	26	27
28	29	30				

Public Relations

BILL STOLLER, PUBLISHER OF Free Publicity (publicityinsider.com) and renowned public relations expert, came up with the Pictionary® Celebrity Auction for the Multiple Sclerosis Society. When it comes to getting publicity, there are a couple of automatic draws: celebrities and charity. Do something for a good cause and have some star power, and the PR world is yours. Sounds easy if you are Coca-Cola or Disney. But for guerrillas, generating star power can be a challenge. However, Bill's idea wasn't about to be stopped by lack of star power. His idea was to have celebrities make a Pictionary® sketch and then auction it off for the Multiple Sclerosis Society. The celebrities wouldn't actually have to be present. Their star power would be represented in the drawings on display. Through a directory of addresses of the stars found in any bookstore, Bill sent out a plethora of requests to some of Hollywood's biggest names. The sky was the limit. Those that were kind enough to reply were Ronald and Nancy Reagan, Bob Hope, Muhammad Ali, Roseanne Barr, Steve Martin, and Barbara Bush.

The star power associated with this event was massive, and so was the publicity it generated—all because of a little time, a little imagination, and a little energy. All because of a guerrilla marketing mindset and attitude.

Your mindset now is that you're almost two-thirds of the way through your 30 days of guerrilla marketing. Congratulations on making it this far. Granted, any one of the day's subjects can be the basis for its own 30 days worth of study, review, development, execution, and writing. In the spirit of continuous learning and self-improvement, you will spend more than a day on your favorite marketing subject or on ones that are your best money-makers.

By now, you have seen that a few key questions and answers can optimize your marketing in many areas. On this Day 20, we will optimize your efforts in the area of PR.

PR is short for public relations. A lot of the marketing you have read about, studied, and reviewed so far in your 30 days has focused on getting the word out. In marketing there are many ways to do this. PR will definitely get the word out.

According to *Public Relations News*, "Public relations is the management function that evaluates public attitudes, identifies the policies and procedures of an individual or an organization with the public interest, and plans and executes a program of action to earn public understanding and acceptance."

A major part of PR is understanding where you want to get the word out. By definition, PR means getting the word out to the "public." This really means getting the word out to your "public target market."

Getting the word out involves relationships, the second part of PR. There are relationships with an audience as well as with organizations that help you get your word out, (radio stations, television stations, and publications). Guerrillas love relationships.

What the public wants to hear is a good story. Good PR tells a good story. The better the story, the better the acceptance by the public and the better your relationship with the public. The better the relationship, the better your chance of earning public understanding and acceptance, and the easier it is to get the word out. If the story is especially appealing to those that could be your clients, then you could have a PR home run, which will open many doors for guerrilla marketing and selling.

PR's importance is changing, according to *The Fall of Advertising and the Rise of PR* (Harper Business). American marketing strategists Al and Laura Ries argue that public relations has become the most effective way to build a brand. Well-known brands like The Body Shop, PlayStation, and Harry Potter spend little on brand-name advertising, especially when compared to traditional mass advertisers. The same is true for many entrepreneurial companies like yours. Business owners become known in their respective fields of concentration through PR and the associated media exposure. The best part about this weapon is that the cost is zero.

For small businesses, entrepreneurs, and guerrilla marketers, PR is most common and most efficient in newspapers. Typically, this means your daily or weekly local paper, but some publications are regional or monthly. Following them in usefulness for the guerrilla are business digests, business monthlies, and other business periodicals. Newspapers target businesses and consumers. Business publications target businesses.

PR can also be obtained from magazines, radio, and TV, and a new venue has recently emerged in the form of online PR.

Now that we have dissected the public and relation parts of PR, lets look at the communication that needs to take place between you and the respective publications.

Seventy percent of what is published in newspapers is the result of a press release. Press releases are used to communicate news to media outlets. The press release states the who, what, where, when, and why of your news. The key word here is news.

Put yourself in two pairs of shoes: those of the editor of the publication and the reader.

For publications, it is the editor's job (or in the case of radio and TV, the producer's job) to publish or present information and news that is appealing and pleasing to the reader/viewer. If there is no news or information of value to a readership/viewership, nothing will get published or produced. If the information from your business or organization has a news angle, the probability of publication goes way up.

This is where you need to put yourself in the reader's shoes. What information do you like to read in a particular publication or view in a particular broadcast? Why did you buy that printed publication or tune into that channel in the first place? You want to be informed. That is the function of news. You want to learn and remember. That is the function of PR.

Notice in the talk about PR, the word promotion was not used once. PR is not promotion. PR is not advertising. Editors and producers hate promotion. Their jobs are not to put promotions and ads together for their readership and viewership. Their jobs are to inform, educate, and entertain (i.e., share news and information).

Even promotion disguised as news does not please an editor or producer to the point where he will publicize it. Editors usually can spot promotion a mile away.

There are many right ways to craft news for your business. This news, communicated in the form of a press release, will get published or aired. It won't get published 100 percent of the time, but the likelihood is much greater than a promotional news release.

There is definitely a knack to writing a newsworthy press release, even though the ultimate goals are usually awareness and promotion. If you provide reporters with news that appeals to their readers, you'll gain instant credibility and be on your way to forming a valuable PR relationship. This can be very powerful for all of your future marketing.

There's no guarantee that any press release will ever be published, but by taking a consistent, professional, and newsworthy approach with reputable editors of respected publications, the probability is good that you'll get some coverage.

Just because press releases don't get published doesn't mean they are wasted. Press releases are also great vehicles for communicating directly with clients and prospects. Putting them on your website is a very effective means of promoting to your captive markets. They bolster your marketing efforts and presence, keep your customers and prospects informed, and maintain your credibility.

Not sure what you should cover in a press release? Consider which of these ideas apply to your business:

- Starting a new business
- Introducing a new product
- Celebrating an anniversary
- Announcing a restructuring of the company
- Offering an article series for publishing
- Opening branch or satellite offices
- Receiving an award
- Receiving an appointment
- Participating in a philanthropic event
- Introducing a unique strategy/approach
- Announcing a partnership
- Changing the company or product name
- Recognition of the company, product, or executives
- Announcing that you're available to speak on particular subjects of interest
- Issuing a statement of position regarding a local, regional, or national issue
- Announcing a public appearance on television, radio, or in person
- Launching a website
- Announcing the availability of free information
- Announcing that your company has reached a major milestone
- Obtaining a new, significant customer
- Expanding or renovating the business
- Establishing a unique vendor agreement
- Meeting an unusual challenge or rising above adversity
- Restructuring your business or its business model
- Setting up a customer advisory group
- Announcing the results of research or surveys you have conducted
- Announcing that an individual in your business has been named to serve in a leadership position in a community, professional, or charitable organization

- Sponsoring a workshop or seminar
- Making public statements on future business trends or conditions
- Forming a new strategic partnership or alliance

These are just a few ideas to get you started with your PR plan. If a press release is well written, almost any event can be turned into news.

Sending out a press release is just one example of free PR. Doing this on a regular basis is key to keeping your name in front of your customers' and prospects' eyes and in creating top-of-mind awareness for you, your products, and services.

Another angle of Guerrilla PR is tying you, your expertise, your business, or your products and services to something that is going on in the current media or associated with a current event showing up in the news. This sometimes is referred to as hitchhiking off of others' PR. Offering yourself as an expert to the media will result in PR. Editors and reporters love to substantiate their media stories with experts. Offering yourself as the expert of choice will result in a quote, by you, usually listing your name, company, and title. The PR bonanza that could also result is a feature interview by the editor or reporter with you.

Will you get a flood of business or awareness if your name shows up in the media? Not usually because of that one thing but your media appearances substantiate your credibility and positioning and support more touches to the prospects within your target market.

Here are some examples of items in the news that experts have tied themselves to:

- Anyone in the financial business, like real estate and mortgage professionals or financial advisors, can comment on anything related to interest rates, which are reported on almost daily.
- Chiropractors, massage therapists, occupational therapists can comment on the preparation for community marathons, half marathons, 10K runs, 5K runs, charity walks, etc.
- A social worker made an appearance on network television to comment on the effect of prisoner sentences on family lives. It was the day that Scott Peterson got sentenced in the Lacy Peterson case. The social

worker created awareness and subsequent business as a result of her "expert" appearance.

Other Free PR

- *Writing articles.* Writing about how to do something is always of value to readers. Writing articles gives you instant credibility. Submitting online, as well as offline, provides another good chance to get your name in print at no cost. Articles don't have to be long; they just need to be informative. The best articles for your target market readers are ones where you share your experiences, cite your wisdom, tell a story, or offer some type of checklist or top ten list. Figure out your area of expertise and write about it. Be sure to put your contact information in the all-important contact resource box at the end of each article you write and submit for publication.
- *Free reports.* Offering a free report online is a good way to get an e-mail from prospects so you can market to them later. This is the whole basis of permission-based marketing, or opt-in lists. You can do the same thing offline. Offering the report offline is a good way to get a prospect to call or contact you. If you're doing a postcard campaign and you offer a free report, you can get an instant appointment from the postcard or at least a phone call. You can increase the response of a direct-mail program from 1 percent to double-digit percentage returns. The free reports can be enhanced articles, a list, a survey that you've done, or some research-based information. Use your imagination here, and you will experience guerrilla delight.
- *Online forum participation.* There are many online newsgroups and forums in particular subject areas. Participating in these is another way to get your name in front of a prospective buyer. Advertising is not usually permitted. Participating by answering and asking questions will position you as an expert and a resource for others. Expertise will be noticed quickly. Many online forums will let you put an e-mail signature with a link to your website or an affiliate website. Take full advantage of this; these links get clicked often when of interest to the forum participants and readers/browsers.

- *Letters to the editor.* A little-known secret that's a good follow-up to a press release is a letter to an editor. This is free PR. Many times a letter to the editor has a better chance of getting published than the actual press release. Sometimes you'll get a press release published with editorial comments from the editor. The letter to the editor is a great place to respond to editorial comments as well as to further state a position. You'd be surprised how many people read this section in publications. This is also another way to become friends with editors. If they see you enough and match you with a newsworthy press release, then your chances of getting a future press release in print increases.

- *Hosting an event.* Hosting an event for your business or at your business can be the equivalent to getting an article published in a targeted publication. The event can take the form of an open house, a ribbon-cutting ceremony, a seminar, or a guest appearance by a celebrity, political official, or someone else of significance. Publicizing the event is news in the eyes of an editor, producer, or a target market member.

These are just some of the many free PR avenues that can increase the top-of-mind awareness with your target customers and prospects. As good guerrillas always do, make sure this is part of an overall marketing plan with guerrilla measurement and guerrilla follow-up.

PR for the retail world is a little different than PR for the service or manufacturing world, although there are many common characteristics. The goal is still to get the word out about your business and your products or services.

With a retail business, you want your "news," or PR information, to appeal to consumers, not necessarily other businesses or investors. Consumers are usually attracted to retail businesses because of something they've heard or seen. They could have been referred, they might have responded to a coupon, or perhaps they drove by and saw your sign. Using PR to enhance all these things is the key to spreading the word and getting more business.

Retail businesses have the advantage of being able to tie into holidays. The spirit of gift-giving does wonders for retail gift buying and marketing, and there's always an event to tie into. Doing something unique—above and beyond just a standard gift-giving theme—will further accelerate PR.

Special-interest articles on relevant topics, such as "The History of Valentine's Day" or "How the Christmas Poinsettia Came to Be So Popular" can provide newsworthy angles. Feeding the news community this information positions your business not only as the resource for information related to holidays, but also as the place to shop for the respective gifts.

Other PR strategies perfect for retailers are those related to events or contests. The event could be an open house or a "meet the expert," "meet the mayor," or "meet the press" event. Contests could be simple things such as guessing the number of roses in a car or predicting the day the last petal will fall off the rose. Another idea might be for customers to come in and guess the flower by its smell and get 25 percent off their order. These suggestions may sound corny, but hopefully they'll get your imaginative juices flowing.

A how-to session is another newsworthy PR event. For a florist business, classes on flower arranging, flower pressing, growing roses, and so on come to mind. These can be listed in the newspaper's list of community events, which gets your name in front of prospective customers.

Community and philanthropic events are newsworthy, too. For example, get the word out that for every rose purchased for Valentine's Day, your business will donate one dollar to the American Heart Association. Or let customers know when your business is donating flowers to the local church for the 100th Sunday in a row.

At the end of this day, you know that establishing relationships with local reporters and editors will enhance your opportunity to turn your newsworthy ideas into published news. Just as with any other PR, making your story, information, or event as newsworthy as possible will get editors' attention and separate you from a "me too" competitor. PR is just one marketing weapon and should supplement your other marketing. Marketing is made up of many, many things. It takes those many, many things to create the proper awareness with your target markets. One of those things is simple PR.

DAY 20 SUMMARY

■ "Public relations is the management function that evaluates public attitudes, identifies the policies and procedures of an individual or an organization with the public interest, and plans and executes a program of action to earn public understanding and acceptance," according to *Public Relation News.*

■ PR means getting the word out to the "public target market."

■ Businesses and business owners become known in their fields of concentration through public relations and the associated media exposure.

■ For small businesses, entrepreneurs, and guerrilla marketers, PR is most common and most efficient in newspapers.

■ A new PR vehicle has emerged recently in the form of online PR.

■ Seventy percent of what is published in newspapers is the result of a press release.

■ Put yourself in the editor's shoes and the reader's shoes when developing PR material.

■ PR is not promotion. Editors and producers hate promotion. They love news.

■ If you provide reporters with news that appeals to their readers, you'll gain instant credibility and be on your way to forming a valuable PR relationship.

■ Sending out a press release on a regular basis is key to keeping your name in front of your target market's eyes.

■ Establishing relationships with local reporters and editors will enhance your opportunity to turn your newsworthy ideas into published news.

■ ■ ■

Action Steps

1. What publications are read by your specific target market?

2. What radio and TV broadcasts are oriented toward your target markets?

3. What events could be newsworthy and gain media attention for your business?

4. Out of the list of reasons to do a press release (pages 191–192), which ones pertain to you and your business?

5. What wild and crazy idea can you think of that would generate publicity? Think of Bill Stoller's celebrity Pictionary® sketches.

6. Draft two or three press releases, using the who, what, where, when, and why format.

7. Establish the timing of each release.

8. Put each press release on your marketing calendar.

9. Create a database of those to send the release to electronically, by fax, and via mail.

10. Create a list of editors with whom to start a potential relationship.

11. Call and meet with one or two editors or producers.

Marketing Calendar

A MAJOR HOTEL CHAIN WAS quite involved in a frequency program to build customer loyalty. Mailings would go out to customers with an invitation to return and a discount coupon. The hotel had trouble tracking the responses to see if the program was working. They considered a control versus a test group to test the program but eventually abandoned the idea. Instead, they did a phone survey of mailing recipients. Their research showed that a large portion of their list targets had moved and not updated their listing with a new address. Some had changed jobs or were no longer traveling. The little bit of research showed that the loyalty program was wasteful because of the tens of thousands of dollars spent in mailings that went nowhere. Measurement has its benefits.

Since the dawn of civilization, man has kept track of time by use of the sun, the moon, and the stars. Time was broken up into units of days, months, and years, based on the relationship of the heavenly bodies.

This information was needed to know when to plant crops, when to worship, when seasons change, and when tides would rise and fall. This caused early guerrillas to use imagination to produce a calendar, which enabled them to keep track of time and events. Guerrillas are no different today, except they place more emphasis on marketing instead of the sun, moon, and stars.

Since 1792, *The Old Farmer's Almanac* has published useful information, including tide tables, sunrise tables, full moon cycles, and weather forecasts for all kinds of people. An almanac, by definition, records and predicts astronomical events, tides, weather, and other events with respect to time.

Just like *The Old Farmer's Almanac*, the guerrilla marketing calendar also is full of useful information for people in guerrilla walks of life. It also records guerrilla marketing events with respect to time.

Effective guerrilla marketing employs an assortment of weapons. Guerrilla marketers aren't expected to have photographic memories; therefore, organization, and prioritization of marketing is a must. This "must" takes shape in the form of a marketing plan. The chronology of a marketing plan's implementation is a marketing calendar. This visual is just like the useful information provided in *The Old Farmer's Almanac*.

Calendars and almanacs are normally based on astronomical events. Guerrilla marketing calendars are based on your marketing events and actions. They include your timetable on when to initiate and execute your plans.

A guerrilla marketing calendar assists you in launching your marketing vehicles in a way that can drive you to your marketing goals in a structured and well-thought-out manner.

By using a marketing calendar effectively, you will not only be able to successfully coordinate all your marketing efforts, but also be able to effectively budget for all of your marketing ventures.

A marketing calendar can keep you on track, making sure that you are using every opportunity that you have to market without a lapse in your efforts. A marketing calendar can help prevent yo-yo marketing, that is, marketing aggressively when sales are low and marketing less aggressively when sales are high.

With your calendar, you can rest assured that your planning, budgeting, and resource allocation are accounted for. This guerrilla step alone could save you hundreds, if not thousands, of guerrilla dollars.

Marketing calendars can be created to address your specific needs. Most calendars break down the weeks of a year and address the marketing activities that will take place in each week. A calendar will be best used if it is specific, spelling out individual promotions or events. Including the marketing cost for each event rounds out the full use of the marketing calendar. By doing this, it is easy to see at a glance which events and strategies were productive and on target. This aids you in planning your future marketing.

A marketing calendar also crystallizes your focus and allows you to see the investment and value in your marketing program. You are able to build consistency into your planning. This again will aid you in preventing marketing lapses that cause the feast-or-famine effect that many businesses experience.

A marketing calendar does not have to be fancy. Guerrilla marketing isn't fancy. The purpose of the calendar is to see where you're going and where you've been with your marketing. In addition, it gives you a mechanism for grading the effectiveness of each weapon and each day of your marketing.

Your marketing calendar can be segmented by weeks or months, whichever visual provides the best management for you. Guerrilla marketers who do some type of marketing every day will benefit from a weekly marketing calendar. Creating it is simple. List your marketing weapons down the left side column of a chart, matrix, or spreadsheet and weeks or months across the top. Prepare a list of your weapons, your events, and important dates in your industry and for your company. Break these events, activities, weapons, and marketing initiatives into weekly/monthly activities and place them on your calendar accordingly. This is a good time to establish and refine deadlines.

You can include budgets per activity/event/initiative. This will assist you when calculating or estimating the return on your marketing investments and when deciding which to continue and which to cease. Also include in the calendar matrix a place to put the person responsible for each marketing activity. Using the budget information in a calendar will also help prevent unforeseen marketing expenditures. Hit-and-miss marketing is more costly than planned marketing.

The marketing calendar is a management tool. This tool helps you get things done and measure, both key management activities. In a small business, you're not only the guerrilla marketer and the guerrilla light bulb changer, you're the guerrilla manager!

You should implement as much guerrilla marketing as you are comfortable implementing, both financially and emotionally. Your calendar and the subsequent evaluation are great tools to help you measure whether you are at comfortable levels.

Another benefit of the guerrilla marketing calendar is that it helps you plan or spot efficiencies and synergies. Can events or initiatives be combined and thus take advantage of lower unit costs? Can you combine the mailing of your new brochure and a quarterly update letter to customers and prospects? This is where the imagination and energy of guerrilla marketing come into play.

Preventing bunched activities or too great a gap between activities is another benefit of using a marketing calendar. This is where the visual comes in handy. Take a look at your calendar. Is there too much spacing between events? If so, plan a more consistent approach. Are there events and activity stacked on top of one another? If so, spread out the timing between each. Consistent, persistent marketing works. Blasts of marketing are less effective. What is your visual?

Measurement

One of the big differences between the guerrilla marketer and the casual marketer is how the calendar is used for marketing measurement. The results of completed marketing events and activity should be reviewed. Again, it's simple. What marketing worked? What marketing didn't work?

A simple rating of effectiveness from one to ten, with ten being very effective, works. Repeat the marketing that ranks between five and ten and eliminate or revise marketing rated below five. Decide which criteria work best for you. This is the essence of marketing metrics and the guerrilla marketing calendar.

A productive dialogue you can have with every prospect that becomes a paying customer begins with, "How did you learn about us?" At the very least, that's marketing measurement. Documenting and charting these responses on your marketing calendar is the simplest form of marketing measurement. Guerrilla marketers like simplicity.

Simple Steps to Your Marketing Calendar

Many entrepreneurs and small businesses get frustrated with unpredictable sales. One week your sales are at the top of the chart; the next week you are sucking wind. You can quickly fall into a yo-yo marketing trap. The challenge at hand is to stabilize sales. This stabilization begins with the marketing calendar.

Planning properly for increased sales will prevent all of your guerrilla energy going into delivery with no time left for marketing.

All marketing can be placed on a calendar. A great start is using it for frequent marketing activities that repeat and those activities that are scheduled. The simplest approach would include ad placement schedules according to a publication's editorial calendar, press release schedules, holiday event publicity, and direct-mail schedules. The toughest part is inputting the activities on the calendar.

A calendar makes implementing each activity simple. As you implement, you will also be involved in delivery, planning the next part of your guerrilla marketing attack, delighting customers, and firing more marketing weapons. It's easy to lose track, but inputting into your calendar will keep you on track. Pull up the guerrilla bootstraps and use a little guerrilla discipline here. Activities won't appear in your calendar just by dreaming about them. Guerrillas who make dreams happen remember to update their calendars.

Just the mere fact that you are planning and recording guerrilla action in a marketing calendar is a commitment. Consider it a contract with yourself to get something done. Good guerrilla marketers make promises to customers, prospects, and themselves. Good guerrillas keep promises. Your guerrilla marketing calendar will help you keep those promises.

- *Create a yearly calendar.* Start with an overview of marketing plans for an entire year. By doing this step, you will see steadier and more consistent growth in your sales, while avoiding the yo-yo marketing syndrome.

- *Evaluate what works.* Look at the period of time when your sales increased the most. What marketing contributed most in that period? The more you pinpoint here, the more you can repeat and the more sales increases you will experience.

- *Market at regular intervals.* Space out your marketing activity in regular, non-seasonal intervals. Don't bunch your marketing during slow times; otherwise, you will fall back into that yo-yo trap. A continuous, consistent application of your marketing will produce steady sales.

- *Plan for growth and success.* After you create your marketing plan and start using your guerrilla marketing calendar, your sales will grow. Plan for this. It happens to every guerrilla who does things right. Planning will also help you manage your resources consistently. Once again, no yo-yos here.

- *Work the plan.* Anticipate and plan for growth, changes, and unexpected curve balls, which will help you avoid that hand-to-mouth effect from yo-yo sales.

- *Use your marketing calendar today.* Spend time on your marketing calendar every day. It is a living document, a true guerrilla guide. Use it as such, and your guerrilla marketing will be in overdrive.

When thinking back to Day 1 of your 30 days, remember that you planned on thinking about something related to your marketing every day. This can also be translated into doing something marketing-related each day on your marketing calendar. Maybe that means calling a group of prospects, visiting a competitor's place of business, or changing your on-hold message. Sometimes there will be a whole host of activities on a particular day, such as finalizing an ad and calling a publication for placement. Don't restrict activity to once a day. Marketing momentum is a good habit and good fuel for a blitz marketing attack.

Fifty-nine percent of Americans begin their workday by reviewing a daily action plan, and more than half of workers use calendars to keep track of their schedules. Don't be in the minority here even if your competitors are. They aren't using a guerrilla marketing calendar. You will be a step ahead of them when you do.

Robert B. Thomas, the first editor of *The Old Farmers Almanac*, told his readers in 1829: "Our main endeavor is to be useful." So should your guerrilla marketing calendar.

DAY 21 SUMMARY

■ The visual sequence and chronology of a marketing plan's implementation is a marketing calendar.

■ A guerrilla marketing calendar assists you in launching your marketing vehicles in a way that can drive you to your marketing goals in a structured and a well-thought-out manner.

■ A marketing calendar not only effectively coordinates your marketing efforts, but also helps you budget your marketing ventures effectively.

■ The marketing calendar is a management tool.

■ All marketing initiatives and actions can be placed on a calendar.

■ A marketing calendar is beneficial in that it prevents bunched activities or too great a gap between marketing initiatives or events.

■ ■ ■

Action Steps

1. Make a list of all your weapons, marketing initiatives, and marketing activity.

2. Make a list of key industry events.

3. Make a list of key dates for your company (anniversary, new product introduction, reorganization, relocation, etc.).

4. Estimate timing per initiative (e.g., a press release every other month, chamber of commerce newsletter ad once per quarter, direct-mail postcard to a particular segmented audience once a month for six months).

5. Take the timing per initiative estimates and place them visually on a 12-month calendar. Refine timing from there.

6. Input all information related to your other weapons, industry events, and key dates for your company from the lists you compiled. Space them out, don't bunch them or leave too many gaps.

7. IMPORTANT: Put on your calendar "marketing calendar review dates" to grade marketing, revisit initiatives, and revise your calendar.

Sunday	Monday	Tuesday	Wednesday	Thursday	Friday	Saturday
	1	2	3	4	5	6
7	8	9	10	11	12	13
14	15	16	17	18	19	20
21	22 ✓	23	24	25	26	27
28	29	30				

Other Marketing: Speaking, Coupons, and Contests

JEANNIE TRIEZENBERG, A PROFESSIONAL organizer and president of Hire Order (hireorder.com), a professional organizing company in suburban Chicago, used a messy desk contest to generate publicity. The entrants sent in pictures of their messy desks. The winner won free organizing services from her company. Press releases announcing the contest caught the attention of a few editors. As the time approached for the winner to be announced, the media got involved. They wanted to communicate the winner to the public. Hire Order then publicized the unorganized before situation and the organized after situation and gained significant PR just by having the contest. In this case, the PR bang was double: PR announcing the contest and PR announcing the contest winners. In guerrilla fashion, the cost of this contest was zero. The time donated to the winner was considered a sampling and resulted in paid work subsequent to the contest, all guerrilla feats. Contests, however, are just one of today's subjects, coupons and speaking are also covered.

Don't you just love all this marketing? Did you ever think we could cover it all in 30 days? We probably can't, but we will work together and see if we can get you a bang for your marketing buck. On this day we will quickly cover some marketing tactics that work just as well as those we covered in a full day. Some of the weapons described on this day are the only ones used by some guerrilla marketers and quite successfully at that. Just because these are approached in blitz fashion does not diminish their potential effectiveness for you. You have to decide, plan, and implement according to your business, your customers and prospects, your budget, and your guerrilla vision.

Coupons

While the name guerrilla marketing was conceived in 1980 with the first guerrilla marketing book, there is evidence of guerrilla marketers way before that. In 1895, C. W. Post, the cereal manufacturer, offered the first money-off coupon ever issued in the United States. The one-cent-off coupon came with Grape Nuts® cereal. By turn of the century standards, this was very guerrilla-ish, and a lot of money. Today the use of coupons has grown so much that consumers have saved over $4 billion dollars since coupons were invented. Not bad for just a little clipping and redemption. Coupons bring a consumer to a business to spend more than the incentive cost of the coupon. That's the basic concept of using coupons. That's guerrilla marketing.

When you think of coupons, you basically think certificate of redemption. Coupons for guerrillas are used mostly in newspapers and magazines. Sometimes fliers and handbills can include a coupon.

Coupons are viable marketing vehicles for increasing product sales. Couponing is another way to commit people to brands that interest them the most. In the spirit of guerrilla marketing, use coupons in conjunction with other supporting marketing. Coupons are best used to create a short-term blip in traffic to a particular establishment, focused around one simple product or service.

The primary idea behind coupons is for the user to save money. Obviously saving money is an opportunity cost to a coupon, which might not have received the business if it weren't for the coupon. The lifetime value of that customer is well worth the coupon cost if the customer returns to buy more products.

Coupon marketing is easily measured, a valuable component in any guerrilla program. Seeing who redeemed the coupons, where the user found the coupons, and tracking print coupons can pinpoint what ads, marketing vehicles, and communication are working best. All that is required is using different codes for different placements. This can be printed on the coupon itself or coded online with coupon codes or web page tracking. As more internet technology is used in marketing, consumers continue to respond to value online, as well. Those coupons, which can be printed on a desktop printer from an online website, add value by being convenient and easy.

> *Guerrilla Hint: Put a printable or downloadable coupon on your website. Putting a code on that coupon also allows it to be used for phone or online purchases.*

Coupon use is very prevalent in the grocery market. Shoppers who use them consistently pay for a significant portion of their groceries. The same can happen for the purchase of nonretail and nongrocery products or services. Including discount coupons in packaging or thank-you cards for redemption against your service is one way to offer the same value to a potential purchaser of your products or services.

Many nongrocery stores publish their own store coupons both online and in newspapers. You can get coupons for haircuts, shoes, movies, oil changes, and clothing, to name a few. Be creative for your products or services. Consumers are used to the coupon craze. Adapting it, in guerrilla fashion, to products and services typically not associated with coupons and the grocery aisle is an opportunity in front of all guerrillas.

Speaking

One of the best ways for people (potential clients) to find out about you, your company, and your products and services is public speaking. It is a chance for them to get information straight from you. You are your best marketing vehicle. Speaking to groups is nothing more than a large conversation. It is powerful marketing—and efficient marketing.

A number of dynamics take place when you are in front of a group of people. First, you are the center of attention. Each audience member feels as if you are speaking directly to him or her. You're not an envelope that goes unopened. You are not a telemarketing call that comes at dinnertime. You're not a television commercial that gets fast-forwarded. Speaking to a group puts you at the forefront of message delivery and effective communication. You are having a conversation with an audience. Sure, members of an audience can walk out of the room, but of those present, you have their undivided attention. If all marketing could be delivered to "undivided attention," we wouldn't need as many guerrilla marketing strategies and tactics.

As you speak, you are also establishing credibility with an audience. Hopefully, this audience has potential paying clients. If they don't, you shouldn't be speaking to them. You establish yourself as an expert in whatever you are talking about. People like buying from experts. They feel comfortable in their buying decisions.

There are many types of potential audiences. These include community organizations, professional groups, trade associations, or civic groups.

Speaking to a group is marketing, not selling. Your speaking should offer something of value, not a direct pitch. Potential speaking topics that are marketing and value-oriented are things such as (fill in the blanks for your industry or business):

- Top ten mistakes made when buying _____.
- Seven insider secrets of _____.
- Three points to consider when _____.
- The four B's of _____.

Another topic that is not only highly marketable, but also highly memorable, is speaking about a system you invented around an acronym. Each letter of the acronym stands for a value point of your message. For instance a speaker that presents the Opportunity RADAR offers content related to:

- **R**—Re-engineering
- **A**—Attitude
- **D**—Drive
- **A**—Aspiration
- **R**—Relentless pursuit

RADAR is the "system" presented in this speech.

A trainer speaking about goal setting talks about SMART goals related to:

- **S**—Specific
- **M**—Measurable
- **A**—Actionable
- **R**—Responsibility
- **T**—Timing

Speaking to audiences doesn't mean you have to be a paid professional speaker or hired through a speaking bureau or even famous. There are many guerrilla tactics that put you in front of potential targets:

- *Seminars*. You can put on a seminar to teach prospects how to do something that you have expertise in.
- *Demonstrations*. Showing how a product works is beneficial, or a service is always valuable to an audience.
- *Panel discussions*. Being a member of a panel discussion at a forum, public event, or business meeting establishes expertise quickly and generates very good exposure.
- *Coordinating team exercises*. Volunteering to coordinate groups, whether within or outside your company, puts you at the forefront.

- *Reporting from a committee.* Be the one responsible for reporting committee actions to a larger group.
- *Teaching.* Some community colleges, extension programs, and other educational organizations are always looking for experts and those willing to share experiences with their audiences.
- *Presenting an award at a conference.* Presenting an award will get you recognized and is a form of public speaking.
- *Sponsorships.* Sponsoring an organization, meeting, or conference usually gets you a few minutes in the limelight. Take advantage of it, practice what you will say, and knock some socks off.

When members of your audience receive something of value from you, even if it is information, they are grateful. When someone is grateful, you have the beginning of a great relationship, and you already know how guerrillas and relationships go together. Once these relationships turn into long-term buying relationships, you will know the true value of speaking to groups.

Now, here comes the good part that makes every guerrilla stand tall. The cost of using speaking as a marketing weapon is free. The more you can use this weapon, the more audiences you can touch, hook, and start relationships with, and the more trips you will make to the bank with deposit slips in hand.

Contests

There is no free lunch . . . unless you dropped your business card in one of those fishbowls on one of your frequent restaurant visits. Why are restaurants so inclined to always give away a free lunch and push to get those business cards? The answer is that they are guerrilla marketers using their imagination and energy to collect your name at no cost. The purpose of that fishbowl is to accumulate names that will be marketed to later on. This little contest for a free lunch is nothing more than a lead generator. Because the winners will surely brag and talk about how great the restaurant is because they won a free lunch, word-of-mouth advertising and referrals are possible.

The primary purpose of the contest is to gather entrants. The cost for you to get these names is the cost of what the contest winner receives. This price for a targeted, permission-based list is a small investment compared to the potential return. That's the way all guerrilla marketing should be.

Contests work at trade show booths: "Stop by our booth today and enter to win a free Palm Pilot or PDA." All entrants are now permission-based prospects that will be marketed to after the contest.

Another benefit of contests is that they can generate PR.

> *Contests don't have to be fancy. They can be publicized; then they will generate word-of-mouth buzz.*

GUERRILLA HINT. Have more than one winner. The more prospects that can spread the word about how you delight customers, the more potential business you will gain. Sometimes restaurants do this if they spot a key card in their fishbowl of entries. You should, too, if you see hot prospects swimming in your fishbowl.

> *Everyone loves a winner. Making prospects winners will make you a winner in their eyes.*

Today showed you three other guerrilla marketing weapons. They all work for the right business with the right creativity and the right implementation. Take this day to see if you are that right business and how these weapons might fit into your attack.

DAY 22 SUMMARY

- Coupons are viable marketing vehicles for increasing product sales. Couponing is another way to commit people to brands that interest them most.

- The lifetime value of a customer using a coupon is well worth the coupon cost, especially if that customer returns to buy more product.

- Coupon marketing is very conducive to measurement.

- One of the best ways for potential clients to find out about you, your company, or products and services is for them to hear information straight from you in a public speech.

- Speaking to groups is powerful marketing and is very efficient marketing.

- Speaking to a group is not direct selling.

- The primary purpose of a contest is to gather as many entrants as possible.

- All entrants to a contest are permission-based prospects that can be marketed to after the contest.

- Contests don't have to be fancy; they can be publicized. That will generate word-of-mouth buzz.

■ ■ ■

Action Steps

COUPONS

1. What product or service of yours is best suited for a coupon offer?

2. Once that coupon is presented for redemption, what ways can you upsell a prospect?

3. How will you present a coupon to your target market? Printed coupon? Included in packaged products? Included in invoices and statements? Online?

SPEAKING

1. What value could you offer in a presentation that is related to your business or industry or area of expertise?

2. What groups are your target market prospects members of?

3. What topics can you come up with to speak about by filling in the blanks in the example above?

4. What system invented around an acronym can you invent that makes for a valuable presentation/speech?

CONTESTS

1. What kind of contest can you have that you can build publicity around?

2. What other businesses and organizations have contests that you can donate your services to, perhaps as the prize for the winner?

3. What database tracking system will you put in place to compile entrants' contact information?

4. How will you market to the newly formed database after the contest? What communication vehicles will you use? What messages will you communicate?

Online Marketing, Part I

OTE TO READER: A bonus day which in effect is Online Marketing, Part III, has been added since there is so much more to this topic. The bonus day appears after Day 24, so read on!

Roger Parker says in *Relationship Marketing on the Internet* (Adams Media) that "information forms the heart and soul of website and internet marketing success. To succeed you must provide, and continue to provide, meaningful content-information that will help turn prospects into customers, customers into repeat customers, and repeat customers into ambassadors . . . ."

Any time something significant happens in our lives having to do with communication, marketing takes a big leap. Just ask Johann Gutenberg, the inventor of moveable type and the printing press. Just ask Samuel Morse, the inventor of Morse Code for the telegraph.

Just ask Bill Gates. In reality, Bill Gates is the only one alive to ask, but you get the point.

As soon as something is written or read on the internet, it has a high probability of changing. That is the stage of the evolution in electronic communication. Until it reaches maturity, which probably won't be in our lifetimes, businesspeople will be faced with constant change. Guerrillas respond to change and thrive on it. If you fall into this category, here's your chance. On this day and the next, we will scratch the surface of online marketing and give you some weapons that can be used in an environment undergoing rapid and ongoing change. As long as you realize that, there are still online marketing fundamentals that tie in to guerrilla thinking and will produce the guerrilla results that you are becoming used to.

At the risk of sounding like a guerrilla broken record, defining your objectives and having a plan is as important for online marketing as it is for all other marketing. You want a website, but what are you going to do with it? You have e-mail. Do you communicate effectively with it and to the right people? These are the types of things you want in your plan and the types of questions you want answers to in order to go forward with success. Make sure you don't try to do too much with your online marketing, which requires a certain amount of resources to implement and maintain. Only develop what is pertinent and comfortable for you, your business, and your resources. Your internet business strategy should be an extension of your company's existing marketing strategy and well integrated with marketing done offline.

Online marketing is more than a website and e-mail. Choosing what is right for your business, the marketing of your products and services, and what your target market needs will determine your online course of action.

Technology should be used in guerrilla marketing. Never have we been at the point that we are today in using technology in marketing.

Before reviewing online marketing weapons and the various components, let's consider the underlying foundation of online marketing.

- *Traffic.* The name of the game in online marketing is to generate visitors to your website. This is not unlike getting people to your place of business or to take your telephone calls. It is not unlike getting appointments to visit with customers and prospects for direct selling. Online and traditional offline marketing does this.

- *Value.* Forget about directly marketing your product or service for the moment. Your online presence and other marketing efforts must offer value to attract visitors and to encourage them to return. Online value is usually information based.
- *Resource.* One goal online is to become a resource for your prospect/customer. Becoming that resource is the ultimate in networking, loyalty, and marketing. Creating a following is powerful marketing. People follow and buy from resources.
- *Information.* You want to be the preferred source of information. You want to be a reference site while providing value. Providing information to customers and prospects helps to keep you and your business in their minds.
- *AIDA.* There are more internet marketing messages than ever. Just like advertising and printed mail, your job is still to get attention, gain interest, and create desire that leads to action (AIDA).

Technology in marketing starts with two basic weapons: e-mail and a website. Both should be treated as process-oriented marketing, not event-oriented weapons. On this day, we will start with your website. On the next day, we will cover e-mail marketing.

Website

This is going to be a guerrilla summary for your website. For more online marketing, consult Jay Levinson's *Guerrilla Marketing Online* (Houghton Mifflin) and Roger C. Parker's *Relationship Marketing on the Internet* (Adams Media).

A website is an address. It is your base. First, you want people to find your house. Then, you want them to be welcomed and comfortable enough to stay and chat with you. You want to get to know each other. You want to get to know each other to the point of wanting to know more about each other. Once this happens, you want to earn mutual trust so that you can partner together on marketing, sales, and business in general. A website can do all this.

A website can collect the names of the people for this potential relationship exercise. Notice that all this interaction is much more effective and personal than a brochure. A website is a tool to interact with a prospect and/or a customer. You want to supply enough information and value so that prospects leave their name (for you to follow up with later) or they return for another visit. Ultimately, getting a sale is your goal.

A website is another marketing weapon used to create one-on-one relationships with prospects and customers and to keep customers forever. Loyalty and relationship building can be done with a marketing-oriented website. Understanding what information your target market needs is paramount when determining website content.

Basically, your website should be viewed as an effective and efficient communication tool.

More Effective Communication

Individual website pages allow you to communicate more information than traditional print marketing and for much less cost. This communication can be interactive, in the same way that direct sales calls and the telephone are interactive marketing weapons. Interactivity starts and furthers relationships and persuades prospects to become paying clients. Anything you can do to further interactivity in a website will increase its effectiveness. This could include signing up for an e-zine, a newsletter, a free report, or other information.

More Efficient Communication

All of this communication can be done without the costs of traditional printing and reprinting. It can be done without the distribution costs, including postage. Websites can displace traditional media advertising. (Be careful and prudent when evaluating this. You still have to make sure that your target market reads your website as it would read your advertisements.) Communicating more information faster and cheaper is the epitome of marketing efficiency. Keeping this communication fresh and valuable will keep customers and prospects coming back to your site.

Search Engines

Search engines are one of the web's major resources for driving qualified, targeted traffic to websites. Getting listed in a search engine listing is not difficult. Getting ranked high in those listings can be challenging. If a search engine returns 1,121,873 sites for a keyword, chances are that the researcher will not go beyond the top 20 or 40. If your site is returned at a ranking of 86,416, chances are good that your site will go unnoticed by the browser.

The marketing activity reviewed here is submitting your site to a search engine or registering your site with a search engine. Getting listed does not necessarily mean that you will rank high for the search terms related to your business. Getting registered simply means that the search engine knows your web pages exist.

There are many strategies and tactics that will rank your site higher in search engines, but they are beyond the scope of this book. The act of managing the key words and tags in your website is referred to as search engine optimization. Search engine optimization improves the odds of your site being found in those first few listings of a search. Evaluating this worth compared to the cost of the optimization will determine the feasibility of using this strategy with this weapon. Using it right will return right to the guerrilla bottom line. Using it wrong will make the positive numbers disappear.

Pay-per-Click Search Engines

Pay-per-click search engines pay for a particular ranking in search engines. These are a highly effective way to attract cheap, targeted traffic to your site. The most popular pay-per-click engine is overture.com.

These search engines connect you with customers who are searching for what you are selling. Prospects and customers arriving at your site via search engines are highly targeted and usually motivated to buy. This is the ultimate in target marketing.

With a pay-per-click search engine, you pay only when a searcher clicks on your listing and connects to your site. These clicks are also known as click-throughs. You don't pay to list your site.

You list your website by selecting keywords that refer to your product or service. For each keyword, you determine how much you are willing to spend. The higher you bid, the higher you will appear in the search results. The higher you bid, the more you will spend upon each click-through to your site. Pay-per-click search engines can be a laser-focused marketing weapon. Converting clicks to paying customers is the key mission. This must be closely monitored so click costs don't exceed your conversion profits.

Reciprocal Links

Reciprocal links are another highly successful way to get traffic to your website.

Reciprocal links are links with other sites, which are generally related to your business or organization. The concept is that you put a link to a particular website on your site and vice versa.

This method of traffic-building is significant, and it's another free marketing weapon. The key is contacting the right types of businesses or organizations and getting the right types of links. Take the time to find companies related to you through search engine research. A simple letter of request stating your objective and intent should get an affirmative reply.

Major search engines are now using the number of links to a site as a determining factor in the ranking of sites. Search engines consider that the more links a site has to it, the more valuable it must be to internet browsers and researchers.

Finding that ideal business or organization to link to is another example of fusion marketing. Combining guerrilla marketing weapons online and offline will increase both your guerrilla marketing effectiveness and guerrilla marketing efficiency—an ideal combination that can't be beat.

Other Considerations

Your website is not just a place to put your brochures in electronic form. It's not just an advertising medium. Websites have more in common with the telephone than they do with a brochure. Seek out as much interactivity as possible.

Online marketing should be integrated with all other marketing activity. Your site should be connected with your company's offline, more traditional marketing efforts. Driving traffic to a website is done most successfully with a combination of online and traditional offline marketing.

Your website should be an information resource for your prospects and customers. Becoming a trusted resource of high quality information is of tremendous value to you, your business, and your position in the marketplace.

Keeping up with the rapid changes of internet marketing requires a lot of time—almost as much as a full-time job. Guerrillas don't have large staffs to keep up with such things. Unless they are in the internet marketing business, it usually is not what they do best. Guerrillas do what they do best and delegate or outsource what they don't. Find an expert to keep your site fresh and up-to-date. Concentrate your efforts on doing what you do best and you will wear the guerrilla badge proudly.

DAY 23 SUMMARY

- Defining your objectives and having a plan is as important for online marketing as it is for all other marketing.
- Online marketing, while relatively inexpensive, still takes resources to implement and maintain.
- Your internet business strategy should be an extension of your company's existing marketing strategy and well integrated with marketing done offline.
- Online marketing is more than a website and e-mail.
- Understanding what information your target market wants or needs is paramount when determining website content.
- Getting listed in search engines is still one of the best ways to drive qualified, targeted traffic to websites.
- Pay-per-click policies pay for a particular ranking in search engines.
- Reciprocal links with other businesses or organizations are another highly successful way to get traffic to your site.

- Your site is an advertising medium that has more in common with the telephone than with a brochure. Interactivity is the key to website success.
- Online marketing should be integrated with all other marketing activity.
- Becoming a trusted resource of high-quality information is of tremendous value to you, your business, and your position in the marketplace.

■ ■ ■

Action Steps

1. Visit a competitor's site. What do you like from a customer's point of view? What don't you like?

2. Solicit input from your customers about your site. How can you make it more friendly, valuable, and useful?

3. What offline marketing is available to produce traffic?

4. What is your online/website hook?

5. Is your site interactive?

6. What value does your site provide?

7. Do you follow the principle of AIDA?

8. Is there a place for people to sign up for free information on your site?

9. Do you have a way to capture the e-mails of people who sign up for your information?

10. What key search words would you choose to bring people to your website via search engines?

11. Type in keywords related to your business, and see how your competitor's are ranked and what they are doing on their sites.

12. Visit a pay-per-click search engine (like overture.com) and see what costs are associated with click-throughs. Also see what keyword search quantitative information is available.

13. Reconcile against your keywords and see what your break-even point is when using this marketing weapon.

14. What businesses would be logical for you to trade links with?

15. What do your customers want as links on your site?

16. What links are on your competitors' websites?

Online Marketing, Part II

NOTE TO READER: A bonus day which in effect is Online Marketing, Part III, has been added since there is so much more to this topic. The bonus day appears after Day 24, so read on!

On Day 23 you read that technology in marketing starts with two basic weapons: e-mail and a website. Both should be treated as process-oriented marketing, not event-oriented weapons. On the previous day you also learned about websites, search engines, pay-per-click search engines, and reciprocal links. Now that you have information on your site, it's time to apply marketing that does something with your site or with your customers to get them to visit your site. Visiting the site is only half the battle. Conversion from visitation to sales is the ultimate goal of all internet marketing. On the next day we will start with e-mail marketing. We follow it with other weapons within internet marketing that will aid in that conversion goal.

E-Mail

E-mail is the most popular online activity on the internet. Just look at your own e-mail activity. It has exploded in size and use. It has also exploded in abuse. Guerrillas operate within ethical parameters in all marketing, especially e-mail. Do not send spam messages.

For most small businesses, permission-based e-mail marketing campaigns are the most memorable and cost-effective way to reach new and existing customers. This can consist of e-mail newsletters or targeted personalized messages.

E-mail marketing can be a tool for branding, direct response, and building customer relationships. It's cheap, easy to use, and almost everybody surfing the internet has an e-mail address.

E-mail marketing is every e-mail you send to a customer or prospect. This includes sending direct promotional e-mails to interested prospects and providing information to acquire new customers or to sell to existing customers. E-mail marketing can also be used to keep in touch with customers, encourage customer loyalty, and further customer relationships.

This can be done as a direct e-mail message, an electronic newsletter (e-zine), or an online advertisement. One difference between this contact and the print equivalent is that electronic mail must only be sent with permission. Some print marketing is interruptive and thus ignored. Another difference is that it can be interactive.

Guerrillas like e-mail because it subscribes to the principle of using time, energy, and imagination. Sending e-mail is very cost effective and many times free. E-mail is very targeted. Using a hook, response can be higher than regular mail. Keep your promises and play by the rules. Doing so will make you a marketing winner through and through.

> *Guerrilla Hint: Your e-mail signature should include your name, contact information, and website in order to drive interested prospects to you.*

Before blasting e-mails to your target world, do the following:

- Develop your campaign strategy, much like your printed direct mail campaign strategy.

- Develop content and copy. Remember AIDA and value. Keep in mind that the attention span of a web browser is much shorter than a print reader.

- Make sure your list is targeted and permission-based.

- Offer a marketing hook for a better response rate. This could be free information, a report, a download, a CD, or an e-course.

- Make sure you are reaching your target audience. Do they even use the internet? Interested prospects buy, uninterested prospects will skip over you.

- Plan your measurement and track where your browsers come from. Understand what they do once they get to your site. What pages do they land on? How long do they stay there? What do they click on?

- Follow up and plan subsequent e-mails. Remember how many times it takes to get a prospect to the purchasing mode.

- Have a follow-up system. Know exactly what you are going to do when you get a response to your marketing.

A Note on Spam

Responsible e-mail marketing is based on getting permission from the person you are sending it to. This is an issue currently under legislative and ethical review. The general view is that you need an e-mail recipient's permission before you can send them an e-mail marketing your product or service. If you don't get this permission, then you are sending unsolicited e-mail, known as spam. Do not send spam. At the time of this writing, there are legal consequences for bulk spammers. Guerrillas play by the rules. Don't send nonpermission-based e-mails.

Auto-Responders

Auto-responders are programs set up to automatically respond via e-mail when triggered. Most are triggered by a blank e-mail sent to the auto-responder e-mail address (e.g., "for information on guerrilla marketing coaching send a blank e-mail to gmcoach@market-for-profits.com").

When someone sends an e-mail to an auto-responder, the person receives an already prepared e-mail message with the requested information. This happens automatically and almost instantaneously, depending on the internet and e-mail servers.

Auto-responders are e-mail on demand, making your information available to your prospect and customer 24/7. Because of their automatic nature, they can significantly increase sales with little work. Your costs remain low and your profits soar to the guerrilla hall of fame when automating any of your marketing. Auto-responders may be your ticket.

What to offer in an auto-responder message:

- Free report
- Checklist
- Top ten list
- Article
- Free book chapter
- Recipe
- Guide
- Booklet
- E-book
- Chart
- Worksheet
- E-course

Some auto-responder programs can be set up to send a series of e-mails back to a requester. E-courses are an example of this. A blank e-mail is sent to a designated address and a prewritten series of e-mails is sent at designated intervals, all automatically.

Remember how many times prospects must be exposed to your marketing message to get them to a state of purchase readiness. Auto-responders ensure consistent and frequent communication to touch prospects the sufficient number of times.

E-Zines

An e-zine is an online newsletter. Publishing your own free e-zine can bring huge amounts of qualified traffic to your website while helping you increase your profits. E-zines are increasingly common on the internet. Nearly all sites related to marketing offer them to their visitors.

The popularity of e-zines is based on the need for information and the offer of value by the publisher. The number-one reason people are online is because of the desire and need for information, which e-zines provide. E-zines are delivered via e-mail either as html pages or straight text.

An e-zine is a great mechanism to keep in touch with customers and prospects. Constant customer and prospect contact is vital to your marketing success. When considering the six to eight touches required to get prospects into a state of purchasing action, e-zines can be one more touch in an efficient and effective marketing world. Not only will an e-zine allow you to maintain regular contact with your website visitors, but it also acts as a reminder to them to revisit your site.

E-zines can help build trust and start relationships online. E-zines that provide regular quality content of value to your readers will help them begin to trust your opinion and feel as if they know you.

An e-zine is almost a necessity today when selling products or services on your website. Keeping in touch, either online or offline, is a guerrilla action that brings in sales and profits. Think of your e-zine as a profit generator.

Online PR

One of the most cost-effective ways to publicize and market your business is to use the many PR tools, methods, and opportunities that exist online. Many of these are simple and either free or low-cost PR options. With online PR, you're simply taking traditional PR and extending it to the online community. This includes targeting online and traditional media that have a significant online presence. In addition to promoting interaction with individuals, online PR allows for a very wide distribution of news and information.

Online press releases are a great way for your authored content to spread without having to spend too much money. Several online press release sites will let you post your press release free of charge. Some of the more popular and user-friendly press release sites are prweb.com, press box.com, and webwire.com.

Putting PR information on your website is another form of online PR. Once press releases are written and distributed, posting them on a separate Web page gives you more bang for your buck. You can take this a step further by developing keywords for each page these releases appear on and then registering them individually in search engines. Another advantage of posting press releases on your site is that you can add hyperlinks for additional information. Streaming video and sound may also be added to enhance communication of your information.

Because editors, web publishers, and site owners want fresh content, the writing and distribution of feature articles is another way to take advantage of the efficiencies of online PR. Feature article writing is one of the best online or offline marketing techniques. Sending well-written articles to various editors and publications is often done online. The following will accept your online article and publish it on their site or in their e-mail distribution list: editor@saintrochtree.com, Free-Content@yahoogroups.com, Newsletter@web promote.com, and PublishInYours@onelist.com. For more leads, type "article submission" in any search engine, and you'll find additional choices.

Online press kits are becoming more and more popular. An online press kit contains the same items you'd find in a traditional press kit, but in an electronic, web-friendly form. Online press kits are put on your website in an area that is usually referred to as an online pressroom. These pressrooms might contain any of the following: articles about the company that have run in the media, white papers in PDF form, company position papers and statements to the press, industry statistics, and usually the names and contact information for those responsible for PR within your company.

PR on the internet is so widely used because of its ease of distribution, the broad potential of contacts, and, of course, and its cost-effectiveness.

Positioning it as you would your traditional PR will increase the bottom and top lines of your business.

Discussion Forum Participation

Forums are another name for online bulletin boards, online discussion boards, and online message boards. They enable users of a website to interact with each other by exchanging tips or posting conversation and information on the site.

One good thing about forums is that they save information posted on a particular topic for other people to see at any time. This promotes great discussion and interaction. Postings get read over and over again by visitors to the particular forum site.

Forums create online communities. People return to the forum site on a regular basis to keep abreast of the community topics. Participation in these discussions can make prospects aware of you and your business as well as position you as an expert. You can also position yourself as a resource to the community online. You have learned in the past 24 days that people like to buy from experts. Also being a resource furthers relationships. Now do you see how all this guerrilla marketing works together?

Online marketing should be integrated with all other marketing activity. Your site should be connected with your company's offline, more traditional marketing efforts. Driving traffic to a site is done most successfully with a combination of online and traditional offline marketing. Using the tools above and those reviewed on Day 23 will put you further ahead of your competition and closer to your prospects' and customers' wallets.

DAY 24 SUMMARY

■ Conversion from visitation to sales is the ultimate goal of all internet marketing.

- E-mail is the most popular online activity.

- For most small businesses, permission-based e-mail marketing campaigns are the most memorable and cost-effective way to reach new and existing customers.

- E-mail marketing can be a tool for branding, direct response, and building customer relationships.

- Your e-mail signature should contain your name, contact information, and website in order to drive interested prospects to your site.

- You need e-mail recipients' permission before you can send them an e-mail message marketing your product or service. Do not send spam.

- Auto-responders are programs set up to respond automatically via e-mail when triggered.

- Auto-responders ensure consistent and frequent communication to touch prospects the sufficient number of times.

- The number-one reason people are online is the desire and need for information. The popularity of e-zines is based on that need.

- An e-zine is a great mechanism for keeping in touch with customers and prospects.

- An online press release is a low- or no-cost way to spread the word about your news.

- Putting PR information on your site is another use for online PR.

- Online press kits are becoming more and more popular.

- Discussion forums online enable users of a website to interact with each other, exchanging tips or posting conversation and information that is mutually beneficial.

- Online marketing should be integrated with all other marketing activity.

■ ■ ■

Action Steps

1. What frequency do you want to communicate to your targeted e-mail list?

2. How will you obtain your permission-based, targeted list?

3. What messages (content) will you use?

4. What hook or free information do you have to offer in your e-mail marketing?

5. What is your follow-up system? That is, what will you do when you get a response to your e-mail marketing?

6. Do you have an auto-responder system to deliver and manage your e-mail marketing? If not, what system is compatible with your usage and budget? Collect e-zines on subjects you like and by your competition, if you can.

7. What components of each e-zine do you like the most and which ones will appeal to your customers and prospects?

8. What will be the format, title, and content of your e-zine?

9. Who will you distribute it to and how?

10. Visit some online PR sites, such as prweb.com, and review other companies' PR.

11. What online sites is it logical for you to send your online press release to? Type "article submission" in a search engine and find sites to distribute your online feature articles to.

12. What discussion forums cover your area of concentration or interest?

13. What information can you contribute to these forums to position yourself as a resource?

14. What frequency will you visit the forum?

Sunday	Monday	Tuesday	Wednesday	Thursday	Friday	Saturday
	1	2	3	4	5	6
7	8	9	10	11	12	13
14	15	16	17	18	19	20
21	22	23	24	25 ✪	26	27
28	29	30				

Online Marketing, Part III

WHEN JAY REVISED *Guerrilla Marketing* into the current 4th edition, he stated that there is one thing certain about anything related to the internet: Nothing is certain about the internet. As soon as anything is written about this powerful, robust, and many times guerrilla, marketing weapon, it often is already close to obsolete. By the time you read it, it is even closer to being outdated. Technology moves fast.

Since the first edition of *Guerrilla Marketing in 30 Days* was published, more technology has been developed, customers and prospects have grown in technical savyiness, and buying and selling has taken a new course . . . much of it internet based.

The online weapons discussed in Days 23 and 24 of the first edition are still powerful arrows in your marketing quiver. The new material in this bonus chapter addresses additional electronic, online weapons that have come to the forefront of marketing: blogs, podcasts, and more about e-mail marketing.

Blogs

In the old days (five to ten years ago in internet years), a common question asked of small business owners was if they had or planned to have a website in their marketing arsenal. Now having a website is almost a prerequisite to being in business. The updated question is now, "Do you have a blog or plan to have one?" Will we get to a point where having a blog will be a prerequisite to being in business? Probably not as much as having a website but darn important as you continue to strive for those guerrilla relationships that motivate prospects and customers to take action and/or buy.

Blogging requires the discipline of creating, writing, and/or contributing information of value to an interested segment of your target market. If you don't have the discipline, put blogs on your NOT-TO-DO list or enlist the help of a writer to continually update and make postings of your valuable information that people are interested in reading.

I'll assume you know what a blog is, what blogging is, and what constitutes a blogger. If not, for those details, consult *Guerrilla Marketing*, 4th edition, page 221 or put any of those terms in any search engine and click your way to being knowledgeable and conversational.

A blog offers many benefits:

- *A blog can position you even more as an expert.* Blogs typically focus on niche areas of a business or specific topics of interest. Where else can you become an author, publisher, editor, and expert all in one day at little or no cost? That's guerrilla positioning; that's guerrilla marketing.
- *In the spirit of guerrilla marketing, blogs are low- or no-cost.* A small investment in a domain name and a website hosting service will more than put you well on your blogging way.
- *Blogs communicate news and make announcements instantly.* Your prospects and customers are interested in the news you make, the news you share, and the news you announce. Spread your information to the North, East, West, and South, (that's where the word NEWS came from).

- *Blogs allow for the building of communities.* The whole concept of "community" is a recent trend in the dynamics of marketing and targeting. Popular blogs become profitable blogs. Blogs become more popular the same way websites become popular, the same way *American Idol* becomes popular, by marketing them.
- *An extension of the community is developing one-on-one relationships.* One-on-one relationships are very guerrilla like. Talk to your audience as if you are having a one-on-one conversation.
- *Blogs have value.* Customers and prospects want, need, like, and buy value. Information can be very valuable. Don't lose sight of your value proposition along your blogging way. Value also prompts your readers to return; return for more value. Make your audience hungry or find them hungry, feed them, make them happy again, feed them again, continuously, all with your blog.

Like the proliferation of reality television shows, giving you the inside look at people's real lives, a blog can give you the inside look into someone's thought machine—their mind; their brain. Brain-to-brain, inside connections build relationships.

Announce your expertise, contribute your knowledge, have conversations, and enjoy your relationships with your blog. Guerrilla relationships build guerrilla profits.

Happy blogging!

Podcasting

Simply said, distributing audio or video files over the internet has taken hold. It actually has done more than taken hold, it has taken off! In the blogging discussion it was mentioned that providing information of value to prospects and customers will allow you to "cash in" in many ways. Podcasting allows for the distribution of information in the form of audio and video to an audience when they want it, where they want it and how they want it.

Some of your target marketing will be visual learners (video); some learn by hearing (audio). Podcasting addresses both types of learners.

Podcasting can be described as "push" audio content. The "push" is to a targeted audience or an "on-demand" audience; those who want it. Another way to describe podcasting is that it is essentially downloaded audio files intended for listening on the move.

There is no tuning in to stations with podcasting. You don't have to visit a website to find streaming podcasting. Podcasts show up (pushed) when new content is produced. If you are a subscriber, you get the podcast right then. All you need is an iPod or MP3 player of any kind for listening, thus the word podcasting.

It was considered revolutionary when listeners were able to take their music to the beach or the park or in their car, but that typically meant listening to whatever the radio stations were playing. Now, with podcasting, listeners can choose the programs they want to download from the internet and listen whenever they want.

The mindset behind podcasting originated in the world of blogging. Some have even referred to podcasting as "audio blogging." For many, podcasting is a logical next step from blogging. As *Business Week* Senior Writer, Stephen Baker observes: "The heart of the podcasting movement is in the world of blogs, those millions of personal Web pages that have become a global sensation. In a blogosphere that has grown largely on the written word, podcasts add a soundtrack."

People are adding them to blogs and websites daily. Businesses are using them for general communication and training. Capital One gave 40 new employees iPods just to receive the training podcasts that they now use as a primary training tool.

Podcasts are more readily listened to. Receivers, subscribers, and listeners can literally listen to each podcast whenever they want and wherever they are. Wireless connections or online connections are not necessary. They can be listened to in a car, in an airport, in the park, or wherever it is convenient for the listener. Listeners can also repeat a podcast or parts of it for emphasis, clarity, or just for entertainment.

The *Mac Observer* reports that Duke University made headlines in 2004 by giving iPods to all 1,600 incoming freshmen; they repeated this again for the class entering in 2005.

Duke University said it will continue distributing the devices to students next year, "although in a more targeted manner, while also exploring other educational applications of multimedia technologies. The iPods will be part of the new Duke Digital Initiative (DDI)."

Just like written communication of any type or even electronic communication, content is king in podcasts. In the business world, no one really wants to hear their boss preach to them for 20 minutes a week in a podcast. Straight presentation can be long, monotonous, and an inconvenience to a listener, regardless of corporate directives.

Content has to be crafted with the listener in mind; not only his/her interests but his/her listening habits. It is a known fact that a listener's patience is less with recorded content than it is with live content.

To create valuable podcast content, think like a radio producer. Radio producers are always aware that a listener can switch stations at any moment for many reasons. That's why they concentrate on the entertainment value of programming, instantly and frequently. Listeners are usually alone when listening and can change stations or turn the program off when not fulfilled, entertained or informed. The radio producer has to provide value. Value is what the audience will listen to, re-listen to, and listen to with a desire for more or the next program (podcast).

Podcasting is the delivery tool. Content is still king in any communication, especially recorded podcasts. Compelling content ensures continuous listening and not a flip of the power switch.

Podcasting is not the end to all ends in the world of technology or the world of communication. It still takes a proactive effort, a planned approach, creative development, and a targeted push all creating demand. It is truly not a "build it and they will come" approach to communication. It takes work just like the early days of radio, TV, and even the internet.

Podcasting is not a guerrilla panacea, but one more guerrilla marketing weapon. It's one more way to touch a prospect or communicate with a customer.

Podcasting Resources

- podcasttools.com
- audacity.soundforge.net
- internetaudioguy.com (Tell Mike hi!)
- feedburner.com
- odeo.com

Podcasting Pointers

- *Provide information of value.* Value can come in the form of education, information, inspiration, motivation, and entertainment. Don't just broadcast commercials. That would put you in the non-guerrilla category.
- *Conversations work.* This can be accomplished by having someone interview you or participating in a panel discussion. One-person podcasts are less dynamic by definition. Dynamic content sells.
- *Remember the 3 p's of podcasting: Promote, promote, and promote.* Encourage subscribers, sign ups, and raving fans with automatic and periodic updates. Post your podcast availability on your website (with a live link), mention it in your e-mail signature, and enlist in podcast directories, including iTunes and podcast.net.

Podcasting is another marketing weapon in your guerrilla arsenal. Market it, just like a product, a person, a service, a company, etc.

Good luck with this guerrilla weapon and let me know when you hit iTunes. I'll help you tell the world. I may even podcast about podcasts.

E-Mail

The number one use of the internet is still e-mail. That fact does not need revised in this revising. E-mail still is one of the more important ways to get your marketing message to a target market. In *Guerrilla Marketing in 30 Days*, 1st edition, we discussed the ins and outs of e-mail and other online marketing. In this revision, I want to put a direct marketing spin on this guerrilla marketing weapon.

Where else can you:

- Think of what you want to market
- Develop the communication
- Send it to a target list of prospects
- Measure the response
- Process the responses
- Fulfill orders
- Evaluate the campaign

All in one day!?

A question us guerrilla authors get is: How can I get a list of people to send e-mail to? When talking about printed direct mail, I recommend to you that you purchase a list from a list company that is defined by your target market specifications. I do not offer this same recommendation for direct e-mail lists. With the ever-changing SPAM rules, the increased etiquette and reverence of permission-based marketing, and the turnover of e-mail addresses, purchasing an e-mail list is highly inefficient and highly un-guerrilla like.

I recommend that you create your own list. You can do this by capturing the e-mail addresses of those visiting your website. Offer a hook, a special report, an article of value in exchange for the e-mail address. Put that newly captured address into your database of choice and continually market to them (with e-mail and your other marketing) like breathing. Your list is your market.

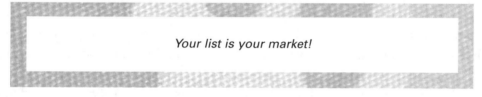

Your list is your market!

Additional e-mail marketing points:

- Keep e-mails short and sweet. On the internet, all readers have IADD—Internet Attention Deficit Disorder. Short copy, to the point, helps to overcome this.
- Provide value three times as often as a commercial message.
- Respect opt-out requests.
- Use links to your websites and other websites of importance for your audience.
- Use the power of an e-mail signature. Use links and autoresponders as well.
- Create and use the most compelling, attention-getting, "in-your-face," e-mail subject line.
- Treat e-mail like printed direct mail when considering:
  - The message

      – The target

      – The frequency

- Make e-mail marketing as automatic as possible using pre-written autoresponder messages.
- Be a resource to your target market, not an annoyance.
- Personalization sells. Talk one-on-one to your receiver.
- Test text e-mails vs. HTML e-mail messages to see what your audience likes best; maybe do a guerrilla thing like ask them.
- Measure delivery rates, open rates, click throughs, and conversions when possible and where practical.
- Simplify the selling and buying process. Make it easy to buy from you or respond to you. Respond back to those that contact you.

■   ■   ■

This completes your Bonus Day of Online Marketing, Part III.

By the time the next revision rolls around, you will hear more about, experience more, and market more with video. That plus more about the always changing subject of search engine marketing and social marketing will be coming your way.

Maybe these three Online Marketing Days (Day 23, Day 24, and the Bonus Day) can be the start of *Guerrilla Marketing Online in 30 Days*. Watch for that on my blog, podcast, or e-mail messages.

Trade Shows and Expos

AVE YOU EVER VISITED a trade show or business expo and walked past a booth of non-guerrillas, chitchatting away in social mode? Do you think these people understand the word "trade" in trade show? Do you think these people are great socializers? Do you think they are more proud of how "pretty" their booth looks than in doing business? Chances are, in a nonguerrilla world, the answers to these last two questions are "yes" and "yes."

On this day, you will learn the guerrilla approach to trade shows. You will learn how to select a trade show and what to do before, during, and after to get the biggest guerrilla bang for your guerrilla buck.

Trade shows are not social events. Your goal, much like in a networking event (see Day 12), is not to pass out as many business cards and brochures as possible. Your goal is not to show off a pretty booth to people walking by. A well-thought-out guerrilla approach to working a trade show can turn this weapon into one with a big bang. Without this thinking you stay in the show off category until you are out of business.

A trade show is an event at which goods and services in a specific industry are exhibited and demonstrated. The key word here is specific. If the specific industry of the trade show is made up of members of your target market, a trade event may be an effective marketing weapon for you. These shows are also known as exhibitions, expos, and trade fairs.

One of the first considerations is to review your target market to determine whether a trade show is an appropriate venue for you and your business. Targeting is a common theme with any of the guerrilla marketing weapons. This one is no different.

Typically a trade show venue is a collection of people with similar interests, ideas, and challenges. Gearing your efforts to these people make trade show marketing effective and profitable, two guerrilla standards.

Planning for a trade show is no different than knowing your destination when you leave on a family vacation. Not knowing it leaves your experience and success to chance. As a guerrilla, you want more of a sure thing; therefore, planning is a given.

Your trade show plan should include (before the show) your objectives for exhibiting:

- Generating leads
- Networking
- Finding partners
- Attending and offering educational sessions
- Assessing competition
- Furthering customer relationships
- Spotting trends
- Meeting with the media
- Demonstrating products

Take some time and define (if you haven't yet done so through other planning) your ideal clients. You want to know their characteristics, needs, and wants in case they show up disguised as a prospect, and what challenges your prospects are at the trade show to solve.

Your objective at a trade show is to make contact with current customers, meet new prospects, and get leads to follow up on. In addition you will want to assess the industry, your market, and your competition. Scoring a judge's "ten" on all of these will make you a trade show champion.

Other reasons for trade show participation include expanding your identity, awareness, presence, visibility, and introducing a new product or service.

Marketing to your target audience before the show brings it to your exhibit. Not promoting will leave your visitors in a "walk-by" status. Have a trade show marketing plan. This includes your objective, theme, message, promotions, marketing vehicles used, follow-up plan, and budget. If you market to a preregistration list for the show, you are marketing to people already committed to attending. If they are committed, your job is to get them to stop by your exhibit. Creative marketing and subsequent PR will attract attendees.

Your event-marketing plan should be done with publicity in mind. This includes seeking media sponsorships, creating helpful media kits, and making it easy for the media to cover the event, especially as it relates to you. Brainstorming story ideas with the media can also result in feature publicity. If you wait until the show to do this, it may be too late to capture the media's attention. You may have missed editors' deadlines.

One simple tactic is to prepare a press release announcing your exhibit and attendance at the trade show. Press releases are a cost-effective way to contact clients and prospects through the trade press, association communications, and the media in general. A preshow press release can announce a new product being unveiled at the show, new personnel, new partnerships, and a whole host of other important information to your targeted audience. Remember, editors will be looking for a newsworthy angle to your presence. Being different and unique will help to get your news published. Give editors and producers specific reasons why they should visit and/or write about you over all the other hundreds of other exhibitors.

You want to be the guerrilla magnet for attendees. You want to create attention for yourself, your company, and your exhibit beforehand so you will get on your prospect's must see list.

This creativity could include a special offer or giveaway in exchange for a visit. This creativity could be the premier unveiling of a new product or service in exchange for exclusive admission. This creativity could be a special audience or meeting with new, key personnel. Creating compelling messages around these offers and communicating them is one of the guerrilla ways you are learning about in these 30 days that will get the necessary attention.

Many companies use celebrities to draw crowds. Announcing celebrity attendees and schedules is done via press release, posters at the event, private invitations, and inclusion in trade show media. Other ideas for announcements beforehand include the following:

- Stop by for your free gift.
- Get your picture taken with . . .
- Stop by for your chance to win . . .
- Meet our CEO.
- Guess the number of jellybeans in the fishbowl to win.
- Test drive our product at our booth.
- Take the Pepsi challenge.
- See how we eliminated the competition.

Trade journals specific to the trade attending the show are a good place for exposure. Watch your costs here and make sure you stand out creatively when using these vehicles. Getting noticed will contribute to your magnetism.

Other preshow marketing planning that must be done is deciding what vehicles will be communicating your marketing message at the show itself. This includes sales collateral, brochures, booth displays, and specialty giveaways, as well as sales messages delivered by booth attendants.

Preshow communication planning includes

- company information.
- contact information.
- featured products and services.
- benefits to attendees.

> *Guerrilla Hint: Market the trade show itself in your communication (e.g., "Come see the National Association of Troubleshooters, premier supplier of training materials, at the NAT annual conference in Las Vegas").*

- personnel attending the show.
- booth locator map.
- special show offers.

Of course, the more you can communicate to your audience and target market before the show, the better the awareness will be for you, your company, and your products and services.

Preshow mailings are effective if done with consistency and impact. If possible, obtain a list of trade show registrants in advance. Don't stop at one mailing to the list. It takes three to four times to get your message noticed and communicated effectively before the show (you learned this on Day 17, Direct Mail).

Don't forget about e-mail and the telephone. Sending an e-mail communication will allow you to send a link to the trade show website as well as your own. You can offer maps, trade information, free articles, appointment schedules, and booth information more efficiently and cost-effectively utilizing your website.

Once you've marketed to your target preshow, it's time to actually show up and work at the trade show. Working the show is work. Here are some guidelines for working smart, not just hard:

- Spot a very targeted prospect by observing name badges.
- Act like a host.
- Talk with people; don't just watch them walk by.
- Speak in sound bites, not long dissertations.
- Always have a business card available.
- Collect names of interested prospects and items of interest to these prospects.

- Look and act professional.
- Don't oversell; start relationships; determine those to follow up with.

Also, understand that trade show goers are attracted to unique exhibits. This includes the use of models, live shows, and interactive displays as well as celerity appearances. Put your guerrilla creativity hat on when using this marketing weapon.

Trade shows open doors and pave the pathways to building strong business relationships with customers, prospects, distributors, the media, and other partners in your industry. Meeting and greeting is as important as the follow-up after the show.

According to the Center for Exhibition Industry Research, 80 percent of exhibitors do not follow up on leads. That presents an absolute guerrilla opportunity for those companies that do the proper follow-up; what a chance to separate you from your competition in a most positive way. Send a note, make a phone call, provide more information, or refer to a website. Even making a personal visit moves you closer to a prospective buyer thinking about your products or services and eventually placing an order for them. Follow up with those most interested in your offerings should happen immediately, within two or three days of the show. Make yourself a guerrilla goal of completing the follow-up in the week after the show.

Establish a system for follow-up. Manage timelines related to follow-up, create a database for the proper tracking and measurement, and assign sales reps leads for follow-up and hold them accountable. Measuring all of these will determine whether you repeat the use of this weapon, revise its use, or eliminate it from your arsenal.

Putting your mind to having a great presentation and display and a great preshow and postshow communication will ensure a successful use of trade show marketing.

DAY 25 SUMMARY

■ A trade show is an event at which goods and services in a specific industry are exhibited and demonstrated.

■ A trade show is effective marketing if the specific industry or focus of the trade show is made up of members of your target market.

■ Your trade show plan should include your objective for exhibiting.

■ Your objectives at a trade show are to make contact with current customers, meet new prospects, and to get leads to follow up on.

■ Other reasons for trade show participation include expanding your identity, awareness, presence, visibility, and introducing a new product or service.

■ Have a trade show marketing plan that includes your objectives, theme, message, promotions, marketing vehicle used, follow-up plan, and budget.

■ Your event marketing plan should be done with publicity in mind.

■ Other preshow marketing planning that must be done is deciding on what vehicles will communicate your marketing message at the show itself.

■ Trade show goers are attracted to unique exhibits.

■ Trade shows open doors and pave the pathways to building strong business relationships with customers, prospects, distributors, the media, and other partners in your industry.

■ Follow-up with those most interested in your offerings should be immediate, within two or three days of the show.

■ Great presentation and display and great preshow and postshow communication will ensure a successful use of trade show marketing.

■ ■ ■

Action Steps

1. What objectives would you state for trade show exhibiting?

2. Visit a trade show before exhibiting. Choose one in your industry or in a similar industry.

3. At what trade shows do your competitors exhibit?

4. What are the major trade associations in your industry and in your customers' industry?

5. How many people attend the trade shows that might be appropriate for you?

6. What will your message and/or announcement be prior to a trade show?

7. What will make your exhibit/booth different? What one thing do you want prospects to remember about your presence at the show?

8. What follow-up system can you put in place?

9. Will you have any special offers for your products and services?

10. What giveaways will you offer? Information? Promotional items?

11. Buy *Guerrilla Trade Show Selling* (John Wiley & Sons) by Jay Conrad Levinson, Orvel Ray Wilson, and Mark Smith.

Sunday	Monday	Tuesday	Wednesday	Thursday	Friday	Saturday
	1	2	3	4	5	6
7	8	9	10	11	12	13
14	15	16	17	18	19	20
21	22	23	24	25	26 ✓	27
28	29	30				

Newsletters

THE BOSTON PUBLIC LIBRARY FOUNDATION (BPFL) uses newsletters to stay in touch with both its 60-member board and its Young Professionals group. Staying in touch internally and externally is its marketing charge. It uses its newsletters to communicate information like regular updates on fundraising, new library exhibits, meeting reminders, save-the-date communications, and invitations for upcoming events.

Newsletters help BPFL foster and maintain relationships with a large and diverse board. As in many nonprofit organizations, the foundation's board members are both significant individual contributors to library programs and the foundation's voice to the world—in effect its direct salespeople.

With newsletters, BPLF ensures that its board members and young professionals are fully briefed on all activities. Because board members are ambassadors to the public and the people in the community talking about their organization, generating interest, and encouraging donations from new sources, keeping members informed at all times is essential. Newsletters accomplish this.

As humankind entered a more progressive period in history, communication of all kinds became widespread—communication about religion, land ownership, trade, government, and farming. As information about events was disseminated, word spread. This was the early form of "news."

Information came from all directions. It was this basic premise that provides one interpretation of the invention of the word news (North, East, West, South).

Today news is rampant. We hear it on the radio and television 24/7, as well as read it in newspapers and other publications. Many members of our society have turned into news junkies. The same goes for our prospects and customers. They yearn for news about the industry, competition, new products and services, and suppliers. As a supplier or partner, you have an opportunity to satisfy this desire. One of the best vehicles to communicate news and information to the business public (your customers and targeted prospects) is the aptly named newsletter.

Newsletter communication comes in many forms. Regardless of the form or the context, you are generally providing your prospects and customers

Why a Newsletter over an Ad?

- Dartnell Corporation, the training and motivational media company, states that newsletters have four times the readership of a traditional advertisement.

- Newsletters are perceived to be more credible and believable than ads.

- More information can be communicated in a newsletter.

- Newsletters have a longer shelf life and are passed around for others to read.

with valuable information. You are extending your relationship with those that read your newsletter. You are making another guerrilla attempt to maintain and improve top-of-mind awareness with your target market. You are paying attention to those most likely to buy from you. Paying attention can be a competitive advantage.

A newsletter is a simple, low-cost way to communicate with customers and prospects. It is one of the best ways to stay in touch and keep your name in front of customers and prospects in your target market.

Newsletters provide an opportunity to inform your customer base and prospective customers of your opinions, facts, and ideas on a wide variety of matters. Engaging prospects and customers in this type of dialogue can increase your selling efficiency and accelerate selling success.

One of the top reasons customers leave, change suppliers, or stop buying is because of a lack of attention. They feel they are no longer being treated like a customer. They truly feel neglected.

Customer attention is easy and simple, much like all guerrilla marketing, but it is difficult to maintain. Those guerrillas that excel at providing consistent attention excel at having more satisfied customers that stick around for a long time. Guerrillas know that attention is a scarce resource that they can offer in abundance.

Newsletters are great marketing vehicles for

- maintaining credibility and your reputation.

- providing consistent contact with your prospects and customers.

- announcing news and other company information.

- communicating information about you and others in your company.

- offering tips, articles of interest, and other value points to help prospects and customers.

- relating case studies and other successful associations with your company.

- communicating special offers.

Customer attention can simply come in the form of staying in touch. One way to stay in touch is with a regularly published and distributed newsletter.

Newsletters are usually produced on a regular basis in multipage format for the purpose of communicating newsworthy information, company updates, special offers, and points of interest or entertainment for your prospects.

Newsletters only work when they are distributed to your customers on a consistent basis. They should be easy to read, loaded with information, and graphically pleasing. You will get to the ultimate point of newsletter effectiveness when your prospects and customers expect your newsletter each month and/or start asking for the next issue of your newsletter before you publish it.

Newsletters are considered a subtle sell. They offer a friendly communication with value that extends your relationship with a customer while improving awareness of your company, brand, product, or service.

Newsletters can also be used as handouts to prospects and customers and as back-up material for media interviews.

With today's desktop publishing capabilities, newsletters are far simpler to prepare and produce, and all fit within a guerrilla marketing budget, especially when compared to the large commercial print runs of yesterday.

One goal of a newsletter is to make it interesting and valuable enough so that your customers and prospects read it all. You want to provide a great return on your reader's investment of time. In order to do this, you need to know what type of information your prospects and customers need. Do they learn from stories and case studies or step-by-step bulleted lists? What is important to them and what do they read?

Articles should be designed to inform, educate, and answer your readers' most frequently asked questions. Once prospects fully understand the many benefits of your products or services, they will be more likely to buy from you.

Free and helpful tips about your products and services work in much the same way as articles. Free tips position you as an expert in your industry and show your willingness to help others, both advantages when compared to your competitors. Once readers are helped or hooked by these tips, they are

Newsletter Content Ideas

- New product/service information

- News of people within your organization

- Industry news

- Market statistics

- Problem-solving tips/expert tips

- Case studies

- Feature articles

- Surveys/survey results

- Trend information

- Outlook/future comments

- Sales/buying information

- Opinions

- Requests for referrals or other calls to action

- Humor

more likely to read more information supplied by you, seek your help, or purchase from you.

Newsletter Format

By definition, newsletters are meant to be short. A four-page newsletter is the most popular newsletter format and is usually sufficent for most marketing purposes. Roger Parker of onepagenewsletters.com suggests one-page, electronically-distributed newsletters.

Use short stories, bulleted information, lists, tidbits, and other concise forms of information.

Because of the short attention span of your reader, the information should be presented in a very positive light and in an uplifting and humorous fashion.

However, newsletters should be professionally humorous, not amateurish. Stick to the purpose of your newsletter, especially if you mean business. Focus on the specific interests of your readers—your prospects and customers.

Name your newsletter creatively. Make it memorable and unique. This is your chance to grab attention. Remember your identity.

Make sure your newsletter contains no ads. Because you are subtly selling, there's no need to be in the face of your prospects and customers with direct selling.

Write your newsletter in a style that is comfortable to read. Don't overuse technical jargon.

The front page of a newsletter is the gateway. It is the attention-getter that entices the reader to keep reading. Make the design appealing and hard-hitting in order to accomplish this.

Other Format Considerations

- *Graphics.* These can consist of charts, cartoons, illustrations, and sidebars.
- *Photos.* Put your photo in the newsletter. You will be surprised how this simple thing can start and maintain relationships.
- *Layout.* Don't try to put ten pounds of information in a five-pound newsletter. Keep it clutter free. White space is good—neat and professional layout will keep readers reading.
- *Hardcopy or digital.* If hardcopy, you will need to consider paper and ink and the associated costs. If digital, you will need to employ the services of an html expert. Considering color and the "look" is done here, regardless of the medium.

Uses of Newsletters

In all of guerrilla marketing, you are encouraged to use your marketing weapons and vehicles for multiple uses. Newsletters are no different. The more uses you find for your newsletters, the more efficient your marketing will be and the healthier your bottom line will be. Here are several uses of newsletters that contribute to that health:

- Use newsletters as a direct-mail piece to customers and prospects in your target market.
- Give the newsletter out on sales calls.
- Hand them out to guests that come to your place of business or office.
- Pass them out at trade show exhibits to prospects passing by.
- Post newsletters on your website.
- Include newsletters in your information and media kits.
- Include newsletters in other customer/prospect correspondence.

DAY 26 SUMMARY

■ One of the best vehicles to communicate news and information to the business public (your customers and targeted prospects) is a newsletter.

■ With a newsletter, you are generally providing your prospects and customers with valuable information. You are extending your relationship with those that read it. You are making another attempt to maintain and improve your top-of-mind awareness with your target market/reader.

■ Newsletters provide an opportunity to inform your customer base and prospective customers of your opinions, facts, and ideas on a wide variety of matters.

■ Newsletters are usually produced on a regular basis in multipage format for the purpose of communicating newsworthy information, company updates, special offers, and points of interest for your prospects.

■ Newsletters only work when they are distributed to your customers on a consistent basis.

■ Newsletters can be used as handouts to prospects and customers as well as back-up material for media interviews.

■ Free tips in a newsletter position you as an expert in your industry and show your willingness to help others, both advantages when compared to your competitors.

■ The more uses you find for your newsletters, the more efficient your marketing will be.

■ ■ ■

Action Steps

1. What is the objective of your newsletter?

2. If you have a newsletter now, what response do you get?

3. Save newsletters that you receive. What do you like about them? What don't you like about them? Did they inform, persuade, or entertain you?

4. How many pages will your newsletter be?

5. How will you distribute your newsletter? How will you use it?

6. Will your newsletter be a self-mailer or will it be inserted into an envelope for mailing?

7. Does it make more sense to offer a one-page electronic newsletter (onepage newsletters.com)?

8. What are all the uses you will consider for your newsletter? Once you determine this estimate, add up the quantity for each use to get a total quantity. The larger the quantity, the lower the unit printing costs.

Sunday	Monday	Tuesday	Wednesday	Thursday	Friday	Saturday
	1	2	3	4	5	6
7	8	9	10	11	12	13
14	15	16	17	18	19	20
21	22	23	24	25	26	27 ✓
28	29	30				

Marketing Budgets

ACCORDING TO *PHYSICIANS NEWS DIGEST*, the rule of thumb for medical marketing is to allocate an individual budget based on 5 to 8 percent of annual gross revenue. First year's costs will be higher as initial efforts and introductions are launched. Commerce Clearing House states in their Business Owner's Toolkit, "Setting a Marketing Budget":

> *Promotion, advertising, and PR spending (i.e., "marketing support") ranges from less than 1 percent of net sales for industrial business-to-business operations to 10 percent or more, for companies marketing consumer packaged goods. Consumer packaged goods companies may spend 50 percent of net sales for introductory marketing programs in the first year, subsequently lowering the percentage spent to a stable 8 percent to 10 percent within a few years.*

Retail stores that advertise and promote spend 4 percent to 6 percent of net sales for marketing support, on average. Reproduced with permission from CCH Business Owner's Toolkit (toolkit .cch.com) published and copyrighted by CCH INCORPORATED.

Day 27 brings us to the seventh step of the marketing plan we reviewed on Day 7. That's a lot of sevens. A question often asked by small business owners, professionals, and other entrepreneurs is how much they should spend on marketing. They are really looking for a number that represents a percentage of their total sales revenue.

Asking this question is almost like asking how much you should eat. The answer depends on how hungry you are and what nourishment you need. Guerrillas are hungry for market share; therefore, marketing expenditures should be higher than average.

One thing for sure is that guerrillas plan where to spend their money and how much to spend. They do not plan their business, check to see what money is left over, and spend it on marketing. That is "gnitekram allirreug," or guerrilla marketing backwards. Your marketing budget should be viewed as a major business investment just like a piece of equipment, a key employee, and the overhead over your head. No one ever claimed business success by marketing with what was left over—certainly no guerrilla ever did.

Here is another word to the wise. If you had a marketing budget last year, don't just pull that one out and add an inflation factor to it. Part of the marketing budget process is understanding where you got bang for your buck, what worked and what didn't, and where marketing dollars can be spent most effectively. A thorough analysis of last year's budget and results is needed for this, rendering an inflationary-adjusted number meaningless.

There is no right answer to the statistical question related to percent of sales revenue spent on marketing. Historically, many internet and other companies in the dotcom era of 2000 spent more on marketing than they had in sales revenue. Most of these companies aren't around anymore, so that level is not recommended.

As you can see in the introductory quote, the percentages vary, and are usually discussed in terms of being an average for the industry. Guerrillas aren't satisfied with average performance. This suggests spending more than these average amounts.

Guerrillas like extra nourishment, too, so they can keep growing. This also suggests above-average spending on marketing. How hungry are you and what level of nourishment do you need?

One of the biggest marketing budget concerns is where to spend the money that's available. Budget items to consider are advertising on the radio and in newspapers and magazines, websites, marketing communication materials, PR, direct sales, and more. The secret to a marketing budgeting is deciding what items to spend on, their priority, and the amount available from the company till. Once those decisions are made, you have found the secret.

The most obvious answer to the where-to-spend question is to spend money on marketing that works. Would you rather spend $1,000 to get $4,000 in business, or $250 that results in zero business? The absolute cost isn't always the determining factor; the return on investment is. Sometimes you don't know this until you spend the money on the actual marketing vehicle.

The Small Business Administration (SBA) says that two of the main reasons small businesses fail is undercapitalization and the absence of effective marketing programs. Many marketing programs aren't effective because they, too, are undercapitalized. This happens often because small business owners don't have the proper marketing mindset. You have it because you went through Day 1 of this book.

Budgets depend on:

- *Your target market size.* If you have a national versus a regional or local market, your marketing budget will be higher.
- *The actual marketing weapons used.* A heavy TV, radio, and print advertising campaign will cost more than a marketing campaign comprised of PR, networking, and referral strategies. A guerrilla will use a mix, keeping profitability in mind.
- *The required frequency to persuade prospects to purchase.* If your prospects are hard to reach or your products or services are complex, you will need more frequent touches to a prospect.

- *The identity required.* Some businesses need an identity that is first-class and full of bells and whistles and ornamentation. Others may be in an identity-rebuilding mode. Each will require different budget amounts.
- *How focused and tight your market niche is.* If you compete in a general market with lots of competition, you may have to wage a larger campaign than if you are in a tightly focused niche with few competitors.
- *The age of the business.* A startup business that no one has heard of will require more marketing dollars than the 25-year-old business that everyone in the market knows about.
- *New products or services are being introduced.* Anytime this occurs, more marketing money is required. New business may come from expanding product sales by attracting new users for the new products, converting prospects to your business from the competition, and converting current customers to users of new products and services.
- *Growth goals.* Growing a business in any way requires more marketing and a corresponding increase in the marketing budget.

If you are the new competitor in the marketplace, you will have to spend more aggressively to establish your market share objective.

If your business is several years old, one way to determine your marketing budget is to review the marketing expenses of prior year(s). Once these lists are accumulated, assign the costs for each marketing item. Understanding marketing expense patterns of previous years will help formulate future requirements.

Once you land on an amount to spend, you should lock it in. Yes, guerrillas are flexible and budgets require flexibility. However, in this case, locking in means sticking to it directionally. Stick to it like paying rent, the light bill, or breathing. Marketing budgets aren't expenses, regardless of what your accounting intuition tells you. They are only expenses if they don't work.

If the economy turns down, do not cut your marketing budget. If you start building profits, guerrilla style, don't overload your marketing budget. Yo-yo marketing will eat a budget and not provide ample returns. There is too much lag factor and inefficiency in marketing when not applied consistently. The same goes for the marketing budget.

A marketing budget in conjunction with a well-thought-out guerrilla marketing plan will be your road map to the future. It is essential to the success of your company and venture. The more successful you are, the easier it is to budget subsequent years and the prouder you will be that you have developed this marketing road map.

DAY 27 SUMMARY

- Good marketers plan where to spend their money and budget how much to spend.
- Part of the marketing budgeting process is understanding where you got bang for your buck. Ask yourself what worked, what didn't, and where marketing dollars can be spent most effectively.
- Spend money on marketing that works.
- Understanding marketing expense patterns of previous years will help formulate future requirements.
- Marketing budgets aren't expenses, regardless of what your accounting intuition tells you. They are only expenses if they don't work.

■ ■ ■

Action Steps

1. What marketing items did you spend money on last year, or so far this year?
2. What worked and what didn't?
3. What would you repeat and what would you budget for it?
4. What new products or services do you plan on introducing?
5. What marketing will need to be budgeted for these?
6. What other expansion or improvement plans do you have that will need marketing (people/facility/product/service)?

7. How would you spend 10 percent of last year's sales dollars on next year's marketing?

8. How many marketing ideas or weapons can you use that cost nothing?

9. What are other uses that you can use the major parts of your marketing for?

10. What is your highest return (on investment) marketing vehicle?

11. Survey competitors in a different geographical region than you trade in to see what their marketing budgets are or have been as a percent of revenue.

12. What will be your marketing budget review process?

13. Put review dates on your marketing calendar.

Sunday	Monday	Tuesday	Wednesday	Thursday	Friday	Saturday
	1	2	3	4	5	6
7	8	9	10	11	12	13
14	15	16	17	18	19	20
21	22	23	24	25	26	27
28 ✓	29	30				

Plan Execution and Implementation

OMPETITORS CAN COPY MARKETING strategies. Marketing plan implementation usually is not as likely to be copied. The more effective implementer wins out. Josia Go, president and CEO of WATERS Phillipine, a well-known figure in the Philippine marketing and business communities, said in a speech to the AGORA marketing conference in October 2002 that effective marketing implementation becomes a competitive advantage, especially if your competitor doesn't have it.

In *7 Habits of Highly Effective People* (Free Press), Stephen Covey says:

> *All things are created twice. There's a mental or first creation, and a physical or second creation of all things. You have to make sure that the blueprint, the first action, is really what you want, that*

you've thought everything through. Then you put it into bricks and mortar. Each day you go to the construction shed and pull out the blueprint to get marching orders for the day.

Guerrilla Marketing in 30 Days is your blueprint. It's now time to visit your guerrilla construction shed, grab the tools that you have developed over the past 27 days, and go to work.

> *As stated in* Mastering Guerrilla Marketing, *"the plan is your guide and you are the master."*

Marketing strategies typically don't fail in the mental creation. They fail in implementation. You haven't come 28 days to fail. Failure is not an option. That's why we devote this whole day to the physical creation (implementation) that Covey refers to. Ensuring the effective implementation of marketing strategies is one of the highest impact ways of marketing success.

In the dotcom heyday, ideas were a dime a dozen. The lack of execution is what spelled doom for many of them. A successful marketing plan will never produce results without successful execution behind it.

Marketing implementation is simply managing marketing activities. Measuring and control are parts of good management. Using a simple chart to monitor initiatives will increase implementation effectiveness. If you don't have a chart, use the plan itself as a review mechanism or develop a marketing management accountability checklist.

A simple accountability system can consist of a spreadsheet with the following column headers: date, action, details, cost, person responsible, target completion date, date completed, and resources required.

The key to a successful implementation of a marketing plan is the execution, the actual "doing" of the planned marketing activities.

Initiatives don't get completed by stating them on paper—they require action, management, and follow-up.

Now that we know what is required of an effective guerrilla marketing plan implementer, let's look at reasons why marketing implementation fails or is substandard:

- Deadlines aren't specified.
- Responsibilities aren't specified.
- Deadlines are skipped over, ignored, or constantly changed.
- Quality/productivity standards and other expectations aren't set or communicated.
- Budgets are too low; funds or other resources are not available.
- Company culture is not consistent throughout the organization—buy-in by all involved is not present.

Successful marketing implementation requires

- effective and efficient coordination of activities—who is doing what and by when.

- deflection of distractions or objections—focus on the tasks at hand and where your time is best spent.

- attention to detail—guerrillas love details and thoroughness.

- attention to responsibility. Never assume someone else is doing something. Guerrillas never assume. It's that simple.

- elimination of procrastination—no waiting allowed. If it's good enough to do later, it's good enough to do now.

- prevention of territorial and not-my-job syndromes—internal politics will bring down a house faster than external politics.

- overdelivery and underpromising—delighting your customers will turn your marketing into sales dollars.

- doing what you do best and outsourcing or delegating the rest—unless you have more than 24 hours in a day, you can't do it all, and you certainly can't do it all well.

- Territorial issues and internal politics are killers.
- No leadership—effective plan implementations starts at the top.
- No follow through—effective plan implementation continues with good management.
- Lack of execution skills—plan implementation is also a function of competent management, either by you or others.
- Unbalanced delegation—don't overload your enthusiasts or yourself.
- Outside influences—telephone calls, meetings, and routine nonproductive tasks. What is the best return on your time investment?

The solutions to overcoming implementation roadblocks are

- organization
- budget
- skills
- resources
- leadership

> *Many business schools teach all about the business, but fail to teach how to get things done in business.*

Accountability is a good marketing habit. Plans fail because those responsible for getting certain things done aren't held accountable. This includes one-person, entrepreneurial businesses. The leader or leaders of the organization must know who is responsible for what tasks. They must manage those that are responsible for getting things done. They must monitor the specific responsibilities for the specific tasks related to each and every marketing plan component.

For example, who is in charge of writing press releases and when they will be finished and issued are questions that the marketing leader/manager should be asking. Who is going to update the website and when will it be done? Who will be researching our main competitor and when will each stage of the research be completed? Following up and checking due dates on a regular basis will help you practice the habit of marketing accountability.

The absence of follow-up and holding people accountable to due dates will almost ensure a lack of implementation and success. If you are the CEO, the marketing manager, or the chief implementer, you have to hold yourself accountable to ensure implementation. This is tough sometimes for one- and two-person businesses because of the distractions, deliveries, and everyday business routines that have to be done.

Poor implementation can usually be traced back to lack of follow-up and tracking, which are basic management tools. You should develop all parts of your marketing plan with management in mind. Think about the whole human element of your plan when developing it and especially when implementing it.

One other implementation initiative comes into play and is indirectly related to the human element. That initiative is outsourcing. If you simply don't have the manpower, talent, or resources internally to get something done, then hire someone. The job could be a support function or the actual delivery function of the product or service. Careful consideration of profitability in this arena needs to be done before proceeding.

Common implementation initiatives to consider in blending the human element with the systems element of a company:

- *Benchmarking.* Establish standards, either yours or ones set by the industry.

- *Culture changes.* Your company's human element must be suited to the plan implementation.

- *New procedures.* Something is going to have to change to get things done in a different way.

- *New processes.* The overall system must be reviewed along with procedures.

- *New policies.* If cultures change along with procedures and processes, policies must soon follow.

Once you have the plan, you must follow up and respond to changes in the market, changes in customer demands, competitive influences, technological advances, and new ideas. This is a dynamic process and vital to successful implementation.

You have come from mindset on Day 1 to implementation on this day. You have progressed from putting a course of action into writing and now are ready to take action on a consistent basis.

As you are seeing on this day, mastering guerrilla marketing requires taking action. You can't sit through a classroom lecture and expect to absorb the insights. You won't gain productive use of the learned material until you do something with it. Action is at the core of learning, and it is at the core of guerrilla marketing. Without action there are no results. You certainly didn't come 28 days to see no results.

One thing to keep in mind as you approach the end of your 30-day journey is that you cannot, at least now, complete everything mentioned in all of the 30 days of Guerrilla Marketing. I can't do them all nor can other marketing professionals do them all. One way to relieve this pressure from your implementation goal is to pick only those things you can implement completely. Maybe it's only one or two of these 30 days. Maybe it's a top-ten list. The point is to pick a few to concentrate on, implement completely, and start seeing the results of your actions.

If you're wondering when to start your implementation, the answer is easy: Now. Don't wait until you have the perfect plan or you feel perfectly ready. "Done" is better than "perfect" in the world of guerrilla marketing.

Be fair to yourself. You have spent your most precious commodity—time—developing a valuable guerrilla marketing plan and related activities. It is only right to give an honest attempt at making your plan a success. Eliminating the roadblocks and paying attention to detail will help with your own accountability. Plans that are attempted are more valuable than plans in filing cabinets. The quality of the results will be judged more than the quality of your plan.

The success of your marketing is dependent on one individual: You. You are in charge of your own actions. You are also in charge of your own inactions. You are the one that says when to start and when to move forward. To succeed takes courage and little bit of risk. If that frightens you, you are normal. Each mistake is a lesson in the making. Just make sure your successes outnumber your lessons. If they do, you will be the best guerrilla in the land.

If you have the best plan and put it in your best filing cabinet, you will have an example of the best marketing failure.

DAY 28 SUMMARY

■ A successful marketing plan will never produce results without its successful execution.

■ Marketing implementation is simply managing marketing activities.

■ The key to implementing a marketing plan is the execution, the actual "doing" of the planned activities.

■ Accountability is a good marketing habit.

■ Poor implementation is usually traced back to lack of follow-up and tracking.

■ If you simply don't have the manpower, talent, or resources internally to get something done, then hire someone.

■ Once you have the marketing plan, you must follow up and respond to changes in the market, competitive influences, technological advances, and new ideas.

■ Mastering guerrilla marketing requires taking action. Taking action is implementation.

■ Now is the time to start implementation.

■ You are in charge of your own actions.

■ ■ ■

Action Steps

1. What reporting system will you use to monitor implementation?

2. Appoint miniproject managers.

3. Recruit a project "champion."

4. Set weekly follow-up meetings to check due dates and responsibilities, even if you run a one-person business.

5. Write a success story of your successful plan implementation. (Think with the end in mind here.)

6. Put review dates on your marketing calendar.

7. Publicly state your intentions to someone.

8. Hire a marketing coach to hold you accountable and to guide you through your plan implementation.

Sunday	Monday	Tuesday	Wednesday	Thursday	Friday	Saturday
	1	2	3	4	5	6
7	8	9	10	11	12	13
14	15	16	17	18	19	20
21	22	23	24	25	26	27
28	29 ✓	30				

Expansion/New Markets/New Income Streams/New Products

A T G.E. CAPITAL, SENIOR LEADERSHIP meets once a week for a half day just to discuss, toss around, and brainstorm new business ideas. Anyone at any rank within the company can get on the agenda. Sometimes people at different levels can see things that higher-ups don't see—the old forest for the trees syndrome. G.E. Capital believes that good ideas, innovation, and development don't necessarily follow an organizational chart.

Richard Branson has built the Virgin brand into a respectable empire. He certainly believes opportunity is there for the grabbing. He also knows where to look. He encourages employees within his companies to phone him directly with new ideas, anytime, anywhere. Yes, he gives his number out. There is no complacency in this guerrilla organization!

Without progress or advancement, there is stagnation. In the business world, this leads to eventual demise. Why must businesses grow and prosper? What if they get comfortable doing what they do best? Why do they need to pursue opportunities and develop new products and services? The answers to these questions lie in the fact that businesses cannot afford to get complacent.

Complacency is a killer because things change all around you. Customers demand change, economics change, and competition dynamics change. We have heard over the past 28 days how guerrillas are responsive to change.

Not being responsive to change puts your sales on that line that usually heads straight down—very unguerrilla like.

One way to overcome complacency, ensure company growth, and be responsive to market changes and influences is to develop new products, product improvements, new services, and new streams of income and to tap new markets.

Half the current growth in the U.S. economy alone comes from companies that didn't exist ten years ago. Worldwide, in industry after industry, the companies creating new wealth aren't simply executing better. They're radically changing the rules of the game, and they're creating situations, environments, products, services, markets, and experiences that produce opportunities. These companies are a true testament of "innovate, create, or get out of the way." New products and services, expansions, and new markets are the only way to better times.

Progress and advancement are the lifeblood of guerrilla companies. If you are not seeking progress and advancement, your company stands to face stagnation, complacency, and eventual demise. This challenge, in no uncertain terms, represents what laypeople categorize as a problem. When thinking like a guerrilla, any act or process of solving a problem is a solution. Solutions are market opportunities. True, there are times when pursuing opportunities don't work out, but in the total scheme of things, all successful companies have succeeded because they went looking for an opportunity, spotted one, and acted upon it. They progressed and advanced as a result. Their problem—whether it was lack of growth, market share, or anything else—was solved because the opportunity sought panned out. Thinking along these lines will deliver your future success.

Every major industry is a growth industry at the beginning and often through the product/service maturation phase. Industries ride a major wave of enthusiasm, but end up in decline or in a no-growth mode. The reason growth is threatened, slowed, or stopped is not because the market is saturated or plans aren't fulfilled; it is because there has been a failure to find new opportunities or look at business in a different way.

The railroad industry did not stop growing because the need to transport people or goods declined. The railroads have suffered because other transportation opportunities arose. Cars, trucks, and planes took over. The railroads failed to view their role and the ensuing activity as an opportunity for transportation. They viewed themselves as being in the railroad business rather than in the transportation business. They had tunnel vision and were railroad-oriented, not transportation-oriented. They were product-oriented, not customer- or market-oriented. They needed to recalibrate their views, thoughts, attitudes, and actions.

The movie business almost suffered a similar fate. Hollywood studios viewed themselves as being in the movie business when they were actually in the entertainment business. When television came along, Hollywood was threatened. Hollywood was product-oriented. Had movie moguls focused on providing entertainment rather than making movies, more opportunities would have presented themselves.

Part of discovering opportunity is understanding what business you are really in. The circus doesn't sell tickets; it sells thrills. Optometrists don't sell eyeglasses; they sell vision. The daily newspaper doesn't sell paper and ink; it sells news and information. Viewing your businesses with this perspective keeps you fresh, on the leading edge, modern in your customer's eyes, and more open to opportunities that present themselves along the way.

Leadership within a particular industry is a competitive advantage and an indicator of a higher probability of success. Leadership itself is about taking people through "uncharted waters" to places that have not been explored and that they probably wouldn't have arrived at without your leadership. Opportunity along the traveled road is just one path in a world of infinite possibilities. These infinite possibilities represent a multitude of points. The path to success depends on how these points are connected (just like connecting the dots in a child's puzzle) along the way to opportunity. Opportunity depends on how the forces are marshaled along the way.

Consider companies that lead in their industry today. Black & Decker is a leader in the home/consumer tool market. A Black & Decker engineer connected the dots, in a different way, on the way to an opportunity. One of these dots represented a customer need. A need existed for a hands-free, rechargeable work light that could wrap around the area being worked on or around objects near a workplace. The Snake Light debuted in 1994. The company originally projected sales of 200,000 units in year one. The result was sales of over 600,000 units. The demand far exceeded supply. Black & Decker demonstrated its opportunity leadership with this innovation.

Sometimes it's a need like the Black & Decker inventor saw. Sometimes it's a competitive strategy. Other times opportunity happens because someone stumbled upon something. Anyone can do this stumbling. It doesn't have to be a research department; it doesn't have to be a product development team. Opportunity is available to anyone just for the grabbing. Opportunity is actually everywhere, all the time. You just have to know where to look, and sometimes how to look. Brainstorming sessions are good for churning out new ideas. Some companies, consultants, and organizations even have formal brainstorming departments called think tanks.

Even some of the tried and true traditional industries can still find opportunity, new products, and new markets. Who would have thought that prepackaging, pre-chopping, pre-tossing lettuce would propel that mature industry from $100 million in revenues to $1.1 billion in seven years? Someone somehow saw an opportunity. In this case, it was mostly related to packaging. Sometimes it takes repackaging, refining, redevelopment, or turning something old into something new. The question at hand is how you can recreate your product or service to stand out and even influence customers and prospects in new and different ways. Most times the answer to this question represents the market opportunity in front of you.

In business boom times, companies are marketing, spending money on new product development, instituting new processes and procedures, and creating environments to spur creativity. In an economic downturn, companies switch from an innovative mode to a survival mode. Development has less of a priority; new products aren't as abundant. Budgets for marketing are slashed. Opportunities seem to diminish as a result, and with that comes a slow business growth. This is inevitable in some or even most businesses and is conventional wisdom. But it is not necessarily the best course when pursuing growth goals and opportunity. In fact, the opposite is what should be happening. Guerrilla companies and individuals can build strength during downturns that can help them emerge on top of the competitive pack. Those companies seeking and managing growth will realize more opportunities than those managing costs, slashing expenses, and eliminating development. Growth depends on opportunity.

This opportunity or expansion comes in the form of developing new streams of income.

Sandra Barry of Marketing Fuel (marketingfuel.com) realized this when planning the future of her income streams. As a marketing services company seeking to expand its work in niche markets, the company started a new division called Adoption Voice (adoptionvoice.com), specializing in helping potential adoptive parents find a child. This new market opened up a new stream of income for the company. Marketing Fuel has been very successful with this new direction, which required evaluating other possible opportunities.

Many companies use product diversification to create the multiple streams of income effect.

Product Diversification

Production diversification is a popular way of finding new income. Just look at the following innovations:

- Diet Cherry Coke
- Double-Stuf Oreos, Fudge Mint Oreos, Mini-Oreos, and Oreos stuffed with peanut butter
- Gap/Baby Gap
- Limited/Limited Too
- Toys 'R' Us/Kids 'R' Us

While these examples are from larger companies, let's look now at some guerrilla examples:

- An accounting and tax firm becomes an accounting, tax, and financial planning firm.
- A printing company evolves into a printing and marketing company.
- A professional speaking and training company adds seminars, books, and tapes for sale.
- A dry cleaning company adding alteration services.

Others juggle activity after activity creating business venture after business venture. As an example, many speakers will run multiple revenue stream businesses that include consulting, writing, publishing books, tapes, and CDs, and seminars. Given the cyclical nature of business, the cash flow of one revenue segment may hold steady while another dips or rises. This provides a continuity that is not present in a business that has only one stream of income.

If you look at most guerrilla companies that are very successful financially, one thing you will find is that they don't put all of their eggs in one basket. In the beginning, diversification of revenue streams gives you a lot more work and details to handle, but in the long run, it also offers greater peace of mind and greater security.

Another benefit of creating such a multifaceted business is that it is good for the creative spirit of the business owner. Guerrillas possess this creative spirit.

The multiple revenue stream business model has gained more credibility with the advent of e-commerce. Most successful websites generate their revenues from more than one product or service. However, some clients still believe that a business should focus on one or two areas of specialization. Businesses with too diverse a dossier may be seen as flighty or unfocused. It is obvious in this circumstance how important target marketing is in order to avoid confusion in the marketplace.

Robert Allen, author of *Multiple Streams of Income* (John Wiley & Sons), compares his approach to mountain streams. There are multiple streams of runoff water from the mountains that feed a lake. If one dries up, the lake doesn't go away because other streams continue feeding it.

Income streams in a business can be anything that brings in more money than it costs. Having more than one, not depending on each other or interfering with each other, will protect the bottom line of your company. There is a feeling of control and security when this state exists. Not having these multiple streams is fine as long as you are willing to take the risk that your only stream might dry up. The risk is up to you. Guerrillas don't mind risk, but they do mind when the bottom line dries up. Developing other streams, finding new markets, and expanding product lines ensure consistently flowing income.

Expansion Opportunity Rules

Let's look at six principles of this expansion perspective:

1. *Understand what business you are in.* There is no such thing as a mature business when you expand your views beyond the traditional definition of your industry, marketplace, or customers.
2. *Volume is not necessarily growth.* Windfalls, spurts, one-time pieces of business, and getting the order versus getting the business can all disguise the lack of business growth. Make sure your growth is profitable and sustainable.
3. *A growth/expansion/diversification attitude starts at the top of the organization.* Think of where your company's vision is created. Who is looking out for where the company is going? Sometimes growth takes a fresh perspective, a new point of view, or a new idea.
4. *Growth should be long term.* Sustainability and profitability will keep a business alive for a long time. Taking care of the core, the infrastructure of the business, and the markets maintain the necessary foundation for growth.
5. *A sustainable growth strategy and an attitude based on customer needs, benefits, and targeted marketing* will increase market share and company profits much more quickly than always responding to competition or reacting to low sales.
6. *Don't think in terms of making something or having a service available and then selling it.* Think in terms of discovering new needs and wants and designing your business and expansion around that. Don't sell products and services people buy. Develop, provide, and have available what people want and need most.

Much of this expansion is evolution: planned and unplanned. In the mid 1970s there were many waterbed retail stores. Those that thought like "Day 29" are still in business, albeit in a different form. Those that did not are out of business. Here is an example of how such a business evolved to the business they are in today (over 30 years' time):

- Waterbeds (start up in the mid—1970s)
- Other beds
- Futons
- Mattress design
- Space-saving furniture
- Children's furniture
- Specialized beds from Europe and America—(the look of the business in 2008/2009)

On this day and in your subsequent thinking, your challenge is to build a deep capability for business concept innovation with an expansive perspective. The ongoing mindset and guerrilla guiding light is to think that what works today probably won't work tomorrow. Finding tomorrow's solution is satisfying tomorrow's customer. Expanding toward those solutions could be your next guerrilla success.

DAY 29 SUMMARY

■ One of the ways to overcome complacency and ensure company growth and responsiveness to market changes is to develop new products, product improvements, new services, and new streams of income and to tap new markets.

■ Companies creating new wealth aren't simply executing better; they're radically changing the rules of the game. And they're creating situations, environments, products, services, markets, and experiences that produce opportunities.

■ Progress and advancement are the lifeblood of guerrilla companies.

■ Sometimes progress and improvement take the form of repackaging, refining, redeveloping, or turning something old into something new.

■ How you recreate your product or service to stand out and affect customers and prospects in a new and different way is the improvement question at hand.

■ Opportunity or expansion comes in the form of developing new streams of income.

■ Many companies use product diversification to create multiple streams of income.

■ ■ ■

Action Steps

1. Do you have the potential to serve global markets?

2. Can you expand beyond your current service area?

3. Does that take more locations?

4. What other resources would be required to do this?

5. Do you need to change, tweak, or re-evaluate your ideal customer?

6. Are there other customer profiles that you could target with your current offerings?

7. What new products and services can you bundle with current products and services?

8. Can you bundle your products and services with someone else's to offer more value to the collective group of customers?

9. Are there pricing, distribution, or service strategies that can be developed around what you are currently doing?

10. What strategies in these areas can be developed that are radically different from what you are currently doing?

11. What is your Baby Gap, your Snakelight, or your Double-Stuf Oreo opportunity?

	Sunday	Monday	Tuesday	Wednesday	Thursday	Friday	Saturday
		1	2	3	4	5	6
	7	8	9	10	11	12	13
	14	15	16	17	18	19	20
	21	22	23	24	25	26	27
	28	29	30 ✓				

New Plan—The Next 30 Days and Beyond

CONGRATULATIONS! YOU ARE AT DAY 30 of *Guerrilla Marketing in 30 Days*. You have come a long way. You have allowed yourself to soak up an immense amount of guerrilla marketing knowledge. You are much better off on this day than on any previous day. Stop reading for just ten seconds and pat your self on the back. It feels good, doesn't it? You're finished—or are you?

You know the answer to that question. You just read 30 days of guerrilla marketing tips, methods, ideas, and values that have taught you that you just spent 30 days on an ongoing experience. You know it wasn't a 30-day event. You have just begun a process. So what's next?

This is a question that every business and every guerrilla marketer should ask every day. Where do you go from here? How can you improve upon what you have already done? What other successes do you want? The answers to these questions are your renewal factor. They contain the impetus behind your re-engineering. What are you doing every day to re-engineer yourself? These answers are the building blocks to that proverbial next level that you want to achieve.

At the end of these 30 days you will have completed action steps and developed plans. The paramount question at hand is, What would you do differently over the past 30 days if you had to relive them? Or if you were starting this book all over?

There is good news! You get to relive them, starting now. Your answer to the previous question is your starting point for the next 30 days—the next 30 days of learning, planning, applying, and progressing.

This time around you will know where your strengths and weaknesses are. You will have a feel for what works and what doesn't, all leading to more focus.

With a foundation in place, you now can think beyond your current scale. How do you make your guerrilla marketing efforts more productive and more profitable?

With a foundation in place, you can now learn and apply more. What have you learned about yourself in the past 30 days? What were some roadblocks along the way? What resources could you use more of? These are common questions to follow-up planning. Although you are asking these questions on Day 30, they should be ongoing questions.

You are in control. You will dictate the next 30 days and beyond. You will have an advantage, too. Chances are that your competitor didn't read this book. You will be ready for the changing markets, the changing customer demands, and the positive changes that occur in your own company as a result of implementing guerrilla marketing principles.

Things will not stay the same. Markets will change, you will change, and marketing itself will change. The fundamentals will remain the same. You have a good guerrilla base.

This book is only 30 days worth of ideas and information. Every thing was not covered, but you have plenty to rocket toward success. There is more that you will learn and apply on your own and more that you will learn from us. There will be another 30 days of guerrilla marketing.

Marketing is changing even as you are reading this and even as you plan new activities. With current legislation under review for Do Not Call regulations and anti-spam rules, marketing will surely change and always be under review. Technology will continue to evolve and change the way we market our products and services. You will start to see more progress in the area of instant messaging (and related regulations). Integration of systems, whether marketing or other, will be a point of emphasis as companies strive for more efficiency and effectiveness. Marketing will continue to progress toward more automation. Information will become even more abundant, changing the way we research and classify our target markets. Demographics will become more refined, which will have great implications on how we market, what we say, and to whom we say it.

Regardless of the advancements of technology, one thing is for certain. The importance of relationships in all guerrilla marketing will never go away. It will still take a buyer and seller to make a transaction happen. As long as there are two people left standing on this earth, relationships will be important. Relationships will be part of a growing emphasis on customer focus. Your guerrilla knowledge has already put you in position to capitalize on this.

Customers will become more interested in their total experience in dealing with you, not just in a transaction. Delightful experiences will breed intense loyalty. Loyalty will provide sustainability for companies, which in turn will contribute to profitability and success.

Regardless of these future trends and your roadblocks in the past 30 days, the bottom line is (guerrillas love healthy bottom lines) you are in charge. You are the planner. You are the marketer. You are responsible for your own implementation. To gain the most, you will have to prioritize what can and cannot be done. Make your to-do and your not-to-do lists. Not only is accountability a good marketing habit to leave these 30 days with, but so also is prioritization. Make it a habit.

Guerrilla marketing is not rocket science. It's not a cakewalk either. The most important ingredient in guerrilla marketing is you. Without you (u), you have "gerrilla" marketing, and we all know that is incomplete. Where you are challenged, seek help. Many guerrilla marketers are givers. Find another guerrilla marketer today and give to each other.

You started off your guerrilla program understanding that guerrilla marketing uses time, energy, and imagination instead of a blank checkbook. These 30 days have contributed to your imagination. You will develop even more ideas from your learning and doing. Ideas breed ideas. Guerrilla marketing breeds more guerrilla marketing. Put these ideas to work. Some will be successful, others will not. Never get to a point where you are saying to yourself that you wish you had done something you haven't. Henry Ford said, "Whether you believe you can do something or can't, you are probably right." Believe in yourself. Believe in all the hard work you have put in over these 30 days and believe in your future successes.

From Guerrilla Marketing, we leave you with:
"There has never been a better time than right now to give wings to our dreams through marketing. There has never been a better way to market than with the insights and attitudes of the guerrilla."

Happy marketing!

DAY 30 SUMMARY

- Your starting point for the next 30 days is the answer to the question of what would you do differently over the past 30 days of learning if you had to relive them.

- With a foundation in place, you now can think beyond your current scale.

- Marketing is changing even as you are reading this and even as you plan new activities.

- Integration of systems, whether marketing or other, will be a point of emphasis as companies strive for more efficiency and effectiveness.

■ Customers will become more interested in their total experience in dealing with you, not just in a transaction.

■ "There has never been a better time than right now to give wings to our dreams through marketing. There has never been a better way to market than with the insights and attitudes of the guerrilla."

■ ■ ■

Action Steps

1. Write out your thoughts on the question of what is next. Include in this your thoughts on the question of where do you go from here.

2. How can you improve upon what you have just done during the past 30 days?

3. What other marketing successes do you want?

4. How do you make your guerrilla marketing efforts more productive and more profitable?

5. What did you learn about yourself?

6. What were some roadblocks that came up during your 30 days of guerrilla marketing?

7. What resources can you use more of? How can you get them?

8. List your top three guerrilla marketing priorities for the next 30 days. Just three. You will have more than this, but for focus and this action step, just list the top three.

9. Who can you recommend this book to?

10. What other guerrilla titles would you like to see?

	Sunday	Monday	Tuesday	Wednesday	Thursday	Friday	Saturday
		1	2	3	4	5	6
	7	8	9	10	11	12	13
	14	15	16	17	18	19	20
	21	22	23	24	25	26	27
	28	29	30	★			

Referral Strategies

GO AROUND THE ROOM AND ASK all the small businesses represented where most of their business came from or will come from and the majority will undoubtedly give the same answer. If you're not in a room now, ask around the next time you are in one. The answer most often heard is "word of mouth."

Ask family, friends, and neighbors (family and friends can still be neighbors) how they chose their family doctor, their dentist, or their preferred plumber. Most will say, ". . . by recommendation of family member, friend, or neighbor."

Referrals are those recommendations of others. Getting those recommendations can be easy, viral, automatic and, in the guerrilla world, profitable. Knowing how to make this all happen is even more guerrilla like. This bonus day will give you that referral know-how.

Referrals can "just happen" but the more you can formalize the process or put a process in place to make them happen, the quicker you'll realize increased, word-of-mouth sales.

Let's look at the fundamental components of this BONUS DAY.

Ask for Referrals

The number-one way, without question by any guerrilla, to get referrals is to simply ask for them. Yes, it can be done simply but many still are challenged by this simple step to obtaining referrals. Potential "referrers" can't always read your mind.

I often ask business owners how their referral program is doing and sometimes their response to me is that their program is not going so well; certainly not as well as planned. Upon further investigation it becomes quite obvious that the main reason the program is not going well is that the person wanting to be referred or wanting a referral is just not asking for them. They typically have no process in place to ask for or obtain referrals.

Jay talks often about the chiropractor front office staff who is trained (key words: "who is trained") to ask one simple question of their patients that generates an avalanche of never-ending referrals. The question they ask, usually on the phone, when a patient or prospective client calls for an appointment is, "Is this appointment for you or another member of your family?" Just a mention of another possibility or different scenario is enough to make the possibility of a referral a reality.

Other related questions to drive referrals or a referral mind-set could be the following:

- Is this for this week's supply or for the whole month?
- Have you considered the same purchase as a gift for your friends and family?
- Will one be enough or will you need more in case of loss, breakage, or usage faster than planned?
- Would you like to buy one for a friend at a discount?
- Would you like to sign our guest book along with friends and family members to receive special offers?

You will generally find that most people like to give referrals. Giving referrals is helping others. People generally like to help. The law of reciprocity is also present with the notion: Give before you get; very guerrilla like. Giving referrals usually means receiving referrals subsequently. Just don't forget to ask for them.

Narrow the Universe

Another fundamental point of referral-based guerrilla marketing is narrowing the universe of those you ask. If I ask you, "Who else do you know that could benefit from my products and services?" I am asking you to think of everyone you know. Since everyone generally knows between 150 and 250 people, each, I'm then asking you to think of all those people at one time. Your reply will probably be, "I don't know right now. Let me think about that and get back to you." Typically, neither happens.

Now, try the same line of questioning, but narrow the universe of the person you're asking. Phrase your question differently. Ask, instead, "Who do you golf with on Sundays that might be interested in my products or services?" What you are essentially doing is asking someone to think of 4 or at most a dozen people that might be good referrals for you instead of 150 to 250. You, many times, will get one referral from this narrowed line of questioning. Would you rather have 1 out of 12 as a good referral or zero out of 250? Narrowing the universe of those you ask will yield this type of positive result.

There is also a side benefit to this narrowed approach. The next time your referrer attends the same type of event with the same narrowed audience, they will often associate your line of questioning with their group and think further about your referral solicitation.

Ask at the Point of Enthusiasm

You probably are pondering right now, as you are making a guerrilla head dive into this chapter on referrals, about when the best time to ask for a referral is: The answer, since this is a book of answers, is when your customer, prospect, or associate is at the peak of their enthusiasm; when they are in the most positive frame of mind possible.

If you exceed customer expectations and they compliment you or exclaim that what you did for them was awesome, they are undoubtedly in a positive frame of mind. As this happens, don't waste time. Jump on this opportunity. This is a guerrilla opportunity. Ask right then and there, who else they know (narrow the universe if you can) that could benefit from your products or services.

People generally want others, especially their friends, family, and associates to feel good and experience positive benefits. They will generally want to share your positive service or the positive experience you provide them with others.

Another point or moment of positive enthusiasm is when people pay you; when they hand you a credit card or write out a check to you. Once again, don't waste time, pounce and ask for that referral.

One way to manufacture this peak enthusiasm is with a customer satisfaction survey. Most customers, when filling out such a survey, will provide positive replies to such a survey. The last question on a satisfaction survey should be related to asking for referrals. In the spirit of guerrilla marketing, this is no- or low-cost marketing and can be leveraged as your referral funnel fills and even, sometimes, overflows.

Asking at the right time is crucial to getting referrals. Customers are more loyal when giving referrals. Taking care of someone is a typical human response and attitude. Take advantage of these, and feel free to refer guerrilla marketing to your narrow universe. Who else do you know in your network who could benefit from receiving a copy of this book?

Referrals do not necessarily happen automatically. A good product or service is certainly necessary but point number one suggests that you need a proactive referral program in place. Hoping and wishing for referrals are not strategies or actions that will necessarily increase your bank account.

The highest level of referral is when a referring associate sends out a letter of introduction for you, referring you to their sphere of influence before you enter that sphere. Once you then enter that sphere, a cold referring situation has become warmer because of the proactive letter writing by your referring associate.

Who in your sphere of influence would you like to tap for referrals? Who in your sphere of influence would be willing to proactively write a letter referring you? People like to do business with those they like, know, and trust. People like to refer people they like, know, and trust.

Having a proactive referral program in place is only half of the job in getting high-quality referrals. To increase the probability of getting successful, high-yield referrals, you need to give high-quality referrals. Act interested in your networking associate. Find out more about them so that you may refer them more and properly. A great line of questioning is to ask, "What is a good referral for you?" When you ask this question, you are hoping for an attitude of reciprocity to kick in. You want your networking associate to then ask you what a good referral is for you. This is your chance to communicate your detail accordingly. Do not forget to talk about how best to deliver a referral to you. This also is a chance to suggest the proactive letter writing campaign to warm up cold referral situations.

A cold lead is not a referral. Referrals should be warmed up, qualified, and researched if possible. Knowing these differences will enhance the results you get from this form of guerrilla marketing.

Proximity Referrals

You can simulate the warm-up letter writing in advance by writing your own letters. This works well when trying to market and solicit business in the same geographic area or the same office building in which you are already doing business. Your letter can mention (by name) the fact that you are already in that area or in that building doing business. There would be many benefits to expand business in the same proximity. I call this a Proximity Referral Program—marketing to others in the same geographical proximity.

As biased as we are, a marketing plan should be a major portion of a business plan. Within a marketing plan, you should have a networking plan and within that networking plan, a referral program plan. Set a goal, establish contacts, develop the methods of communication, convert to business, measure, and repeat. This all sounds simple but it does require your effort. This sounds like common sense but it is not common practice. Best of all, in the spirit of guerrilla marketing, we didn't have to discuss any associated cash investment or budget with this bonus day.

About the Authors

Jay Conrad Levinson

Jay Conrad Levinson is the author of the bestselling marketing series in history, *Guerrilla Marketing*, plus 29 other business books. His books have sold 14 million copies worldwide. His guerrilla concepts have influenced marketing so much that today his books appear in 39 languages and are required reading in many MBA programs worldwide. Jay taught guerrilla marketing for ten years at the extension division of the University of California at Berkeley, and practiced his skills in the United States as senior vice president at J. Walter Thompson and in Europe as creative director and board member at Leo Burnett Advertising.

He has written a monthly column for *Entrepreneur* magazine, articles for *Inc.* magazine, and monthly online columns for the Microsoft website, as well as occasional columns in the *San Francisco Examiner*. He also writes online columns for several internet websites, including Netscape, America Online, Fortune Small Business, and Hewlett-Packard.

Jay is the chairman of Guerrilla Marketing International, a marketing partner of Adobe and Apple. He has served on the Microsoft Small Business

Council and the 3Com Small Business Advisory Board. "Guerrilla Marketing" is a series of books, audiotapes, videotapes, an award-winning CD-ROM, an internet website, and a breakthrough online marketing tool called "The Guerrilla Marketing Network." It is a marketing support system for small business owners that allows them to spend less, get more, and achieve substantial profits.

He has one child and lives north of San Francisco.

Al Lautenslager

Jay Levinson once described Al Lautenslager as a true guerrilla marketer with a passion for marketing that is second to none. He went on to describe how Al's strong desire and uncanny ability to share his knowledge and experience with others usually results in their success.

Alfred J. Lautenslager is an award-winning marketing/PR consultant, direct-mail promotion specialist, author, speaker, and entrepreneur. His knowledge has helped hundreds succeed in their own businesses. He is the principal of Market for Profits, a marketing consulting firm in Chicago, and the former president and owner of a small business, The Ink Well, a commercial printing and mailing company in Wheaton, Illinois. Al recently appeared on radio as a marketing expert to review Super Bowl commercials. He has also appeared on TV.

Al has started up businesses and closed them down. He has walked the walk of a guerrilla marketer. He is a multi-winner of Business of the Year awards from various organizations. His articles can be read on more than 100 online sites, including that of *Entrepreneur* magazine (entrepreneur.com), where he serves as a marketing expert and coach.

Al speaks to audiences wanting to learn more about building their businesses through low- or no-cost marketing tactics. Many audience members leave with strategies and tactics they can use the same day.

His leadership has extended to past community involvement as a member of the board of directors of numerous nonprofit organizations, including two chambers of commerce. Al also is a Certified Guerrilla Marketing Coach and can be reached at al@allautenslager.com.

Index